Landmarks in Rhetoric and Public Address

Quintilian

ON THE TEACHING OF SPEAKING & WRITING

TRANSLATIONS FROM BOOKS ONE, TWO
& TEN OF THE *INSTITUTIO ORATORIA*

SECOND EDITION

Edited by **James J. Murphy**
& Cleve Wiese

Southern Illinois University Press • Carbondale

Copyright © 1987, 2016 by the Board of Trustees,
Southern Illinois University
This book is a revised and enlarged version of *On the Early Education of the Citizen-Orator*, published by Bobbs-Merrill Company, Inc., in 1965.
First Southern Illinois University Press edition published 1987.
Second edition 2016.
Printed in the United States of America

19 18 17 16   4 3 2 1

Library of Congress Cataloging-in-Publication Data

Quintilian, author.
[Institutiones oratoriae. Selections. English]
Quintilian on the teaching of speaking and writing : translations from
  books one, two, and ten of the "Institutio Oratoria" / edited by James J.
  Murphy and Cleve Wiese. — Second edition.
    pages cm — (Landmarks in rhetoric and public address)
Summary: "Translation, with introductory material and other critical
  apparatus, of 'Institutio oratoria' (The Education of the Orator),
  by Roman rhetor Quintilian (Marcus Fabius Quintilanus, ca. A.D.
  35–98?)." — Provided by publisher.
Includes bibliographical references and index.
  ISBN 978-0-8093-3440-7 (paperback)
  ISBN 978-0-8093-3441-4 (e-book)
1. Oratory—Early works to 1800. 2. Rhetoric—Early works to 1800.
  I. Murphy, James Jerome, editor. II. Wiese, Cleve, editor. III. Title.
PA6650.E5M87 2015
808.5'1—dc23   2015023462

Printed on recycled paper. ♻

The paper used in this publication meets the minimum requirements of
  American National Standard for Information Sciences—Permanence
  of Paper for Printed Library Materials, ANSI Z39.48-1992. ∞

CONTENTS

ON THE ADULT EDUCATION OF THE CITIZEN-ORATOR
Book Ten of the *Institutio oratoria*

PREFACE

This is a book about how a lesson once learned can be used again.

It is also a book about future writing and speaking, about preparing for discourse that is yet to be.

It takes advantage of the longest-lasting teaching process in Western civilization, which was devised by Roman schoolmasters more than a century before the birth of Christ. Over the next two thousand years, this teaching process influenced figures as diverse as Cicero, Saint Jerome, Erasmus, Martin Luther, John Milton, John Stuart Mill, Winston Churchill, and John F. Kennedy. The Roman schools prepared a carefully crafted learning sequence based on a close relationship between the four factors of listening, reading, speaking, and writing.

Toward the end of the first Christian century, the best features of this system were distilled into a comprehensive work titled *Institutio oratoria* (*The Education of the Orator*). The author was Marcus Fabius Quintilianus (circa A.D. 35–98), one of Rome's most famous teachers, who had flourished under three emperors and then devoted two years of his retirement to describing and explaining his educational program.

This volume offers translations from the three key sections of the *Institutio oratoria* in which Quintilian provides the rationale for an education that looks to future writing and speaking.

Modern readers, it is hoped, will find his ideas as useful today as they have been in many countries for nearly two thousand years.

PART ONE

THE DIDACTIC PHASE:
LEARNING ABOUT QUINTILIAN

*This phase acquaints the reader with Quintilian,
his place in history, and the main principles of his
educational program for the promotion of literacy.*

Quintilian in the History of Western Education

In one sense this is the story of a centuries-old successful approach
to the teaching of speaking and writing, and in another sense it is
the story of the one ancient book that best typifies that approach.

To understand the story, we have to start at the beginning.

The Concept of "School"

What became Roman education began, as did so much of Roman
culture, in ancient Greece. Democratic education in ancient Greece
was necessarily of a collective character because it aimed to provide
learning opportunities to all free men. This goal led to the creation
and development of a remarkable social tool—the "school."[1] It is
often difficult for the modern student and the general public to understand that the concept of "school" had to be invented. But it was
a deliberate cultural choice at a certain stage in Western civilization,
one that has dominated our subsequent thinking.

Yet there have always been alternatives. It has always been possible for the rich or the reclusive to hire a tutor for a son or a daughter, and on the other hand, for the ignorant or the religious zealot
to reject any learning at all. At the level of trades like carpentry or
masonry, one-on-one apprenticeships have long been popular. Over

the centuries the predominant choice of societies as diverse as the Roman Empire and Christian monasticism has been, nevertheless, to gather young people in groups to receive purposeful instruction in the methods and values dear to those societies.

For the Greeks, and for the Romans who inherited Greek thought, such instruction usually began with the matter that made all other learning possible—that is, it began with language and the uses of language. The interplay of speaking and writing has been an integral part of this instruction from the beginning.

These are historical truisms of Western culture, but they are worth repeating here because they illustrate the central importance of Quintilian's concerns. Quintilian not only describes for us the educational processes that he inherited and that were to be replicated substantially down into our own century, but he also explains to us why these processes are superior to their alternatives and what they can accomplish for society by educating citizens who are both humane and effective. His frequent discussions of alternative ideas provide us with a depth of understanding that could not be reached by a bare statement of a single viewpoint. That is why you need to read Quintilian's own words in these translations rather than trusting someone else's summaries—including our own.

The Romans were a systematic people. Their remarkable feats of hydraulic engineering created aqueducts for the water supply of cities. They built paved roads that, in some parts of the world, are still usable today. The Romans introduced central heating for buildings. They pioneered the mass production of chariots and naval vessels with interchangeable parts to support a carefully designed military force that dominated Europe, Asia Minor, and North Africa for five hundred years. The governmental structure of the Republic was delicately balanced to prevent any one man from seizing absolute power, with paired executives (the consuls), a parliamentary body (the senate), and representatives of the people (the tribunes) having the power of veto; this pattern of government worked so well, in fact, that when the Republic finally succumbed to personal dictatorships it was possible, even then, for the emperors to keep the old mechanisms intact while they wielded the real power. The worldwide system of public administration under the empire was a marvel of meticulous record keeping. In short, the Romans were social engineers as well as mechanical and military experts.

It should not be surprising, then, to discover that the Roman approach to schools was equally systematic. We know that the subject of rhetoric was so highly schematized by the lifetime of Cicero (born 106 B.C.) that even as an adolescent (aged perhaps seventeen to nineteen) Cicero was able to rehearse what he had learned as a student to produce a major treatise on rhetoric—his *De inventione*.[2] This systematization of rhetoric, a product of Hellenistic efforts during the second century before Christ, may well have been a by-product of the increasing standardization of the schools in which rhetoric was the core subject. As George A. Kennedy remarks, "practically all of the additions to rhetorical theory made in Hellenistic times stem from the desire to create an academic discipline, a list which could be memorized, or something which applied to classroom exercises."[3] Naturally, there was a good deal of variety among specific schools, and the official censors closed down at least one rhetorical school in 92 B.C. for promoting "a new kind of study."[4] But there is such a clear overall pattern of subject matter and teaching methodology across many centuries of Roman schooling that it seems fair to think of Roman education as a "system" with identifiable characteristics.

By the time of Emperor Vespasian (A.D. 69–79), the schools had become an instrument of public policy. Vespasian initiated the practice of granting teachers immunity from certain municipal taxes, a practice that was confirmed and expanded by many later emperors, on the grounds that the teachers' service was a benefit to the state.[5] It was also Vespasian who established official professorships to be paid from the state treasury; Quintilian was the first to receive the chair for Latin rhetoric, with its annual stipend of 100,000 sesterces (a large sum, possibly equivalent to a modern half-million dollars).

Quite apart from this kind of official privilege or endowment, a larger social force ensured a close relation between the schools and the world power of Rome. The military administration that enforced Roman rule was founded on permanent garrisons; these garrisons required civilian support by merchants, suppliers, and clerks. In due course garrisons became towns and cities. The parents of children in York, Beirut, Marseilles, Cologne, or Carthage could demand the same educational advantages accruing to residents of Rome itself, and there is ample evidence of municipal support for such schools at least into the sixth Christian century.[6] Where the soldiers went, the schools went as well.

The schools outlasted the empire. While some early zealous Christians such as Tertullian and Cyprian wanted to renounce learning in favor of a simple faith, the fifth-century church decided instead to pursue the values of the educational system already in place.[7] The example of Aurelius Augustinus (A.D. 354–430) shows how firmly embedded was the concept of school. After attending school in his hometown of Tagaste in North Africa, Augustinus taught rhetoric in Carthage but moved to a better teaching job in Rome; once there, he moved again to a position in Milan. It was in Milan that Augustinus went to hear a popular Christian speaker, Ambrose, and through him became interested in Christianity. Ultimately, Saint Augustine became the bishop of Hippo in North Africa, a prolific writer and speaker on behalf of Christianity, and one of the four Latin Fathers of the church. His teaching background led him to write one of the most influential documents of the fifth century, *De doctrina Christiana* (*On Instruction in Christianity*), arguing for the use of rhetoric to promote the faith. His career would not have been possible without the schools.[8]

If the schools outlasted the empire, it was also true that the teaching methods outlasted the Roman schools themselves. The history of medieval education is only now being written, but there is increasing evidence that the basic pedagogy that the Romans had inherited from the Greeks was passed on into the Middle Ages substantially unchanged.[9] The methods persisted long after their sources were forgotten—perhaps because the methods worked well—and were already familiar to the humanists who created in the fifteenth and sixteenth centuries what has come to be called the Renaissance. One of the reasons for the great popularity of Quintilian in the early Renaissance, in fact, was that his work provided an explicit rationale for an educational program in literary culture that was already under way. The English poets William Shakespeare and John Milton, for instance, each had an education remarkably similar to that outlined in Quintilian's *Institutio oratoria*—but remarkably similar as well to that of John of Salisbury in the twelfth century, of Gasparino da Barzizza in the fourteenth, and of Winston Churchill in the nineteenth. The continuity of method depended not on any single book but rather on the pragmatic conclusion that what was successful was worth continuing.

Our modern reading of Quintilian, then, is not a mere antiquarian exercise. His book epitomizes the best of a humane approach to literacy.

Who Was Quintilian?

Marcus Fabius Quintilianus was born about A.D. 35 in Calagurris (modern Calahorra) in Spain.[10] The province of Spain was at that time a famed center of Roman culture, and Quintilian's father may have been a teacher of rhetoric. Spanish schools counted among their pupils such distinguished writers as the essayist Seneca the Elder, the dramatist Seneca the Younger, and the poet Martial.[11] Quintilian may have received his elementary education in Spain, but when he was about sixteen years old, he went to Rome for advanced education.

The young Quintilian attached himself, as was the custom, to one of the famous orators of the day—Domitius Afer, a well-known pleader who held high office under three emperors, Tiberius, Caligula, and Nero.[12] Many years later Quintilian was to "praise him for skill, and for his general manner of speaking, and we need not fear to rank him with the ancient orators" (10.1.118).[13] Domitius Afer had apparently given some thought to the theory of his art, as opposed to the mere practice of it, for Quintilian says that Afer wrote two books on the examination of witnesses (5.7.7).

Quintilian returned to Calagurris when he was about twenty-five, presumably to teach and practice law. Domitius Afer died in A.D. 59, and his death may have made a natural break in the young Quintilian's association with Roman affairs. There is no information about his activities in Spain, but he must have attained some sort of provincial prominence, for he was among those who came to Rome at the end of A.D. 68 with Galba, the governor of Spain who became emperor of Rome in January of 69.

In Rome Quintilian was both teacher and pleader. Among his better-known cases is that of the Jewish queen Berenice, before whom Saint Paul appeared in Caesarea before going to Rome.[14] Quintilian states that he represented the queen in a trial in which she herself was the judge (4.1.19). The young orator's abilities in logical presentation led his peers to rely on him to make the opening statement of the case in trials; both Pliny the Younger[15] and Quintilian (4.2.86) point this out.

His teaching soon attracted attention. In A.D. 72, just four years after returning to Rome with Galba, Quintilian was included among the rhetoricians who were given an annual subsidy by Emperor Vespasian. He rapidly attained preeminence among Roman teachers. His emphasis on moral principle as a factor in education must have made a profound impression in the dissolute society of his time. A famous epigram by Martial, dated A.D. 84, indicates his prominence at that time:

> *Quintiliane, vagae moderator summe iuventae,*
> *Gloria Romanae, Quintiliane, togae.*[16]

The fame of his pupils is another mark of his own position. Pliny the Younger was one of them, and the satirist Juvenal remarks several times on Quintilian's good influence on the young; there has been some suggestion that Pliny's friend Tacitus may also have been a pupil, and the same has been said of another historian, Suetonius. Even after the teacher's retirement, the Emperor Domitian entrusted for a time to Quintilian the education of his two grandnephews. Quintilian amassed sufficient wealth, either from his law practice or his teaching, to regard himself as blessed by fortune, at least economically; Juvenal confirms his judgment.[17]

The peak of public recognition as a teacher came in A.D. 88 when, according to the historian Jerome, Quintilian was placed in charge of the "first public school of Rome" with an annual salary paid from public funds.[18] It was evident that even without this post, he was widely acknowledged as the first teacher of Rome. Quintilian retired from teaching, as he tells us, to secure "rest from my labors, which for twenty years I had devoted to the instruction of youth" (1. Preface 1). This would have been sometime around A.D. 90. During his retirement, Quintilian received still another honor—the dignity of consular rank, bestowed by the Emperor Domitian—which was, for that time, an unparalleled accolade for a rhetor.[19] There is no record of Quintilian after Domitian was assassinated in A.D. 96, and it is probable that he died sometime before the year 100.[20]

It was during Quintilian's retirement that he wrote his major work, the *Institutio oratoria*, or *The Education of the Orator*. In his preface addressed to Marcellus Victorius, he shares that for a long time he had resisted his friends' requests that he write on the art of speaking. And in the opening letter to his "publisher," the bookseller Trypho, Quintilian points out that he had spent two years on research and writing, followed by another period of reflection and, presumably, editing. So the book was written between about A.D. 92 and 95.

Sometime earlier he had written another book, now lost, called *De causis corruptae eloquentiae* (*On the Causes of the Corruption of Eloquence*).[21] Like other famous writers, he suffered from the depredations of literary pirates who copied his lectures (3.6.68) or who falsely circulated books under his name (1. Preface 7). It is known from Quintilian's own testimony (7.2.24) that he published one of his courtroom speeches given in the case of Naevius of Arpinum; in the same passage he takes pains to point out, however, that this is the only one he has ever published and that others being circulated as his contain little genuine material. The flattery of ascription continued even after his death; there appeared two sets of *declamationes*, or fictitious speeches, that were reputed to be his.[22]

Not everything in Quintilian's life was success and honor, however. Tragedy struck the life of Rome's greatest teacher three times, each time in conjunction with his writings. The poignant opening of Book 6 of the *Institutio oratoria* records his grief at the loss, first, of his nineteen-year-old wife and then of a five-year-old son, both apparently about the time of his retirement. He then rested all his hopes on his second son, Quintilian, to whom he had hoped to present the completed book "so that if the fates should cut me off before him, as would have been but just and desirable, he might still have his father's precepts to guide him" (6. Preface 1). His hope was in vain. Quintilian's ten-year-old son died, leaving his father alone to continue his great work, now only for the "studious youth" of Rome to whom he commends the book in the final paragraph of Book 12.

His *Institutio oratoria* (circa A.D. 95)

Quintilian spent only two years writing and one year reflecting and editing this book, but, as one scholar observed, it represents a lifetime of experience in speaking and teaching. Quintilian states his purpose in the preface to Book 1, "We are to form, then, the perfect orator, who cannot exist unless he is above all a good man. We require in him, therefore, not only a consummate ability in speaking, but also every excellence of mind" (1. Preface 9).

This blending of moral purpose and artistic skill is emphasized throughout the whole book. For this reason, the *Institutio oratoria* is perhaps the most ambitious single treatise on education that the ancient world produced. Each section of the book is built around the ideal of the perfect citizen-orator. In fact, Quintilian later defines oratory itself as *vir bonus dicendi peritus*, or "the good man speaking well" (12.1.1)

The *Institutio oratoria* has been described as four major works blended into one: a treatise on education, a manual of rhetoric, a reader's guide to the best authors, and a handbook on the moral duties of the orator.[23] The work is divided into twelve books. Quintilian's own outline of it gives a good overview and a keen sense of its moral basis.

The first book, therefore, will contain those particulars which are antecedent to the duties of the teacher of rhetoric. In the second book we shall consider the first elements of instruction under the hands of the professor of rhetoric and the questions which are asked concerning the subject of rhetoric itself. The next five will be devoted to invention (for under this head will also be included arrangement); and the four following, to elocution, within the scope of which fall memory and pronunciation.[24] One will be added, in which the orator himself will be completely formed by us, since we shall consider, as far as our weakness shall be able, what his morals ought to be, what should be his practice in undertaking, studying, and pleading causes, what should be his style of eloquence, what termination there should be to his pleading, and what may be his employments after its termination. (1. Preface 21–22)

Thus Quintilian intends everything—both rhetorical technique and good morals—to work toward the formation of the citizen-orator. As he says in Book 1's preface, "Nothing is unnecessary to the art of oratory" (1. Preface 5). Nevertheless, Quintilian wrote his book during the reign of the Emperor Domitian, a man whom the historian Tacitus calls a "monster," and repressive political conditions limited such an orator's opportunities to speak: the Roman senate had survived in structure but was beginning to deteriorate into a huddle of terrorized sycophants existing at the pleasure of imperial military power.[25] There was no longer any safe public position in Rome for the outspoken citizen of the type that Cicero represented in the days of the Roman Republic. Part of Cicero's fame as an orator stems from his public denunciations of enemies of the state—of Catiline, the senator who attempted armed revolution, and later of the Antony who quarreled with Octavian over control of the Roman state. Even though Cicero's enemies eventually triumphed over him, hunting him down and killing him, his speeches were listened to and his judgment respected in the Roman senate and forum.

Not so in Quintilian's day. In the year after he arrived from Spain, A.D. 69, three emperors rose and fell in one year: two were killed and one committed suicide. Vespasian and Titus provided a fairly calm period from A.D. 69 to 81; but during the reign of Domitian (A.D. 81–96), an active secret police preyed on the Roman population, and even senators were encouraged to inform on each other. Death or exile was the punishment for the crime of *laesa maiestas*. In Cicero's day this had been a crime of treasonable lessening of the authority of the people or their officials, but under Domitian even the slightest suspicion of disrespect for the emperor became a capital crime. Nor was Domitian merely opposed to political conspiracies; he went so far as to expel philosophers from Rome in A.D. 95.

Even Quintilian felt the breath of jealous tyranny. As he states at the beginning of Book 4, the Emperor Domitian entrusted his two grandnephews to him for their education. But by the time Quintilian finished the *Institutio oratoria*, the two young men—potential rivals to a shaky throne—had vanished into exile. This episode in particular must have made a painful impression on Quintilian. Certainly, his allusions to social corruption are veiled and circumspect, and he draws his examples of virtue and vice from Rome's glorious past rather than its more ignoble present. But his continuous concern with moral virtue can best be understood in the context of an age in which public morals seemed to have descended to a savage low. In a supreme act of irony, the Emperor Domitian became *censor perpetuus* (perpetual censor), making himself responsible for public morals. It is a final indication of the age's temper that in A.D. 96 Domitian was murdered in a conspiracy that not only involved his secretaries and his personal praetorian guard but his wife Domitia as well.

Yet Quintilian is not wistfully looking to a bygone day. He has great hopes. He envisions his citizen-orator displaying eloquence "on trials, in councils, at the assemblies of the people, in the senate, and in every province of the good citizen" (12.11.1). Elsewhere he declares that "the orator must above all things study morality" (12.2.1). It is thus that careful people give advice under a dictator. Quintilian's clear implication is that a skillful citizen with a strong moral sense can only act to improve society. But he is never more explicit than that, so that his reflections on good citizenship retain a charming generality that have made them easily applicable to ages other than his own.

What to Look for in Reading Quintilian

As we have noted, reading Quintilian today can be misleadingly easy. His words flow easily, producing what might be called a user-friendly text. He is a master of transitions, providing frequent links between ideas so that the reader is led along with him as if he were speaking rather than writing. (See, for example, the clarity of his outline for the whole book in his preface, sections 21–22.) Quintilian gives additional dimension to his own ideas by frequent discussion of other writers' ideas and his opinions of them, as in his praise of music at the beginning of chapter 10 in Book 1.

Even so, the modern reader can identify three levels of understanding in these translations.

The first and easiest level is Quintilian's concern for the way his students learn. His text is studded with remarks about the necessity of variety, the value of competition, the care needed in correction, the use of memory in learning, the consequence of differences in age, the role of listening, the place of vocabulary, and the like. Quintilian is not an educational theorist in the sense of announcing grand precepts; instead, he explains at every turn why he prefers this or that practical mode of instruction, often with comments about other people's ways. A careful reader, therefore, can adduce from these texts the overriding principles he has in mind.

The second level of understanding is at the practical level of individual teaching methods. As we have noted earlier, virtually every individual exercise was inherited from the Greeks but "Latinized" by the Romans. Most of the time Quintilian tells us precisely what he has in mind, as when he discusses the value of gymnastics for body control (1.11.15), but sometimes he takes for granted things that now require explanation in notes, as in his rapid discussion of chreia, or anecdote (1.9.4). Nevertheless, the modern reader may come to appreciate individual classroom activities as he lays them out for us.

The third level of understanding is the most difficult, since it calls on the reader to appreciate the architectonic nature of the whole apparatus. Everything is intended to fit together. Nothing is to be wasted. Quintilian warns us about this from the very beginning: "For myself, I consider that nothing is unnecessary to the art of oratory" (1. Preface 5). If, then, the modern reader cannot at first glance understand some point—meditation in Book 10, for example—a rereading is in order, to see how the point fits into the grand plan envisioned by the author.

This three-dimensional aspect of the translations offered here does of course pose some challenges to the modern reader, but Quintilian points out that "there is no one who has not gained something by study" (1.1.3).

Books One and Two: Early Teaching Methods

With the *Institutio oratoria*'s structure in mind, it is easier to understand the role played by the first two books. On the surface, the books deal merely with the training of a young boy who will someday be a public orator; in reality, they embody Quintilian's whole theory of education, his concept of the moral citizen, and his prescriptions for the technical training of an oratorical artist. These first two books are the keystones of the whole *Institutio oratoria*: The long discussion of rhetoric that fills the middle of the work depends upon the early education described in the opening books. Book 10's methods for the adult learner and the ideal orator sketched out magnificently in Book 12 cannot exist without the double discipline of technique and morals of Books 1 and 2.

Education for Quintilian begins in the cradle and ends only when life ends.[26] And he is quick to note that every experience can educate, for good or ill. In fact, Quintilian declares that attention to such details is vitally necessary. Together with painstaking attention to the details of young students' lives, the author provides a series of gradually intensifying rhetorical and literary exercises calculated to sharpen their writing and speaking talents. It is also significant that the prescribed readings are chosen for their moral as well as their technical value. "Care is to be taken, above all things," he admonishes, "that tender minds, which will imbibe deeply whatever has entered them while rude and ignorant of everything, may learn not only what is eloquent, but, still more, what is morally good" (1.8.4). Consequently, Homer and Virgil rank high with Quintilian as exemplars of both artistic excellence and moral probity. And the infant's nurse is even seen as an educational influence worthy of careful selection for speech and morals.

Quintilian's remarks are so humanely sensible that any type of summary or outline can only give a false impression of their contents. The *Institutio oratoria* is not a schematic, rigidly organized textbook stating its author's views in dogmatic terms. He discusses each major point fairly, noting contrary opinions where they exist, always explaining his own viewpoint on the basis of experience or precedent. For example, readers should note at the outset of Book 1 his careful discussion of public schools as opposed to private tutoring. No bare outline of even this brief passage could give an adequate indication of the personality that shines through here as it does in so many other parts of the work.

There is, nevertheless, a careful framework to these first two books. Book 1 deals with early or pre-school training, and then with the subjects to be taught by the *grammaticus*, or teacher of "grammar." This subject for Quintilian includes both the rules of syntax and what we would today call "literature." Book 2 takes the student into the classroom of the *rhetor*, the teacher of rhetoric who leads the young boys through further exercises culminating in the *declamatio*, or the presentation of speeches on fictitious themes. (As Stanley F. Bonner has pointed out, girls may have been present in some grammar schools, but rhetorical training was exclusively for the young male.)[27]

Quintilian's basic organizational pattern is the developing educational progress of the young pupil. Book 1 begins at the cradle, and the education of the future citizen proceeds by acquaintance, first with letters, then with sentences, and finally with whole poems and speeches. The early exercises (*progymnasmata*) of the teacher of grammar (*grammaticus*) begin with the simple and add complexity at each stage. The teacher first has the student recast fables and poems, thus reworking the ideas of other people. Then the teacher advances to asking the students to express their own ideas in the amplification of weighty aphorisms (*sententiae*), and in the explanation of anecdotes (*chreiae*). In later essays the pupil learns to discuss the characters of people in the exercise known as *ethologia*. During this period, the student also takes lessons from a professional teacher of enunciation—from an actor, in fact. The pupil studies other arts, like geometry, music, and bodily control from a gymnast.

Quintilian does not go into extensive detail about the specific sequence of the preliminary exercises, but he may not have needed to: they likely formed such an essential part of the school curriculum of his day that he could reasonably expect his readers to already know them well. Despite his brief treatment, the *progymnasmata* (though he doesn't use that term) form an important foundation for the educational program that he outlines. Greek in origin, the earliest surviving textbook illustrating their use was written by Aelius Theon of Alexandria in the latter half of the first Christian century, about the time of Quintilian. The two most popular Greek textbooks on the *progymnasmata* came later, and were written by Hermogenes of Tarsus (second century) and Aphthonius of Antioch (fourth century), respectively. Both had an impact that extended into the Middle Ages, the Renaissance, and beyond; in fact, the influence of Aphthonius's text, the more popular of the two, reached even to the schools of colonial America.

These preliminary exercises were so named because they were meant to pave the way for the more complex exercise of declamation, the fictitious speeches that were the main form of practice in the rhetoric school themselves, but Quintilian evidently had a higher opinion of their importance and complexity than many of his contemporaries. In fact, when he discusses in Book 2 the proper provinces of rhetoric teachers and grammarians, he criticizes the common practice of relegating the preliminary exercises entirely to the grammar school, arguing instead that the teacher of rhetoric "does not shrink from the earliest duties of his profession" (2.1.8).

His insistence on this point probably follows from the importance he placed on gradual progress in a student's early studies. Quintilian admonished teachers to not, "through ostentatious haste, begin where they ought to end, and, while they wish to show off their pupils in matters of greater display, retard their progress by attempting to shorten the road" (1.4.22). Quintilian believed that if students were able to master the skills contained in narrowly delimited exercises, they would ultimately be able to transmute them into a habitual way-of-being that functioned effectively in the complexities of real-world situations. Indeed, the relationship between specific skills of the sort taught by individual *progymnasmata* and the cultivation of an overall rhetorical habit is a fundamental principle in Quintilian's pedagogical approach. While describing the exercise of paraphrase, for instance, he notes that whoever "shall successfully perform this exercise, which is difficult even for accomplished professors, will be able to learn anything" (1.9.3). Clearly, Quintilian believed that the *progymnasmata* added up to something greater than the sum of their parts.

This effectiveness depended largely on the exercises' sequential structure, each building on the last and leading to the next. The following, a brief overview of twelve *progymnasmata* exercises common in Quintilian's time, gives a sense of this clear progression.

1. *Fable.* In this first and simplest exercise, the student retells a well-known fable in his own words. Part of the challenge involves changing the length and detail of the original story by either focusing on its most important elements or by adding additional, imagined dialogue and action.
2. *Tales.* In this slightly more complex exercise, the student recounts an event drawn from either history or literature.
3. *Chreia.* For this exercise, the student elaborates on the words or actions of individual characters (such as those he was dealing with more generally in the previous two exercises).
4. *Proverb.* This is another exercise in amplification similar to *chreia*, but here the student speaks about an aphorism rather than a character's words or actions.

5. *Refutation and confirmation.* Like the fable and tale stages, this exercise focuses on a narrative. But here an additional argumentative element is introduced, as the student must prove or disprove an account of an event.

6. *Commonplace.* In this exercise the student is given an established fact and asked to "color" or—in contemporary terms—to "spin" it, casting an either positive or negative light on the fact by the way it is explained.

7. *Encomium.* This exercise utilizes similar skills of praise and blame but in a more integrated and ethical sense. Rather than focusing on an isolated fact, here the student must praise or criticize a subject's virtue or vice.

8. *Comparison.* This exercise builds on encomium, but here the student must not only praise or blame a single person or thing but compare the virtues and vices of two subjects in a single composition.

9. *Impersonation.* Here the student is asked to go a step further in his understanding of complex characters by not only praising or blaming their virtues or vices but by *playing* them directly, composing imaginary speeches that such characters might plausibly have given in particular situations.

10. *Description.* In this exercise in vivid description (*ecphrasis*), the student describes a place or a scene as vividly as possible with the goal of "bringing before the eyes"—a phrase used by Theon, Hermogenes, and Aphthonius, as well as Quintilian.

11. *Thesis.* In this exercise, the student composes a complex response to a "general question" (*quaestio infinita*)—that is, a question about general principles rather than individual characters, such as "Should a man marry?" or "Should one fortify a city?"

12. *Laws.* In this last and most difficult *progymnasmata*, the student composes an argument in favor of or opposition to a law. This exercise comes last because it is so complex. As Quintilian notes, "The praise or censure of laws requires more mature powers, such as may almost suffice for the very highest efforts" (2.4.33). In other words, if the student can succeed in this exercise he is almost ready for the final step in his educational progress: declamation.

When the pupil graduates to the teacher of rhetoric (*rhetor*), he does not abandon these elementary exercises but rather adds to them the more advanced drills he now takes up. These include narration, refutation and confirmation, encomium and invective, commonplaces, and criticism of laws. Thus, there is a direct link to early training. Composition becomes a more complex matter at this second stage, with the student taking up plot summaries of tragedies and comedies; he also begins the analysis of legendary and historical narration. In a manner analogous to what happens under the *grammaticus*, the pupil first studies the speech and writing of others before spreading his own wings to undertake original composition.

The difference is that the materials studied are far more complex. Eventually, the student is asked to deliver elementary panegyrics and comparisons as a prelude to actual amplification of typical propositions of a general nature (*loci communes*, or "commonplaces"). Later the *rhetor* provides speech outlines that the students are to use as the basis for their own speeches. The final preparatory exercise is criticism of laws, a preparation for reality outside the classroom.

The culmination of all this preparation is the *declamatio* (the "declamation"), or speech on a fictitious theme. Today we might call declamations "case studies," asking students to solve an assigned problem. At this stage, the young man is deemed ready to take up the two main types of declamation: the fictitious court case (*controversia*), or the imaginary political or deliberative problem (*suasoria*). In these exercises the student is given a statement of a problem and asked to prepare an appropriate speech giving his solution. Obviously, this requires all the student's abilities in thought, organization, phrasing, and oral presentation. The declamation, involving all his talents, thus makes a fitting climax to the preparation of the citizen-orator.

The declamation, as the ultimate preparation for real life, is purposely difficult. Abstruse questions of inheritance law, sibling rivalry, and pirate ransom are common in the records that have survived. A modern example might be this kind of challenge: Your sister has been kidnapped, and her abductors say they will kill her if you tell the police. Prepare an explanation of your response. Or another might be this: You find an unmarked envelope on the sidewalk containing fifteen one hundred dollar bills. Explain your decision whether to turn the money in to the authorities.

Another major feature of this educational program is imitation (*imitatio*)—the careful following of models until the student is prepared to branch out into his own inventions. Quintilian proposes this method under both the teacher of grammar and teacher of rhetoric, keeping in mind all the while that the very presence of the living teacher supplies the student with still another object of imitation. "It cannot be doubted," he says, "that a great portion of art consists in imitation" (10.2.1). This principle underlies much of what he asserts throughout the first two books; he is conscious of the power of imitation, even while the child is still in the cradle listening to its nurse, and it colors his judgments even about such matters as deciding whether a student should be corrected in front of his classmates. It helps him decide, too, that ancient writers, like Homer and Virgil, are the best exemplars for the student to keep in mind, either for speaking or for writing.

This ancient practice of imitation is misunderstood today. Some people mistake it for plagiarism, the copying of another person's words and style. Yet the basic principle is that the student can absorb new methods and even thoughts by emulating what someone else has already done. The object is not to plagiarize Homer, for example, but to learn by emulating the best of that writer's capacities. A modern example might be to ask a student to prepare a funeral oration in the way Abraham Lincoln did in his Gettysburg Address. In all of these classroom drills, there is a constant interplay between the three types of expressions—reading, writing, and speaking, with critical listening as an important, assumed fourth adjunct. Sometimes this interplay involves translation from Greek into Latin, or Latin into Greek; sometimes it involves paraphrase, as when Aesop's fables are abstracted from the Greek into shorter Latin narratives. Even the reading itself is connected to oral expression; the young boy learns very early to read aloud, first by hearing his teacher (*praelectio*), and then by reading the same passages himself (*lectio*). Quintilian later commends the judgment of Cicero that writing is the greatest molder of oral skill.

Textual criticism is a constant tool of education for Quintilian. His sensible comments on various authors appear throughout the whole *Institutio oratoria*—there are eleven hundred references to Latin literature and two hundred to Greek[28]—but in the early books he gives very explicit methodological direction to the reader. For instance, he outlines the critical duties of the teacher:

But let the tutor, above all things, impress upon the minds of his pupils what merit there is in a just disposition of parts, and a becoming treatment of subjects; what is well suited to each character; what is to be commended in the thoughts, and what in the words; where diffuseness is appropriate, and where contraction. (1.8.17)

While he gives only brief directions in the early books as to choice of models for study (see 2.5.18), he does devote a considerable portion of Book 10 to a discussion of specific orators and writers (10.1.30). It is clear from what he says in Books 1 and 2 that a similar array of models would be available for the elementary education of the young.

The connection of sound and sense is always one of Quintilian's preoccupations. He is convinced that adequate linguistic training is a prerequisite for any user of language: hence his insistence on a careful study of word formation and pronunciation, his lengthy treatment of etymology and analogy, and the other minutiae that sometimes exasperate the modern reader. At first glance, chapters 4 through 7 of the first book may seem unnecessarily tedious in their detail, but even the modern reader can learn something of Quintilian's method from these pages. Why, for instance, does he discuss such things as *solecism* (fault in one or more words) and *barbarism* (fault in a single word) in these chapters? He tells us two reasons: both to increase knowledge and to "sharpen the wits of boys" (1.4.6). Even more basic, however, is his conviction that grammar is the fundamental science. Without it, no reading, no writing, no speaking is possible.

Quintilian's famous defense of grammar (that is, including "literature") early in chapter 4 may serve to justify his handling of the many details that follow the statement.

Those, therefore, are not to be heeded who deride this science as trifling and empty; for unless it lays a sure foundation for the future orator, whatever superstructure you raise will surely fall. It is an art which is necessary to the young, pleasing to the old, and an agreeable companion in retirement. Alone, of all the departments of learning, it has in it more service than show. (1.4.5)

If this is grammar's importance in his eyes, it is not surprising that his careful treatment of it bears out his promise in the preface that

"I shall not shrink from stooping to those lesser matters, the neglect of which leaves no place for greater" (1. Preface 5). His first example in the fourth chapter is indeed on the very narrow, yet fundamental, question of whether the Roman alphabet is complete enough. He warns that no man should look down on the elements of grammar as a small matter.

Again, it should be remembered that in Quintilian's day there was no standard textbook of Latin grammar to which he could refer. Therefore, he is obliged to make his own detailed expositions of grammar.

This painstaking attention to detail is balanced by a remarkable sensitivity to individual differences in his pupils. After delivering some general observations at one point concerning the proper means of correcting students, he adds this judgment: "Different ages, however, are to be corrected in different ways, and work is to be required and amended according to the degree of the pupil's abilities" (2.4.14). Even his criterion for sending the boy to the *rhetor* is a reflection of the same concern for individual differences. He asks when the boy should be advanced to the second teacher, and answers, "When he shall be qualified" (2.1.8). It is evident that in a given set of pupils, Quintilian would have some advancing at different rates of speed.

Sometimes a brilliant flash of psychological insight, breaking out of an otherwise sober passage, gives us a brief glimpse of the master teacher as a human being who must have delighted in his pupils. In the second book, for instance, he slips imperceptibly away from a discussion of narration into a series of revealing opinions about the natural exuberance of boys, the danger of a "dry master," and the bad effects of too much correction of the young. Then, as if catching himself up, he labels all this a digression and returns to his technical exposition.

The *Institutio oratoria*, then, is much more than a dry exposition of an experienced teacher's reflections on education. Significantly, he begins the book with advice to fathers to have only the highest aspirations for their sons. Throughout the work he exhorts his readers not to despair of perfection merely because perfection is difficult. His own goal—to make possible "the good man speaking well" (12.1.1)—calls for the highest artistic aspirations on the part of both teacher and pupil. And yet his program calls for severe discipline in the practical details of the art of expression, so that mere hopes can never be allowed to act as a substitute for artistic skill founded on good training.

Perhaps Quintilian's own statement on the nature of "rules" would make a fitting résumé of his whole attitude toward the education of the citizen-orator.

But let no man require from me such a system of precepts as is laid down by most authors of *books of rules*, a system in which I should have to make certain laws, fixed by immutable necessity, for all students of eloquence . . . for rhetoric would be a very easy and small matter, if it could be included in one short body of rules, but rules must generally be altered to suit the nature of each individual case, the time, the occasion, and necessity itself. Consequently, one great quality in an orator is discretion, because he must turn his thoughts in various directions, according to the different bearings of his subject. (2.13.1–2)

The liberal education of such a man of discretion—that is the subject of the whole *Institutio oratoria*. Rhetoric, or the theory of effective communication, is for Quintilian merely the tool of the broadly educated citizen who is capable of analysis, reflection, and then powerful action in public affairs. Thus it is that Quintilian refuses to provide rigid rules for the education of the citizen-orator; instead, he aims to develop the minds and talents of young men who can themselves decide their own actions in the public arena.

Quintilian's text is so easy to follow, and his advice so sensible, that it may be tempting for some readers to overlook the fact that what he describes is, in fact, a rigorous and carefully constructed sequence of learning exercises. If there is indeed an art that conceals art, Quintilian has an art that almost conceals method.[29]

Quintilian did not invent these teaching methods. For the most part, the use of particular exercises dates back to the fourth century B.C. The French educational historian Henri Marrou comments about one device (textual analysis) that "there is not much to be said about the actual method of teaching beyond the fact that it was the Hellenistic method all over again."[30] British classicist Donald A. Russell says of another mode (declamation) that "everything about the exercises makes it clear that they were a Greek invention. . . . Greeks did not learn from Romans, least of all in rhetoric."[31]

Many of the names (*chreia*; *prosopopeia*, or impersonation; *thesis*) come directly into Latin usage from the Greek, while Quintilian himself frequently reminds his readers of the Greek background—for example, "What the Greeks call *orthography*, we may call the art of writing correctly" (1.7.1)—and he remarks in one place about "the Greeks, who are more happy [than we are] in inventing names" (1.5.32). He recognizes the antiquity of exercises in speaking on fictitious cases (2.4.41).

However, the Roman contribution was architectonic. The school described by Quintilian was not a cafeteria of assorted items, to be picked up or discarded at random or by the whim of the teacher. Just as the basic form of the building arch was known in Mesopotamia as early as 4000 B.C. but was adopted by the Romans as an integral part of their architecture, so the Romans took from the Greeks the elements of educational process, which they then shaped into an integrated system. That system, as we have seen, worked so well that it outlasted its architects.

Isocrates, rather than Plato or Aristotle, is the ultimate inspiration for this Roman collation of methods. Stressing a trilogy of talent, education, and practice, Isocrates promoted a broad educational program using language study as a means of preparing for citizenship as well as for the communicative skills themselves.[32] By Cicero's time the Roman study of rhetoric, technical though it might have been when taken by itself, was already embedded in a larger sociopolitical framework for which the schools were the training ground.[33] Each teaching unit, in other words, was not used for its own sake alone but was intended as part of a larger whole. Effective oratory for public citizenship was the aim, and even though history shows that the ideal of citizenship was stifled under the empire, the schools continued to provide thorough training even if their later graduates often had oratorical objectives of which Isocrates and Cicero would not have approved.[34] It is this effective system that Quintilian describes.[35]

Space does not permit a detailed analysis here of all the methods used. A great deal has been written about Greco-Roman teaching, of course, and there are especially valuable treatments in Baldwin, Bonner, Clark, Gwynn, Little, Marrou, Parks, and others listed in the Suggestions for Further Reading.

The section below on Quintilian in the modern classroom presents a brief listing of the main methods that appear throughout the text of the *Institutio oratoria*. Each method is defined either in the text or in the preceding section of this introduction, but it may be easier for the reader to grasp the extent of the terms' coverage when they are seen as a list.[36] They fall into five categories: (1) precept, (2) imitation, (3) composition exercises (*progymnasmata*), (4) declamation, and (5) sequencing.

Perhaps the most important aspect of these methods is their coordination into a single instructional program. Each is important for itself but takes greater importance from its place within the whole. The outline below may illustrate how these elements fit together in the first two books of the *Institutio oratoria*.

BOOK ONE

Preface: The purpose is to form the perfect orator.
A. Earliest lessons in speech (education begins in cradle; begin with Greek; public education, not private)
B. Studies with *grammaticus*
    1. In diction as usage
    2. In diction as style, learned through reading
        a. Reading by the pupils
        b. Detailed analysis of poetry (*praelectio*) with reading aloud (*lectio*)
    3. In composition
        a. Retelling of fables
        b. Paraphrase of poetry
        c. Writing of aphorisms (*sententiae*)
        d. Formal amplification of anecdotes (*chreiae*)
        e. Character descriptions (*ethologiae*)
    4. In contributory subjects (music, geometry, astronomy) necessary for the perfect orator
    5. In enunciation (lessons from an actor)
    6. In several varied studies simultaneously

BOOK TWO

C. Studies with *rhetor*
    1. Learn from his example (ideal teachers' qualifications)

   2. Exercises in composition
       a. Rehearsal of events
            I. Summary of the plot of a tragedy (*tabula*) or a
               comedy (*argumentum*)
           II. Summary of historical event (*historia*)
       b. Elementary analysis of statements of facts (refutation
          and confirmation of narration)
            I. Analysis of legends
           II. Analysis of history
       c. Elementary panegyric (*laudatio*) and parallel (*comparatio*)
       d. Amplification of typical proposition (*loci communes, theses*)
   3. *Rhetor*'s analysis of models (*praelectio*)
   4. *Rhetor*'s reading of speeches (*lectio*)
   5. Speeches from assigned outline (*praeformata*)
   6. Memorization of models (not students' own compositions)
   7. Advice to teachers on correction and promotion (individual
      treatment of pupils)
   8. Speeches on a hypothetical case (*declamatio*)
       a. Deliberative (*suasoria*)
       b. Forensic (*controversia*)

Book 2 concludes with a discussion of the nature of oratory and
rhetoric, preliminary to a detailed treatment of the five parts of
rhetoric—invention, arrangement, style, memory, and delivery—
which occupies Books 3 through 9 and all of Book 11. Book 10 deals
with the relation of reading, writing, and speaking; and the final one,
Book 12, describes the ideal orator as "a good man speaking well."

Book Ten: Adult Self-Education Methods

Some modern scholars are perplexed by the fact that after com-
pleting the lengthy discussion of style that occupies Books 8 and 9,
Quintilian turns in Book 10 to a fervent defense of self-study instead
of going on in the customary fashion to begin a treatment of the
next two "parts of rhetoric," memory and delivery.[37]

   Nevertheless, there is good reason for the position of Book 10. Its
subject is *facilitas*, or the readiness to use language in any situation.
All the precepts of invention, arrangement, and style have been

rehearsed in the preceding books; these are things that children begin to learn. How does the adult acquire the deeply ingrained capacity for improvisation? Quintilian's answer is that the adult must consciously undertake a continuation of the interrelated learning activities once forced on him by the schoolmaster when he was too young to understand the process he had to undergo in the school. If the adult learner does not do this, he will not benefit from the precepts of memory and delivery that are shortly to follow.

In this sense, Book 10 is an adult's commentary on Books 1 and 2 because here Quintilian explains in greater detail the "why" of the school regimen. The difference is that the adult must now know the why of what he does, while as a child he needed only to follow the directions of his master. As he says,

I am not here saying how the orator is to be trained—for that has been told already, if not satisfactorily, at least as well as I could—but by what kind of discipline an athlete who has already learned all his exercises from his master, is to be prepared for real contests. (10.1.4)

Consequently, the modern reader should take all three books together to gain a clear picture of Quintilian's plan for learning how to speak and write. Book 10 is not just another parallel to the earlier books but is additional material to be piled on top of them, just as the second story of a building is piled on top of the first floor.

The most important thing he says in Book 10 is that writing, reading, and speaking are inseparably related.

I know that it is often asked whether more is contributed by writing, by reading, or by speaking. This question we should have to examine with careful attention if in fact we could confine ourselves to any one of these activities; but in truth they are all so connected, so inseparably linked with one another, that it [if] any one of them is neglected, we labor in vain in the other two—for our speech will never become forcible and energetic unless it acquires strength from great practice in writing; and the labor of writing, if left destitute of models from reading, passes away without effect. (10.1.1–2)

What may be less apparent to the modern reader is that Quintilian includes listening as one of the key elements here. Listening is closely related to reading, not only because the way of learning by hearing is analogous to learning by seeing, but because in ancient times the act of reading itself had an audible aspect. The silent reading to which we are accustomed is largely a phenomenon caused by the introduction of mass-produced printed texts in the fifteenth century. When there were fewer texts, read more slowly and carefully, it was common to vocalize while reading—that is, to pronounce the words as they were read.[38] When printing with movable type made it possible to produce very large numbers of texts,[39] it was no longer feasible to read in such a slow, vocalized manner, and silent reading has been the norm ever since.

Listening for Quintilian is not a passive act. It requires as much conscious application as reading, speaking, or writing. In imitation, for instance, the student is asked to hear a model text read aloud, then asked to hear the text dissected by the master; he is also expected to listen to his colleagues' paraphrases and transliterations and to the master's corrections of those exercises. Quintilian argues that a good stock of words comes not from a memorized vocabulary but from "reading and listening to the best language" (10.1.8). While what is read is easier to remember than what is heard "because the perception of the eye is quicker than that of the ear" (11.2.34), it must be remembered that the whole educational program begins with the child listening—listening to a nurse, a parent, or a *paedagogus* (schoolmaster)—long before he is entrusted with the visible letters of the alphabet.[40] The adult is to continue, on his own, to utilize active listening just as he continues purposefully to read, to write, and to speak so he may gain that *facilitas*, which is the purpose of all his self-training.

Quintilian states quite clearly in chapter 1 that the purpose of Book 10 is to explain how to secure *copia rerum et verborum*, or the "supplies of matters and of words," which when coupled with practice will make *facilitas* possible (10.1.5). This facility, this power of improvisation in any situation, he calls a "habit" (Greek *hexis*). In other words it is to become an almost innate characteristic, and knowledge of the precepts is not enough.[41] Consequently, he takes up the principles of imitation (*imitatio*), which enable the reader to identify the best in what is modeled.[42] He then moves on to the value of practice in writing, including self-correction and meditation as aids, and the value of practice in extempore speaking. At every stage there is correlation between the four elements of listening, reading, writing, and speaking. Quintilian is especially interested in the writing-speaking relationship. For example, he says at one point that "By writing we speak with greater accuracy, and by speaking we write with greater ease" (10.7.29). At another point he says, "In writing are the roots, in writing are the foundations of eloquence" (10.3.3).

Book 10 would be difficult to summarize briefly, just as the rest of Quintilian defies easy summary. His sensible advice about practical matters—where and when to write, for instance, or how much weight to give to correction of drafts—is best seen in his own text.[43] The important point is that he clearly regards Book 10 as an integral part of the lifelong educational plan for which the whole *Institutio oratoria* is composed. Book 10 is the adult counterpart of the child's Books 1 and 2. The rhetorical principles (*praecepta*) of the intervening books only make sense when employed in the real world by a well-taught, and self-teaching, writer-speaker. For these reasons Book 10 deserves as much attention as the first two books, since it completes and supplements, at an adult level, what was provided for the young boys at the beginning of the *Institutio oratoria*. For example, the concept of "meditation" that he introduces here is a process that would have been unsuitable for boys learning the mechanics.

Quintilian in the Modern Classroom

The recent renewal of interest in the *Institutio oratoria* takes its place in the work's long history of adaption and use for a variety of cultural contexts. Although it has never entirely dropped from sight, the influence of the *Institutio oratoria* has reached three great peaks during the two millennia since its composition. In each of these three instances, the book has seemed to reflect the spirit of a whole age and has declined in popularity only when the humanistic tradition itself has suffered a decline.[44]

Quintilian's Influence

Quintilian's immediate influence on his pupils is noted in the regard that Juvenal and other contemporaries have for him; the *Dialogue on Orators* of Tacitus is so close in spirit that some modern scholars have conjectured that perhaps Quintilian and not Tacitus is the true author. In the sense that Quintilian captures the essence of the Roman educational system, it might be said that the schools formed from Roman conquest were another sphere of influence. Indeed, one modern student has declared that a fairly adequate knowledge of Greek and Roman rhetorical education could be based on Quintilian alone.[45] Roman schools, after all, trained such Christian leaders as Origen, Ambrose, Jerome, and Augustine. Saint Augustine, as we have seen earlier, was a teacher of rhetoric in a school following Quintilian's program.

Perhaps the most famous early instance of direct influence is Saint Jerome's noted Letter 107, addressed to Laeta, concerning the education of a Christian girl. The Roman rhetorician Julius Victor, writing in the fifth century, absorbed so much of Quintilian into his own *Ars rhetorica*[46] that some modern editors have used it to correct the text of the *Institutio oratoria*. This seems to have been the peak of ancient influence.

Early medieval citations are rare. Isidore of Seville (560–636), author of a very popular encyclopedia of knowledge known as the *Etymologia* or *Origines*, looks to Quintilian for his discussions of music and of grammatical analogy. Another encyclopedist, Cassiodorus (485–585), eulogizes him. Servatus Lupus (805–62) sought a copy of the *Institutio oratoria*; and Charlemagne's aide, Alcuin, quotes the book apparently through Julius Victor. At some time in the eighth or ninth century the original text of the *Institutio oratoria* was mutilated and shortened, so that later readers did not even have a complete text.

The second major phase of Quintilian's influence took place in twelfth-century France as part of what has been called "The Renaissance of the Twelfth Century."[47] There are a number of references to Quintilian by Wibald of Corvey, Alexander Neckam, and Ulrich of Bamberg. Alain de Lille mentions the spurious declamations in his *Anticlaudianus*.[48] But it is the schools of Chartres and Bec that lay claim to a Renaissance of classical culture in the twelfth century.

John of Salisbury leaves us, in his *Metalogicon* (1159), a graphic description of his own education at Chartres under Bernard, Thierry, and William of Conches. The program was simply that of

Quintilian, as John points out in his praise of *praelectio* and *lectio*.[49] But the resurgence of humane studies was short-lived—even the *Metalogicon* praises the study of dialectic, which was to dominate medieval university training for five centuries. About 1225, Quintilian again slipped into obscurity, this time for a century and a half. It will be remembered that there was, at the time, not even available a complete text of the *Institutio oratoria*.

By the end of the fourteenth century humanist scholars like Gasparino da Barzizza were attempting to fill in the obvious gaps in the mutilated text then available. The poet Petrarch so admired Quintilian that he included a letter to Quintilian among his letters to dead authors. Quintilian's analogy of the whetstone reveals Petrarch's esteem so well that it bears repeating here.

> Thou has performed the office of the whetstone rather
> than that of the knife, and thou hast had greater success in
> building up the orator than in causing him to excel in the
> courts; thou wert a great man, I grant, but thy greatest merit
> lay in the ability to ground and to mold great men.[50]

Meanwhile the humanists' interest in careful literary education was spurred by such events as the official appointment in 1396 Florence of the teacher Chrysoloras. Chrysoloras and his pupils—Leonardo Bruni and P. P. Vergerio among them—advocated minute attention to the basic matters of grammar and literature. The stage was set for the third and most important major period of Quintilian's influence, one that was to last in various forms for more than four centuries.

In the year 1416 the Italian book-hunter Poggio Bracciolini discovered a complete text of the *Institutio oratoria* in an old tower at the monastery of St. Gallen in Switzerland. Poggio wrote to a friend that the priceless manuscript was lodged at the bottom of a dusty tower, which he declared was not even fit for a condemned criminal. So excited was he by the discovery that he personally sat down and copied the entire manuscript. Reaction to the discovery was immediate. Leonardo Bruni wrote to Poggio as follows:

> We have now the entire treatise, of which, before this
> happy discovery, we had only one half, and that in a very
> mutilated state. O what a valuable acquisition! What an

unexpected pleasure! Shall I then behold Quintilian whole and entire, who, even in his imperfect state, was so rich a source of delight? I entreat you, my dear Poggio, send me the manuscript as soon as possible, that I may see it before I die.[51]

An impressive roster of Renaissance educators and literary lights interested themselves in Quintilian after this discovery. Vittorino da Feltre so admired and imitated the author that he became known as *Quintilianus redivivus*, or "Quintilian living again." Lorenzo Valla wrote a commentary on the entire *Institutio oratoria*. Erasmus built his own educational theory around ideas from the book. Juan Vives also borrowed heavily from him. Martin Luther declared that he preferred Quintilian to almost all other authorities on education: "For while he teaches he gives us a model of eloquence. He teaches by a happy combination of theory and practice."[52] Philip Melanchthon, the German educator of the early sixteenth century, also took up some of his ideas. "It will be clear from all this," says F. H. Colson, "that the influence of Quintilian, especially with writers and thinkers on education, was throughout this period immense."[53]

Certainly the printing history of the *Institutio oratoria* indicates that it was a popular book. It was one of the first rhetorical texts to be printed, with two editions published in 1470 in Rome, one edited by Andreas and the other by Campanus. An even one hundred editions were published over the next eighty years, together with a rash of commentaries and summaries; many editions are accompanied by the *Declamationes*, which are falsely ascribed to Quintilian.[54]

Perhaps one of the most telling indications of Quintilian's reputation during this period was the fact that the French educational reformer Peter Ramus, having published attacks on Aristotle in 1543 and then on Cicero in 1547, felt obliged to attack Quintilian as well. It is clear that he regards the three ancient authorities as the triple foundations of an old order that he hopes to overturn in favor of what he terms the true "Method." His *Rhetoricae distinctiones in Quintilianum* (*Arguments in Rhetoric against Quintilian*) was published by Matthew Davis in Paris in September 1549.[55] "The dialectical and rhetorical arts of Aristotle, Cicero, and Quintilian," he says in the preface, "are fallacious and confused in their treatment of the dialectical and rhetorical usage of reason, and then of speech."[56]

Ramus begins by attacking Quintilian's definition of an orator as "a good man speaking well," then proceeds to criticize all twelve books of the *Institutio oratoria* in order. Ramus was widely influential in both Europe and America, and his own *Rhetoricae* went through 103 editions in the century following publication.

In England there was already evident use of Quintilian in Sir Thomas Elyot's *The Book Named the Governor* in the sixteenth century. "In every discipline," he says, "example is the best instructor."[57] Roger Ascham did not seem to share the general enthusiasm for Quintilian; but, on the other hand, Richard Mulcaster, in his *Positions*, praised his rules for choosing writers to study. Ben Jonson paraphrased Quintilian in his *Discoveries*. Perhaps the longest-lasting English influence, however, lay not in the citation or quotation by individual authors, but in the form that literary training took in England from the sixteenth century to the nineteenth century. While many other influences besides those of Quintilian were at work during the Renaissance, it is difficult to examine the early training of someone such as John Milton without concluding that the Roman author's theories had much to do with shaping the curriculum. The young Milton, for instance, undertook the very kind of translation, paraphrasing, and rewriting that Quintilian recommends.[58]

A couplet by the eighteenth-century poet Alexander Pope is often cited as evidence of continuing English use of the *Institutio oratoria*:

> *In grave Quintilian's copious works we find*
> *The justest rules and clearest methods join'd.*[59]

English rhetoricians in the eighteenth and nineteenth centuries, of course, continued to make extensive use of the rhetorical sections, ranking Quintilian along with Cicero and Aristotle. Hugh Blair, George Campbell, and Richard Whately use him to varying degrees in their works on rhetoric. The modern reader of *Tom Brown's School Days* will recognize some of Quintilian's exercises described in the nineteenth-century English school that young Tom attends. At least as late as Whately's *Elements of Rhetoric* (1828), then, Quintilian remained a powerful figure among English writers on education and rhetoric. Benjamin Disraeli and Thomas Macaulay give evidence from the middle of the nineteenth century that he was still read by literary men. John Stuart Mill, as a matter of fact, states in his

Autobiography that "I have retained through life many valuable ideas which I can distinctly trace to my reading of him even at that early age."[60] It might be noted also that Quintilian would have approved readily of John Henry Newman's proposals for "Elementary Studies" in his *Idea of a University* (lectures delivered 1854–56). Newman's principle is "a little, but well," and he actually opens his discussion with an infant greeting the world.[61]

In America, Quintilian's direct influence seems to have been slight during the early colonial period, though the Cambridge University curriculum imported by colonists from England in the 1630s to found New College at Harvard was still influenced by European traditions. By the middle of the eighteenth century, however, his work had achieved some circulation.[62] The American popularity of John Ward's *System of Oratory*, based largely on Quintilian, was another factor. The greatest stimulus probably came, however, from the lectures of John Quincy Adams, who took up the first Boylston Chair of Rhetoric at Harvard in 1806. His lectures, published in 1810, consisted of restatements of the doctrines of Aristotle, Cicero, and Quintilian. By the middle of the nineteenth century, however, the classical rhetorical tradition had lost much ground, although a few schools continued to teach the ancient authors for some time.

The third major period of direct influence, then, beginning with the Renaissance, gradually disintegrated in the nineteenth century. Its indirect force, however, remained in educational programs, especially in England.

Now, at the beginning of the twenty-first century, there is renewed appreciation of Quintilian's importance. As one recent essay declares,

There is no substitute for reading the primary sources! Since we are fortunate to have a comprehensive treatment by a successful orator and teacher, who includes surveys of other theorists' opinions and his own reflections on rhetoric and its pedagogy, the obvious place to start is Quintilian.[63]

Current Views of Quintilian

Since Quintilian has, like rhetoric itself, meant many things to many people, perhaps the best place to begin an evaluation of his current influence on rhetorical pedagogy is at the end—the ultimate goal of a rhetorical education as he envisioned it.[64] As discussed above, Quintilian aimed for the production of the perfect orator, even if he considered that goal to be ultimately unattainable. Lofty as this ideal might have been, it was, nevertheless, highly practical and deeply entwined with a concrete vision of active, effective, and ethical citizenship.

> For I cannot admit that the principles of moral and honorable conduct are, as some have thought, to be left to the philosophers. This is true because the man who can duly sustain his character as a citizen, who is qualified for the management of public and private affairs, and who can govern communities by his counsels, settle them by means of laws, and improve them by judicial enactments, can certainly be nothing else but an orator. (1. Preface 10–11)

Contemporary rhetoric teachers often have similarly civic ideals. Indeed, cultivating "citizenship" has become such a widely shared pedagogical goal that, as Amy Wan has recently argued, the meaning of the word has grown somewhat ambiguous.[65] This ambiguity is potentially problematic because the project of teaching citizenship entails often-implicit value judgments about the kinds of skills necessary for students to become the *right* kinds of citizens.[66] In Quintilian's world, a broadly shared ethical and civic ideal was perhaps a reasonable concept, even if the moral realities of ancient Rome were increasingly complex and violent.[67] Quintilian's students all came from similar social backgrounds and were all being trained for comparable social roles—were all striving, in other words, for the same kinds of social capital.[68]

Contemporary writing teachers can make no such assumptions about their students' backgrounds or their goals. Nevertheless, many teachers continue to think of "citizenship" as a broadly applicable, if ill-defined, ideal—a situation that, according to Wan, can make it easy to "imagine that every student's access to citizenship is equal, and that it is merely a matter of activating a desire to practice citizenship," although "that is not always the case."[69] This notion of equal access may have been much more defensible in the context of an ancient rhetoric school than it is today, and this perhaps marks a point of tension between ancient tradition and changing classroom exigencies.

From a modern perspective, there also seems to be a disconnect between Quintilian's ideal vision of the perfect orator and his highly pragmatic approach. He was, for example, very critical of classroom techniques that he did not see as good training for real, civic practice, and he argued that if an exercise such as declamation were anything other than "preparation for the forum, it is merely like theatrical ostentation, or insane raving" (2.10.8). At the same time, he thought that a rhetorical education should be boundlessly (perhaps impossibly) broad, encompassing not only rhetoric but everything from music (1.10.12) to geometry (1.10.49), a sweeping vision that corresponds to the universal qualities of the perfect orator. Needless to say, modern composition teachers tend to be more constrained in their goals.[70]

Still, some scholars have seen connections between Quintilian's universal vision and the practically focused but cross-disciplinary movement known as Writing across the Curriculum (WAC). In this now well-established and influential approach, writing is situated within the contexts of a variety of other disciplines rather than taught as an independent subject, and students learn to write for specific academic fields rather than in a more general or civic sense. Unsurprisingly, whether or not scholars see Quintilian's program as commensurate with the WAC model largely depends on their view of the end or ideal purpose of a rhetorical education.

Andrew Bourelle has gone so far as to argue that WAC is a direct descendent of the Quintilian tradition.[71] He claims that WAC is the best preparation for an actively engaged civic life precisely because its "ultimate goal is to have students do a lot of writing, in many classes, and in every major" so that writing and rhetoric itself become—in Quintilian fashion—an integral part of learning at every level.[72] Conversely, David Fleming has argued that if all teachers in all disciplines are "theoretically" responsible for writing, "there's always the risk that ultimately *no one* will be responsible for it, and discourse will become, once again, transparent to both teacher and student."[73] More fundamentally, Fleming contends that because "civic discourse is underrepresented at present by a traditional content area," moving rhetoric into independently established disciplines undermines its essential role in the formation of active citizens.[74]

This debate is perhaps most notable for its illustration of the different and often conflicting ways ancient rhetorical pedagogy can be adapted and interpreted by contemporary teachers. In some cases, the overarching spirit or intention of ancient rhetoric is aligned with current pedagogical trends.[75] In other cases, scholars call for a revival of specific ancient practices, often as a response to pedagogical trends that they are calling into question. Either way, such arguments are usually grounded in claims about the relationship between ancient exercises and larger civic goals. Fleming, for instance, argues that a revival of the ancient *progymnasmata* exercises can be a counterweight to approaches such as WAC if the focus is less on the content of the specific exercises themselves than on their larger intention to "make of rhetoric not just a theory or art or an historical and cultural artifact or a sociocognitive process but rather a complete and developmentally attuned curriculum in written and spoken discourse" with the ultimate goal of inculcating "a set of deep-seated verbal habits and dispositions oriented to public effectiveness and virtue."[76] Similarly, Robert Terrill argues that imitation—one of the pillars of Quintilian's pedagogical program—has transhistorical value not just because of the specific rhetorical skills that it fosters but also of the way it cultivates "a set of habituated attitudes toward fellow citizens."[77]

Imitation is a particularly interesting point of comparison between ancient and contemporary approaches to writing pedagogy in part because of how it seems to fly in the face of many long-standing assumptions about authentic expression and sincerity. Peter Elbow, for example, famously claimed in his influential 1973 book *Writing without Teachers* that writers have a distinct, innate "voice" that is "the main source of power in your writing."[78] According to Elbow, this voice can be trained and adapted, but it can never be fundamentally replaced or abandoned because "it's the only voice you've got. It's your only source of power."[79] The practice of imitation and the notion of innate voice appear to be completely contradictory ideas. And while many postmodern scholars have taken issue with Elbow and the "expressivist" movement of which he was an important part on exactly these grounds,[80] the question of where Quintilian would come down on pedagogy that emphasizes students' authentic personal expression is a more complex question than it might initially seem, and is perhaps best approached through an examination of specific classroom practices.

One of the most influential practices advocated by Elbow is "free-writing," an exercise in which the composer simply writes without stopping for a set period of time. During freewriting, there must be no reflection about the best way to word something, no editing, no reading of what has been written. The immediate goal of the practice is to break through mediating layers between thought and language—to simply "put down whatever is in your mind."[81] The ultimate purpose is twofold: First, to clear away inhibiting thought processes (including many learned in school), thereby gaining access to one's authentic and natural "voice"; second, to actually generate ideas and even to produce usable pieces of writing for subsequent drafts.

The first use—predicated on notions of authentic "voice" and identity—is less evident in most newer composition textbooks even if its influence lingers in more subtle ways. Needless to say, Quintilian would probably also oppose any notion of innate or essential voice, especially given his emphasis on imitation. Freewriting is more frequently used for the second purpose, though, particularly as part of the brainstorming or prewriting process. Similar techniques were practiced in the ancient world.

Quintilian, however, did not approve. In the *Institutio oratoria*, he writes,

Of those who wish, first of all, to run through their subject with as rapid a pen as possible, and, yielding to the ardor and impetuosity of their imagination, write off their thoughts extemporaneously, producing what they call a rough copy, which they then go over again, and arrange what they hastily poured forth; but though the words and rhythm of the sentences are mended, there still remains the same want of solid connection that there was originally in the parts hurriedly thrown together. (10.3.17–18)

In this passage, Quintilian is speaking of adult orators rather than students; in the rhetoric school itself, techniques as antithetical to the careful and precise writing process that he has outlined elsewhere in the work would have simply been prohibited by the guiding hand of the teacher.

Related impulses create similar problems, though, even for much younger students: Where the adult may fall into freewriting as a faulty mode of invention, a precocious youngster may, in "striving to attain the command of pure and correct language," err by way of "extemporary garrulity, without waiting for thought, or scarcely taking time to rise," all before a firm foundation in grammatical correctness has paved the way for such speed (2.4.15). Both kinds of faults follow from closely related perversions of the same mental process discussed in both Books 2 and 10, since the generation and selection of content as well as a certain amount of preliminary editing must, according to Quintilian, take place in the mind, before anything is actually cast in words. For the young student, his advice to this effect in Book 2 focuses on correctness and precision in language; for the fully grown orator, his advice in Book 10 focuses more on invention, arrangement, and style. In either context, though, he is referring to work that takes place in the mind rather than on the page.

Let us search for what is best, and not allow ourselves to be readily pleased with whatever presents itself; let judgment be applied to our thoughts, and skill in arrangement to such of them as the judgment sanctions; for we must make a selection from our thoughts and words, and the weight of each must be carefully estimated; and then must follow the art of collocation, and the rhythm of our phrases must be tried in every possible way, since any word must not take its position just as it offers itself. (10.3.5–6)

For Quintilian, then, the composing process takes place primarily in the mind, while, for many process-oriented, modern rhetoric teachers, it takes place in the mind and on the page as well. This is one reason that, in Book 10, Quintilian draws such clear connections between writing, thought, and memory. Writing is important, he argues, not as a way of channeling unmediated thought (as in freewriting), but as a method through which, with sufficient discipline and practice, one can acquire a more powerful and controlled "*form* of thinking," a transformation "which in a great degree depends on memory" (10.6.3).

To be fair, Elbow does not present freewriting as a way to produce final drafts, and he does advocate disciplined revision as part of the writing process. As Jacquelyn Hoermann and Richard Enos note in their review of Elbow's most recent work, *Vernacular Eloquence*, freewriting in the early stages of a writing project must be balanced with careful editing in later stages.

There are times when freewriting "frees up" the author so that she or he can draw from the comfort zone of speech. There are, of course, times for rigorous editing, what some teachers call "polishing the diamond." Overall, Elbow's treatment of speech and writing stresses a pedagogical point: all levels of writing are best learned after we've convinced the student to care. Freewriting, as Elbow points out, does not mean careless writing.[82]

Nevertheless, there is a marked distinction between the way contemporary writing teachers sometimes use such techniques such as freewriting to liberate students' thoughts from inhibiting mental habits and the way Quintilian teaches writing as method of tempering and molding the mind's habit, or *hexis*. This difference probably follows, at least in part, from the de-emphasis in most modern approaches to rhetoric instruction on oral delivery or performance.[83] For contemporary theorists such as Elbow, freewriting is a way of helping students to access the resources of natural speech for purposes of writing well; for Quintilian, writing was always already bound up with speech or oral delivery.

Still, Quintilian's view is somewhat more moderate than it may initially seem. To begin with, he is aware of the dangers of excessive editing, caution, and fear of fault, noting that "it is often the case even with young men of talent, that they wear themselves away with useless labor, and sink into silence from too much anxiety to speak well" (10.3.12). He is also aware of the value of sudden inspiration, though he is far more suspicious of it than many modern writing teachers. "At times, however, if a gale bear us on, we may spread our sails to it, provided that the license which we allow ourselves does not lead us astray" (10.3.7). Furthermore, he definitely believes that writers, young and old, should approach their task by way of a process or method. In one of his more timeless images, Quintilian warns against wallowing in writer's block, waiting in vain for a burst of inspiration rather than employing techniques of methodical investigation.

But to enable us to write more, and more readily, not *practice* only will assist (and in practice there is doubtless great effect) but also *method*, if we do not, lolling at our ease, looking at the ceiling, and trying to kindle our invention by muttering to ourselves, wait for what may present itself, but, observing what the subject requires, what becomes the character concerned, what the nature of the occasion is, and what the disposition of the judge, set ourselves to write like reasonable beings—for thus nature herself will supply us not only with a commencement but with what ought to follow. (10.3.15–16)

Although practices such as imitation might seem directly opposed to many persistent if controversial notions in modern writing instruction, it could be argued that imitation, like freewriting, gave students a way past the overwhelming and crippling anxiety that sometimes hampers acts of writing and speaking—a problem that Quintilian was well aware of.

It is also worth noting that the most important object of imitation, according to Quintilian, is the teacher. As one recent essay points out, "Quintilian comments that teachers of composition should themselves be skilled in composition, and his reasons are as applicable to us as to his Roman audience."[84] Quintilian claims that students are able to most effectively imitate what they directly witness and feel, so the teacher must

speak much every day himself, for the edification of his pupils. Although he may point out to them, in their course of reading, plenty of examples for their imitation, yet the living voice, as it is called, feeds the mind more nutritiously—especially the voice of the teacher, whom his pupils, if they are but rightly instructed, both love and reverence. (2.2.8)

Furthermore, Quintilian sees this dynamic as a two-way exchange: Teachers are more effective when addressing "a large number of hearers" because the crowd's excitement in turn *excites* them, inspiring them to higher levels of eloquence (1.2.30). This is because "eloquence depends in a great degree on the state of the mind, which must conceive images of objects, and transform itself, so to speak, to the nature of the things of which we discourse" (1.2.30). According to Quintilian, then, teachers achieve rhetorical power in the classroom by intuitively imitating the excited mind-set of their listening students—who, in turn, intuitively imitate (because of their excitement) the very rhetorical power they helped inspire in the teacher.

From the point of view of modern approaches to writing pedagogy, though, this very dynamic may seem problematic. As David

Fleming notes, "The triple onslaught of print, capitalism, and romanticism has made us moderns deeply suspicious of imitation; and, in our teaching, we stress nothing so much as the writer's exclusive rights to his or her own language."[85] Nevertheless, cognitive scientists such as Shaun Gallagher would seem to support Quintilian's view about its fundamental role in learning; indeed, Gallagher asserts that imitation is the earliest and most important mechanism of identity formation, occurring even in neonates.[86] Furthermore, the research of cognitive scientists, such as Vittorio Gallese and David Freedberg, indicates that prerational imitation in what they call the "Mirror Neuron System" of the brain underlies most of the emotional and aesthetic experiences that occur throughout the course of a person's life. "We propose that a crucial element of [a]esthetic response consists of the activation of embodied mechanisms encompassing the simulation of actions, emotions and corporeal sensation, and that these mechanisms are universal."[87]

According to Gallese, systems in our brain mirror the actions or feelings of others as if they were our own; we enact "representations" of other people's experiences on a direct, "pre-linguistic and pre-theoretical" level.[88] As such, we imitate an external other before (or below) the distinction between self and other even arises, and this kind of performance actually constitutes the self. What Gallese calls "embodied simulation" is a game we can't not play: imitation literally makes us who we are. Gallese and linguist George Lakoff have further argued that this kind of involuntary imitation plays a very important cognitive role in language use and have even suggested that language itself may be founded on embodied simulation structures.[89]

Since Quintilian's students—unlike many of their contemporary counterparts—delivered their work orally, the implications of this line of research are particularly relevant to the performance that his curriculum involved. Amy Cook, a scholar working on the border between cognitive cultural studies and performance theory, has analyzed how the mirror neuron system affects the experience of not only watching but also performing in live theater. Because of the physical presence of both audience and actor in live theater, she contends, in the mirror neuron system creates a particularly powerful "shared neural substrate linking imagination and understanding, doing and feeling, fact and fiction, actor and character, me and you."[90] Presumably the same would be true in Roman rhetoric schools both when teachers gave demonstrations and when students delivered their own compositions. This dynamic would have served a pedagogical purpose because it would have deepened the students' experience of the rhetorical skills they were trying to acquire and also facilitated the transfer of rhetorical habit from teachers to students and from students to peers, both when students were watching speeches and when they were delivering them—a process very similar to what Quintilian describes.

But intuitive imitation is grounded, in Quintilian's curriculum, by concrete, modular exercises and precepts such as the *progymnasmata*. Modern cognitive science seems to provide support for these kinds of techniques as well. For example, the emerging field that researchers Shinobu Kitayama and Jiyoung Park call "cultural neuroscience," and in particular their concept of "cultural tasks" seems to offer scientific grounding for the idea that repetitive, systematic exercises can have a measurably formative effect on a person's identity. These scholars define cultural tasks as "conventions, routines, and socially shared scripts for action" that, through systematic engagement, actual modify and create "neural processing pathways." In other words, repeated participation in socially scripted forms of behavior—cultural tasks—has been shown in MRI studies to actually change the neural structure of the brain. Such culturally instantiated neural structures in turn facilitate the seamless performance of further "cultural tasks designed to achieve a culture's values," thus "anchoring" "the self and identity in the cultural world." This effect is particularly marked during a "second peak" of neurogenesis that occurs around puberty—the traditional age of Roman rhetoric students.[91]

From another point of view, many scholars studying the pedagogical value of games and play have come to similar conclusions about the value of systematic, carefully structured approaches to teaching and learning—a development Quintilian might well have supported. After all, he was in favor of productive forms of play: "There are some kinds of amusement, too, not unserviceable for sharpening the wits of boys, as when they contend with each other by proposing all sorts of questions in turn" (1.3.11–12).

Jane McGonigal has recently argued, for instance, that games are such effective and compelling mechanisms in part because of their modular, graduated structures.

Satisfying work always starts with two things: a clear goal and actionable next steps toward achieving that goal. Having a clear goal motivates us to act: we know what we're supposed to do. And actionable next steps ensure that we can make progress toward the goal immediately.[92]

Games are so fun and rewarding, she writes, because they are "designed for us to learn them, get better at them, and eventually be successful. Any gamer who puts in the effort can't help but get better."[93]

This bears comparison to Fleming's observation that

the virtue of the ancient system of rhetorical "practice," centered as it was on the progymnasmatic exercise cycle, was not the specific tasks assigned but the way that program provided students with the subcomponents of expert rhetorical performance, broke each component down into teachable patterns or topics, made ample room in the curriculum for a wide variety of such components, ordered them into a thoughtful developmental sequence, and attempted both within each exercise and in the program as a whole to give students practice in the full range of rhetorical activities.[94]

At this point it is suggested that the reader reread the preface that begins this volume. A lesson once learned can be learned again. Ideas do not have any chronology; they can be used again and again.

Notes

1. Two older surveys are still valuable: Henri-Irenée Marrou, *A History of Education in Antiquity*, trans. George Lamb (New York: New American Library, 1964), 68. See also Stanley F. Bonner, *Education in Ancient Rome: From the Elder Cato to the Younger Pliny* (Berkeley: U of California P, 1977), 34–75. And now see the readings in Y. L. Too, ed., *Education in Greek and Roman Antiquity* (Leiden, Netherlands: Brill, 2001).

2. *Cicero, de inventione. De optimo genere oratorum. Topica*, trans. H. M. Hubbell (Cambridge, MA: Harvard UP, 1960). For this development see Robert

N. Gaines, "Roman Rhetorical Handbooks," in *A Companion to Roman Rhetoric*, ed. William Dominik and Jon Hall (Oxford, UK: Blackwell, 2007), 163–80. See also Malcolm Heath, "Codifications of Rhetoric," in *The Cambridge Companion to Ancient Rhetoric*, ed. Erik Gunderson (Cambridge, UK: Cambridge UP, 2009), 59–76.

3. George A. Kennedy, *The Art of Rhetoric in the Roman World: 300* B.C.–A.D. *300* (Princeton, NJ: Princeton UP, 1972), 116. Marrou adds, "There was no real Latin rhetoric. It was an art that had been invented and developed and brought nearer and nearer to perfection by the Greeks" (*History of Education* 383).

4. Quoted in James J. Murphy, Richard A. Katula, and Michael Hoppmann, *A Synoptic History of Classical Rhetoric*, 4th ed. (New York: Routledge, 2013), 124–25. The edict notes that "our ancestors arranged what they wished their children to learn and to what schools they wished them to go."

5. Some details of what Vespasian calls "an active policy of intervention in the matter of schools" may be found in Marrou, *History of Education*, 403–11. Marrou also notes a policy of "Romanization," which included taking provincial children as hostages and putting them into Roman schools (393ff).

6. For the case of one specific province, see Theodore Haarhoff, *The Schools of Gaul* (Oxford, UK: Clarendon, 1920).

7. This debate is summarized in James J. Murphy, *Rhetoric in the Middle Ages: A History of Rhetorical Theory from St. Augustine to the Renaissance* (Berkeley: U of California P, 1974), 48–64.

8. Augustine's contemporary, Saint Jerome, remarks at one point that "we have been rhetoricated" (*Rhetoricati sumus*). Quoted in Charles Sears Baldwin, *Ancient Rhetoric and Poetic* (New York: Macmillan, 1924; rpt. Gloucester, MA: Peter Smith, 1959), 96.

9. See the chapters by Carol Dana Lanham, and Martin Camargo and Marjorie Curry Woods in Murphy, ed., *A Short History of Writing Instruction: From Ancient Greece to Contemporary America* (New York: Routledge, 2012), 77–113, 114–47. See also John O. Ward, "Quintilian and the Rhetorical Revolution of the Middle Ages" *Rhetorica* 13.3 (1995): 231–84.

10. For Quintilian's biography see Kennedy, *Quintilian*, 2nd ed. (New York: Sophron, 2013). Kennedy places his birth around A.D. 40, though all such estimates are based on extrapolations from indirect evidence, such as later remarks by Quintilian or by the age at which he may have studied rhetoric in Rome. Also see William Peterson, *M. Fabii Quintiliani institutionis oratoriae liber decimus* (Oxford, UK: n.p., 1891; rev. ed., New York: Sophron, 2013), 1–13; F. H. Colson, ed., *M. Fabii Quintiliani institutionis oratoriae liber I* (Cambridge,

UK: Cambridge UP, 1924), 9–20; and Charles Little, ed., *Quintilian: The Schoolmaster*, 2 vols. (Nashville, TN: George Peabody, 1951), 2, 9–14.

11. For biographical and literary information about these and other ancient figures, consult M. Gary et al., ed., *The Oxford Classical Dictionary* (Oxford, UK: Clarendon, 1949).

12. Quintilian himself recommends this practice in *Institutio oratoria*:

> Let the young man, then, who has carefully learned skill in concep-
> tion and expression from his teachers (which will not be an endless
> task if they are able and willing to teach) and who has gained a
> fair degree of facility by practice, choose some orator, as was the
> custom among the ancients, whom he may follow and imitate; let
> him attend as many trials as possible, and be a frequent spectator
> of the sort of contest for which he is intended. (10.5.19)

13. For Quintilian quotations not included in this edition, see *Quintilian: The Orator's Education*, ed. and trans. Donald A. Russell, 5 vols. (Cambridge, MA: Harvard UP, 2002), Loeb Classical Library.

14. See Acts 25:13. Queen Berenice was twice in Rome, having formed an attachment to the youthful Titus who later became emperor.

15. Pliny the Younger, *Epistles* 2.14.10.

16.   O Quintilian, supreme guide of unsettled youth,
                  Glory of the Roman toga, O Quintilian.
                  (Quoted by Colson, *M. Fabii Quintiliani* 13)

17. Juvenal, *Satire* 7. And see *Institutio oratoria* 6. Preface 4, where Quintilian laments his loss of family but notes that he is otherwise fortunate.

18. *Quintilianus, ex Hispania Calagurritanus, primus Romae publicam scholam ac salarium e fisco accepit et claruit.* The salary was 100,000 sesterces per year. The date given by Jerome may be incorrect, since Vespasian (A.D. 69–79) had subsidized some rhetoricians during his reign, and the date of A.D. 88 would place the event under Domitian (A.D. 81–96). In either case, the fact is clear and signalizes the eminent public position of Quintilian.

19. Kennedy describes this as "an honorary tribute roughly analogous to the order of merit" (*Art of Rhetoric* 493).

20. Marrou places Quintilian's death in A.D. 95, though he does not present his evidence for that conclusion (*History of Education* 351).

21. Quintilian himself gives it this title (6. Preface 3 and 8.6.76). Early editors of Quintilian conjectured that the *Dialogus de oratoribus* (usually attributed to his contemporary, Tacitus) was really the book named in these

two passages. Tacitus is now generally accepted as its author. There is a good description of the *Dialogus* in Kennedy, *Art of Rhetoric*, 515–23, where it is assigned a date of A.D. 101.

22. See the discussion of *declamatio* in the section on teaching methods (lx). Some modern scholars believe that the declamations circulated in his name represent the lecture notes of a scholar who either was using Quintilian's system or had actually been trained by him.

23. Little, *Quintilian*.

24. These are the five elements or "canons" of rhetoric. Taken together they form a complete textbook on the subject as it was taught in Roman schools.

25. For a graphic description of the decline of free speech under the emperors, see Chester G. Starr, *Civilization and the Caesars* (Ithaca, NY: Cornell UP, 1954), especially 121–62.

26. For instance, he praises Marcus Cato the Censor for having learned Greek "in the very decline of life" (12.11.123).

27. Bonner, *Education in Ancient Rome*, 135–36. See also Kristina Milnor, "Women," in *The Oxford Handbook of Roman Studies*, ed. Allessandro Barchiesi and Walter Scheidel (Oxford, UK: Oxford UP, 2010), 815–26; and Elaine Fantham et al., *Women in the Classical World: Image and Text* (New York: Oxford UP, 1994).

28. There is a useful summary of Quintilian's citations and quotations in Little, *Quintilian*, 2, 165–200. For instance, Little quotes Virgil 150 times. See also Little's section on the role of Book 10 of the *Institutio oratoria*.

29. For a more detailed description of the teaching methods, see Murphy, *Short History of Writing*, 36–76. Quintilian sometimes assumes knowledge on the part of the reader. See, for example, the opening paragraph of Book 1, chapter 9, which runs rapidly over the main elements of imitation. Quintilian no doubt relies here on the fact that his readers would readily recognize the exercises they had undergone themselves in their own schooling.

30. Marrou, *History of Education*, 375.

31. Donald A. Russell, *Greek Declamation* (Oxford, UK: Oxford UP, 1983), 3.

32. There is a brief account of what Marrou terms "the educational rivalry of Plato-Isocrates" in his *History of Education*, 119–36. See also Murphy, Katula, Hoppmann, *A Synoptic History*, 50–55. Isocrates's educational ideals are best expressed in his two "speeches," *Antidosis* and *Against the Sophists*, in *Isocrates*, trans. George Norlin, vol. 2 (Cambridge, MA: Harvard UP, 1954). The best single summary of Isocrates's influence on Roman

rhetoric and education is Harry M. Hubbell, *The Influence of Isocrates on Cicero, Dionysius, and Aristides* (New Haven, CT: Yale UP, 1913). Bonner, however, gives Isocrates less credit for his contributions to Roman practice; see especially his *Education in Ancient Rome*, 81, 292.

33. The adolescent Cicero, for instance, defines rhetoric in his *De inventione* (1.5) as a branch of political science. See *On Invention*, trans. H. M. Hubbell (Cambridge, MA: Harvard UP, 1949).

34. The term "Second Sophistic" is often used to describe the period under the empire (roughly A.D. 50 to 400) in which the skills learned in the schools were employed for oratorical display rather than for citizenship as Cicero would have understood it. Greek, more than Latin oratory, flourished in this period, partly as a result of differing political circumstances in eastern portions of the empire. See the account in Kennedy, *Art of Rhetoric*, 553–607. See also Graham Anderson, "Rhetoric and the Second Sophistic," in *A Companion to Roman Rhetoric*, ed. William Dominik and Jon Hall (Oxford, UK: Blackwell, 2007), 339–53.

35. The conservatism of rhetorical teaching over such a long period makes it possible to give an account of it as a system, based on the late textbooks which survive, without feeling that one's conclusions are likely to be fundamentally wrong for the earlier period. Quintilian is undoubtedly the best guide. (Russell, *Criticism in Antiquity* [Berkeley: U of California P, 1981], 119)

Bonner, in fact, devotes 162 pages to what he describes as "the Standard Teaching Programme" (*Education in Ancient Rome* 165–327).

36. It may be useful to compare this brief summary with the outline of Books 1 and 2, which precedes the translation, and then to trace the various devices in the text itself.

37. For example, "It seems rather strange, therefore, to find the whole discussion inserted into the middle of the account of style" (Kennedy, *Art of Rhetoric* 500). Even though he does not take a clear stand on the issue, Kennedy does posit the possibility that Quintilian purposely places Book 10 in this unusual position to emphasize the importance of its subject. For a different view on the purpose of Book 10, see Murphy, "Quintilian's Advice on the Continuing Self-Education of the Adult Orator: Book X of His *Institutio oratoria*" in *Quintilian and the Law: The Art of Persuasion in Law and Politics*, ed. Olga Tellegen-Couperus (Leuven, Belgium: Leuven UP, 2003), 247–52.

38. Note, for instance, the auditory considerations involved in the discussion of "reading" in chapter 8 of Book 1. The Latin word *lectio* makes

no distinction between types of reading, whether for a single reader or an audience.

·39. It has been estimated that as many as a million books were printed in the forty-odd years from the Gutenberg Bible in the 1450s to the end of the fifteenth century. The effect of printing on the listening-reading relationship has not yet been fully assessed despite the work of Marshall McLuhan, Walter J. Ong, and others.

40. The future orator's command of language begins with what he hears even in the cradle: "Let the child not be accustomed, therefore, even while he is yet an infant, to phraseology which must be unlearned" (1.1.5).

41. "But these precepts of being eloquent, though necessary to be known, are not sufficient to produce the full power of eloquence unless there be united to them a certain Facility, which among the Greeks is called *Hexis*, 'habit'" (10.1.1).

42. After laying out the principles of active reading in the first part of chapter 1, Quintilian completes the chapter with a lengthy discussion (sections 46–131) of "the various sorts of reading which I consider peculiarly suitable for those who aim at becoming orators." He begins with Homer and ends with Seneca, treating along the way the virtues and defects of a large number of Greek and Roman poets, historians, philosophers, orators, and essayists.

43. He has advice on many aspects of the composition process, as in his remarks on the rate of writing: "The sum of the whole matter, indeed, is this: that by writing quickly we are not brought to write well, but that by writing well we are brought to write quickly" (10.3.10).

44. Colson, in his introduction to the edition of Book 1 devotes forty-one pages to Quintilian's influence (43–89). This is the best single short treatment of the subject. The following account is based on Colson and Little, unless otherwise noted. However, there is also an interesting survey of Quintilian's influence down into modern times by Otto Seel, *Quintilian, oder Die Kunst des Redens und Schweigens* (Stuttgart, Germany: Klett-Cotta, 1977), 161–325.

45. Donald Leman Clark, *Rhetoric in Greco-Roman Education* (New York: Columbia UP, 1957), 14.

46. Text in Charles Halm, ed., *Rhetores latini minores* (Leipzig, Germany: Teubner, 1863), 373–448.

47. See Charles H. Haskins, *The Renaissance of the Twelfth Century* (Cambridge, MA: Harvard UP, 1927; rpt. New York: Meridian Books, 1957).

48. For a survey of Quintilian in the medieval period see Murphy, *Rhetoric in the Middle Ages*, 123–30.

49. John of Salisbury, *The Metalogicon*, trans. Daniel D. McGarry (Berkeley: U of California P, 1955), 1.24, 65–66.

50. Quoted in Little, *Quintilian*, 2, 21. Quintilian uses the whetstone image (2.12.8), but it also appears in Horace and earlier in Isocrates.

51. Quoted in William Shepherd, *The Life of Poggio Bracciolini* (Liverpool, UK: Harris Brothers, 1802), 105.

52. Quoted in Colson, *M. Fabii Quintiliani*, lxxiii.

53. Ibid., lxxxiii.

54. For the printing history, see Lawrence D. Green and James J. Murphy, *Renaissance Rhetoric: A Short-Title Catalogue, 1460–1700*, 2nd ed. (Aldershot, UK: Ashgate, 2006).

55. See Murphy, ed., *Arguments in Rhetoric against Quintilian: Translation and Text of Peter Ramus's "Rhetoricae distinctiones in Quintilianum"* (1549), trans. Carole Newlands, introduction by James J. Murphy (DeKalb: Northern Illinois UP, 1986).

56. Ibid., 82.

57. Colson, *M. Fabii Quintiliani*, lxxxiii.

58. See Clark, *Milton at Saint Paul's School* (New York: Columbia UP, 1948). For Quintilian's use by Renaissance English writers on rhetoric, see Wilbur S. Howell, *Logic and Rhetoric in England, 1500–1700* (Princeton, NJ: Princeton UP, 1956), 108, 137, 177, 180, 225, 322, 325, 334, 340. See also Clark, *Rhetoric and Poetry in the Renaissance* (New York: Columbia UP, 1922).

59. *Essay on Criticism*, lines 669, 670.

60. Quoted in Colson, *M. Fabii Quintiliani*, back of frontispiece.

61. See John Henry Newman, *The Idea of a University* (New York: The America Press, 1941), Discourse 4, Sections 1–3, pp. 344–79. Earlier in the same book (277), Newman mentions Quintilian in connection with the tradition of Roman studies.

62. The following account is based on articles in Karl Wallace, ed., *A History of Speech Education in America* (New York: Appleton-Century-Crofts, 1954).

63. Heath, "Codifications of Rhetoric," 73.

64. Sharon Crowley and Debra Hawhee's popular textbook *Ancient Rhetorics for Contemporary Students* is a good example of the way ancient rhetorical theory in general, and Quintilian in particular, has recently been adapted for the modern classroom. Many earlier rhetoric and composition scholars paved the way for these developments: Of particular note is Edward P. J. Corbett, whose 1965 book *Classical Rhetoric for the Modern Student* helped reignite scholarly interest in ancient rhetoric as a resource for contemporary pedagogy. More recently, works such as Susan Jarratt's *Rereading the Sophists: Classical Rhetoric Refigured* and Kathleen E. Welch's *The*

Contemporary Reception of Classical Rhetoric: Appropriations of Ancient Discourse have provided useful analyses of the intersections of ancient and modern rhetorical theory and practice.

65. It is particularly common for writing teachers to emphasize public writing and new media composition as valuable ways of teaching habits of citizenship. See, for example, Charles Tryon, "Writing and Citizenship: Using Blogs to Teach First-Year Composition" *Pedagogy* 6.1 (2006): 128–32. Tryon, in his argument for the value of using blogs in writing classes, claims that

> a composition class that nourishes citizenship should convey the connections between the classroom and the so-called real world, which seems to exist everywhere else. In order to foster this notion of citizenship, I have incorporated into my first-year composition courses the requirement that students write, and sometimes read, Web logs. (128)

66. Amy Wan, "In the Name of Citizenship" *College English* 74.1 (2011): 28–49.

67. See pp. xvi–xvii from this book's introduction for a discussion of the political turbulence and violence in Quintilian's day.

68. Robert Kaster has noted, for instance, that one of the primary functions of rhetorical exercises such as declamation was instilling "by sheer repetition, approved values in the still impressionable minds of the next generation of the elite" (325) and thereby ensuring the "social reproduction of the conservative elite who patronized the schools of rhetoric" (326). "Controlling Reason: Declamation in Rhetorical Education at Rome," in *Education in Greek and Roman Antiquity*, ed. Y. L. Too (Leiden, Netherlands: Brill, 2001), 317–39.

69. Wan, "In the Name of Citizenship," 39.

70. Given the short duration of a semester-long class, limited goals are, perhaps, unavoidable. As Wan notes in the article "In the Name of Citizenship," there is just "too much other work to do, too many other demands put upon the course" (46).

71. Andrew Bourelle, "Lessons from Quintilian: Writing and Rhetoric across the Curriculum for the Modern University" *Currents in Teaching and Learning* 1.2 (Spring 2009): 28–36.

72. Ibid., 32.

73. J. David Fleming, "The Very Idea of a Progymnasmata" *Rhetoric Review* 22 (2003): 105–20.

74. Ibid., 106.

75. Bourelle's article is a good example of this approach. See also James E. Porter's article "Recovering Delivery for Digital Rhetoric" *Computers and Composition* 26 (2009): 207–24.

76. Fleming, "The Very Idea of a Progymnasmata," 114. See also Christy Friend's argument about the relevance of declamation exercises for contemporary approaches to critical pedagogy. Friend claims that a "close examination of the declamations and their pedagogical function can inform our current debate over critical teaching, by providing a rich example of politicized pedagogy to which modern rhetoricians may connect their own practice" (302). "Pirates, Seducers, Wronged Heirs, Poison Cups, Cruel Husbands, and Other Calamities: The Roman School Declamations and Critical Pedagogy" *Rhetoric Review* 17.2 (Spring 1999): 300–320.

77. Robert Terrill argues that imitation "cultivates a form of duality that is an especially productive resource for citizenship, and that these doubled attitudes are among the outcomes of a rhetorical education that are its most significant contributions to public culture" (297). "Mimesis, Duality, and Rhetorical Education" *Rhetoric Society Quarterly* 41.4 (2011): 295–315.

78. Peter Elbow, *Writing without Teachers* (Oxford, UK: Oxford UP, 1973), 6.

79. Ibid., 6–7.

80. As Lester Faigley writes, postmodern theory "would situate the subject among many competing discourses that precede the subject" and "understands subjectivity as heterogeneous and constantly in flux" (227). *Fragments of Rationality* (Pittsburgh, PA: U of Pittsburgh P, 1992).

81. Ibid., 3.

82. Jacquelyn E. Hoermann and Richard Leo Enos, "Vernacular Eloquence: What Speech Can Bring to Writing" *Composition Studies* 42.2 (Fall 2014): 167.

83. As Porter notes in "Recovering Delivery for Digital Rhetoric,"

> Because delivery came to be associated almost exclusively with speech situations and with functions of the speaker's body (voice, gestures), it seemed less relevant, if not irrelevant, to written composition than the other canons (particularly *dispositio* and *elocutio*). By the time of 20th-century rhetoric theory and composition pedagogy, delivery had effectively disappeared. It is seldom taught, at least as a distinct topic, in departments of writing, English, or communication. (207)

84. Susan Miller, "Classical Practice and Contemporary Basics," in *The Rhetorical Tradition and Modern Writing*, ed. James J. Murphy (New York: The

Modern Language Association, 1982), 56. See also in the same volume the essays by Nan Johnson and Donald C. Stewart. There are frequent references to Quintilian in Robert J. Connors, Lisa S. Ede, and Andrea A. Lunsford, ed., *Essays on Classical Rhetoric and Modern Discourse* (Carbondale: Southern Illinois UP, 1984).

85. Fleming, "The Very Idea of a Progymnasmata," 108.

86. Shaun Gallagher provides a thorough discussion of neonate imitation in part 1 of *How the Body Shapes the Mind* (Oxford, UK: Oxford UP, 2005).

87. David Freedberg and Vittorio Gallese, "Motion, Emotion and Empathy in Esthetic Experience," *Trends in Cognitive Science* 11 (2007): 197–203.

88. Vittorio Gallese, "Embodied Simulation and Its Role in Intersubjectivity," in *The Embodied Self: Dimensions, Coherence and Disorders*, ed. Thomas Fuchs, Heribert C. Sattel, and Peter Henningsen (Stuttgart, Germany: Schattauer, 2010.), 77–94.

89. Vittorio Gallese and George Lakoff, "The Brain's Concepts: The Role of the Sensory-Motor System in Conceptual Knowledge," *Cognitive Neuropsychology* 22 (2005): 455–79.

90. Amy Cook, "Interplay: The Method and Potential of a Cognitive Scientific Approach to Theatre," *Theatre Journal* 59 (2007): 579–94.

91. Shinobu Kitayama and Jiyoung Park, "Cultural Neuroscience of the Self: Understanding the Social Grounding of the Brain," *Social Cognitive and Affective Neuroscience* 5 (2010): 111–29.

92. Jane McGonigal, *Reality Is Broken: Why Games Make Us Better and How They Can Change the World* (New York: Penguin, 2011), 55.

93. Ibid., 68.

94. Fleming, "The Very Idea of a Progymnasmata," 117.

PART TWO

THE INDUCTIVE PHASE:
LEARNING FROM QUINTILIAN

*This phase invites the reader to become an interactive, self-
educating explorer of both Quintilian's ideas and his words
as found in the translations of Books 1, 2, and 10. We
encourage the use of this outline of teaching methods and the
questions and quotations that follow it to help guide reading
and rereading and to put Quintilian's text in dialogue
with contemporary issues and concerns in education.*

An Outline of Quintilian's Teaching Methods

Perhaps the most important aspect of these methods is their coordination into a single instructional program. Each is important
for itself, but takes greater importance from its place within the
whole. The outline below illustrates how these elements fit together
throughout the *Institutio oratoria*.

A. Precept: A set of rules that provide a definite method and
   system of speaking. Rhetoric as precept occupies eight of the
   twelve books.
   1. Invention: the finding of ideas
   2. Arrangement: placing them in order
   3. Style: putting them into words
   4. Memory: recalling them for use
   5. Delivery: presenting them to an audience
B. Imitation: The use of models to learn how others have used
   language. Specific exercises include
   1. reading aloud (*lectio*);

    2. master's detailed analysis of a text (*praelectio*);
    3. memorization of models;
    4. paraphrase of models;
    5. transliteration (prose or verse and/or Latin or Greek);
    6. recitation of paraphrase or transliteration;
    7. correction of paraphrase or transliteration.

C. Composition exercises (*progymnasmata* or *praeexercitamenta*): A learning ladder of a graded series of exercises in writing and speaking themes. Each succeeding exercise is more difficult and incorporates what has been learned in preceding ones. The following twelve were common by Quintilian's time.

    1. Retelling a fable
    2. Retelling an episode from a poet or a historian
    3. *Chreia*, or amplification of a moral theme
    4. Amplification of an aphorism (*sententia*) or proverb
    5. Refutation or confirmation of an allegation
    6. Commonplace, or confirmation of a thing admitted
    7. Encomium, or eulogy (or dispraise) of a person or thing
    8. Comparison of things or persons
    9. Impersonation (*ethologia, ethopoeia, prosopopeia*), or speaking or writing in the character of a given person
   10. Description, or vivid presentation of details
   11. Thesis, or argument for or against an answer to a general question (*quaestio infinita*) not involving individuals
   12. Laws, or arguments for or against a law

D. Declamation (*declamationes*), or fictitious speeches, in two types:

    1. *Suasoria*, or deliberative (political) speech arguing that an action be taken or not taken
    2. *Controversia*, or forensic (legal) speech prosecuting or defending a fictitious or historical person in a law case

E. Sequencing, or the systematic ordering of classroom activities to accomplish two goals:

    1. Movement, from the simple to the more complex
    2. Reinforcement, by reiterating each element of preceding exercises as each new one appears

Details of these teaching activities may be found in the translations of Books 1, 2, and 10.

A Dozen Questions for Quintilian at the Classroom Door

The Personal First-Day Question: How can I [the teacher] convince a bunch of smartphone-using students to pay attention to such an old book?

The Ultimate First-Day Question: How can I get the students to understand why they are here?

The Identity Question: Are my students different from other students?

The Leap-of-Faith Question: Can these methods be used to help modern students learn how to speak and write?

The Time Question: Do I have enough time to use these methods?

The Sequence Question: Do I have to use every one of these methods to make them work?

The Priority Question: Where do I start?

The Translation Question: How do I put these exercises into words my students can understand?

The *Progymnasmata* Question: Which of these twelve approaches are the best for this group of students?

The Etiological Question: How can I convince these students that speaking and writing are important?

The Societal Question: Are skills in writing and speaking simply the tools used by the elite to keep power?

The Long-Term Impact Question: How can I ensure that my students will continue to think, even after the class period is over?

All answers may be found explicitly in, or inferred from, the translations of Books 1, 2, or 10 in this volume.

Thirty Quintilian One-Liners for Discussion and Debate

"For myself, I consider that nothing is unnecessary to the art of oratory." (1. Preface 5)

"There would be no eloquence in the world, if we were to speak only with one person at a time." (1.2.31)

"It is often difficult to distinguish faults from figures of speech." (1.5.5)

"A graceful and becoming motion of the body, also, which the Greeks call *eurythmic*, is necessary, and cannot be sought from any other art than music." (1.10.26)

"If an orator has to speak (as the next book will show) on all subjects, no man, assuredly, can become a perfect orator without a knowledge of geometry." (1.10.49)

"So much more easy is it to do many things one after the other, than to do one thing for a long time." (1.12.7)

"For divine providence has granted this favor to mankind, that the more honorable occupations are also the more pleasing." (1.12.19)

"Of these professors the morals must first be ascertained." (2.2.2)

"Let him [the teacher] adopt, then, above all things, the feelings of a parent toward his pupils, and consider that he succeeds to the place of those by whom the children were entrusted to him." (2.2.4)

"How much more readily we imitate those whom we like can scarcely be expressed." (2.2.8)

"The master ought not to speak to suit the taste of his pupils, but the pupils to suit that of the master." (2.2.13)

"For my part, I do not consider a man a real teacher if he is unwilling to teach little things." (2.3.5)

"The remedy for exuberance is easy, but barrenness is incurable by any labor." (2.4.6–7)

"For what object have we in teaching them, but that they may not always require to be taught?" (2.5.13)

"Nor will the preceptor be under obligation merely to teach these things, but frequently to ask questions about them, and try the judgment of his pupils." (2.5.13)

"It will be of greater service to point out the right way at first, than to recall those who have gone astray from their errors." (2.6.2)

"For as it is the duty of preceptors to teach, so it is that of pupils to show themselves teachable." (2.9.3)

"One great quality in an orator is discretion." (2.13.2)

"But these precepts of being eloquent, though necessary to be known, are not sufficient to produce the full power of eloquence unless there be united to them a certain Facility, which among the Greeks is called *Hexis*, 'habit.'" (10.1.1)

"For our speech will never become forcible and energetic unless it acquires strength from great practice in writing; and the labor of writing, if left destitute of models from reading passes away without effect, as having no director." (10.1.2)

"Some speeches contribute more to our improvement when we hear them delivered, others when we peruse them." (10.1.16)

"Reading is free, and does not escape us with the rapidity of oral delivery, but allows us to go over the same passages more than once." (10.1.19)

"Indeed, the whole conduct of life is based on the desire of doing ourselves that which we approve in others." (10.2.2)

"We see, in short, that the beginnings of every kind of study are formed in accordance with some prescribed rule." (10.2.2)

"It is dishonorable even to rest satisfied with simply equaling what we imitate." (10.2.7)

"Every species of writing has its own prescribed law." (10.2.22)

"By writing quickly we are not brought to write well, but that by writing well we are brought to write quickly." (10.3.10)

"For it is *habit* and *exercise* that chiefly beget facility." (10.7.8)

"We must study at all times and in all places." (10.7.26)

"I even think that we should not write at all what we design to deliver from memory, for if we do so it generally happens that our thoughts fix us to the studied portions of our speech, and do not allow us to try the fortune of the moment." (10.7.32)

*The amplification of an aphorism (*sentencia*) is one of the twelve exercises in the learning ladder known as progymnasmata.*

Fifty-Five Questions for Quintilian

Is writing better than speaking?

Do adults learn the same way children do?

Is peer criticism better than teacher correction?

Is imitation the same as plagiarism?

Is it possible to plan for future language?

Which is more important, the subject or the learner?

Should a student acquire a good textbook?

Is it important to examine what others have said or written?

How important is grammar?

Which is more important, precept or practice?

Can public correction by the teacher affect self-esteem?

Is writer's block a modern invention?

How often should the teacher lecture to students?

Is it the responsibility of the students or the instructor to make the classroom interactive?

Should students correct other students?

Is writing or speaking as if you were another person a violation of privacy?

Which rules are the most important in speaking and writing?

To what extent can past language be a guide for future language?

How much does it matter that the instructor be a good model for speaking and writing?

Is it best to write a draft first, or to find ideas first?

Is it a good idea to prepare an outline before speaking or writing?

If a good education prepares both speakers and writers for future language use, would a speaker need notes?

Can memory be strengthened by exercise, like a physical muscle?

Why do some people say that you are undemocratic, favoring the elite?

Are games a legitimate teaching tool?

Is transliteration possible in a monolingual society?

Are you in favor of today's English as a second language movement?

Is the modern class period too short to use your ideas?

Hasn't modern psychology refuted your basic learning principles?

Wouldn't using your ideas in teaching speaking and writing require a whole new educational system?

Can society afford to spend so many years teaching people to speak and write?

Are there any good models for imitation today?

Wouldn't your plan require an impractically low student-faculty ratio?

Would modern students tolerate transliteration exercises?

Are modern forms of writing and speaking so different that your types of analysis won't work anymore?

Can your system work in a society with no consensus on the goals of education?

Has modern research invalidated traditional rhetorical paradigms?

Are the twelve exercises of the *progymnasmata* out of date?

Is it impractical to see writing, speaking, listening, and reading as a whole in today's interactive postdigital age?

Aren't speaking and writing skills already fixed by the end of high school?

How is hearing related to writing and speaking?

Would you approve of student group discussions about the principles of future writing and speaking?

Which analogy do you prefer: education is like filling a pail with water, *or* education is like growing a tree?

Is playing with words a virtue or a vice?

Would it be fair to use the term "learning ladder" for what you call *progymnasmata*?

Would it be fair to use the term "case studies" for what you call declamations?

Do you think texting is a good invention?

What influence do parents have on their children's language skills?

Should less literate students be kept out of the classroom
so teachers can work better with those most likely to
benefit society?

Are we facing the death of the old-fashioned writing and
speaking you teach?

How can you keep students thinking after the class period
is over?

How can you keep the attention of sullen, disinterested
students?

How can the teacher concentrate on the learning of the
students and not on his or her own performance?

Is it better to write quickly or to write carefully?

Does every species of writing and speaking have its own
laws?

*Readers are encouraged to search the translations of Books 1, 2, and 10 for
Quintilian's answers to these questions.*

A NOTE ON THE TEXT

The original translation of the Reverend John Selby Watson has been revised in a number of places by the editor of this volume. Changes were mainly to achieve greater clarity, either through modernization of the punctuation or through alterations of the translation itself. Watson's 1856 translation follows very closely Quintilian's own Latin style, which is characterized by the frequent use of lengthy periodic constructions, often involving several parallel structures within a single sentence. In some cases the editor has divided the longer sentences for clarity.

Two modern editions of the *Institutio oratoria* have been used to check the accuracy of the translation, and to verify the form of Latin and Greek terms retained in the text. One edition is that of Ludwig Radermacher (Teubner Series: Leipzig, 1907) and the other is that of Michael Winterbottom (Oxford: Clarendon, 1970). Greek terms have been either transliterated into Roman alphabet or translated where possible. Chapters 4 through 7 contain a number of Latin terms which have been retained without translation, since Quintilian uses them in his first book to illustrate grammatical points best understood in the original forms.

Notes are provided to identify direct quotations and literary allusions. No attempt has been made to treat Latin textual problems except in those cases in which such notes are necessary to understand the translated text.

ON THE EARLY EDUCATION
OF THE CITIZEN-ORATOR

BOOKS ONE AND TWO
OF THE *INSTITUTIO ORATORIA*

QUINTILIAN TO TRYPHO,[1]
WISHING HEALTH

You HAVE prevailed on me, by your daily importunity, to 1
proceed at once to publish the books on the Education of an
Orator, which I had addressed to my friend Marcellus. For
my own part, I thought that they were not yet sufficiently advanced toward perfection. On the composition of them, as you
know, I spent little more than two years, while distracted by
so many other occupations; and this time was devoted, not
so much to the labor of writing, as to that of research for the
almost boundless work which I had undertaken, and to the
perusal of authors, who are innumerable. Following, besides, 2
the advice of Horace, who, in *Ars poetica*, recommends that
publication should not be hurried, and that a work should
be retained till the ninth year, I allowed time for reconsider-
ing them, in order that, when the ardor of invention had
cooled, I might judge of them, on a more careful reperusal,
as a mere reader. Yet if they are so much demanded, as you 3
say, let us give our sails to the winds, and pray for success as
we loose our cable. But much also depends on your faithful-
ness and care in order that they may come into the hands of
the public in as correct a state as possible.

---

1 Trypho was an eminent bookseller at Rome.

PREFACE, ADDRESSED TO
MARCELLUS VICTORIUS

1   WHEN CERTAIN persons, after I had secured rest from my labors, which for twenty years I had devoted to the instruction of youth, requested of me in a friendly manner to write something on the art of speaking, I certainly resisted their solicitations for a long time: I was not ignorant that authors of the greatest celebrity in both languages had bequeathed to posterity many treatises having reference to this subject, written with the greatest care.[1] But by the very plea on which I

2   thought that excuse for my refusal would be more readily admitted, my friends became still more urgent, "since," they said, "amid the various opinions of former writers, some of them contradicting each other, choice was difficult." They appeared, not unjustifiably, to press upon me the task, if not of inventing new precepts, at least of pronouncing judgment concerning the old. Although, however, it was not so

3   much the confidence of accomplishing what was required of me, as the shame of refusing, that prevailed with me; yet, as the subject opened itself more widely, I voluntarily undertook a heavier duty than was laid upon me, not only that I might oblige my best friends by fuller compliance, but also that, while pursuing a common road, I might not tread merely in other men's footsteps.

4   Other authors who have committed to writing the art of oratory have in general commenced in such a manner, as if they were to put the finishing touches to those who were accomplished in every other kind of learning—whether from despising the branches of knowledge which we previously learn, as insignificant, or from supposing that they did not fall under

[1] Quintilian refers here to the numerous Greek and Latin textbooks dealing with the technical aspects of rhetoric. Aristotle wrote a book on rhetoric; Cicero composed seven.

their province, the duties of the professions being distinct; or, what is more probable, from expecting no credit to their ability in treating of subjects, which, however necessary, are yet far removed from display: as the pinnacles of buildings are seen, while the foundations are hid. For myself, I consider 5 that nothing is unnecessary to the art of oratory, without which it must be confessed that an orator cannot be formed, and that there is no possibility of arriving at the summit in any subject without previous initiatory efforts: therefore, I shall not shrink from stooping to those lesser matters, the neglect of which leaves no place for greater, and shall proceed to regulate the studies of the orator from his infancy, just as if he were entrusted to me to be brought up.

This work, Marcellus Victorius, I dedicate to you, whom, 6 as being most friendly to me, and animated with an extraordinary love of letters, I deemed most worthy of such a pledge of our mutual affection. Not, indeed, on these considerations alone, though these are of great weight, but also because my treatise seemed likely to be of use for the instruction of your son,[2] whose early age shows his way clear to the full splendor of genius: a treatise which I have resolved to conduct, from the very cradle, as it were, of oratory, through all the studies which can at all assist the future speaker, to the summit of that art. This I designed because 7 two books on the art of rhetoric were already in circulation under my name, though neither published by me nor composed for that object. After holding two days' discourse with me, some youths, to whom that time was devoted, had caught up the first by heart; the other, which was learned indeed in a greater number of days (as far as they could learn by taking notes), some of my young pupils, of excellent disposition, but of too great fondness for me, had made known through the indiscreet honor of publication. In these present books, accord- 8 ingly, there will be some things the same, many altered, very many added, but all better arranged, and rendered complete, as far as I shall be able.

2 Geta.

9   We are to form, then, the perfect orator, who cannot exist unless he is above all a good man. We require in him, therefore, not only consumate ability in speaking, but also every
10   excellence of mind. For I cannot admit that the principles of moral and honorable conduct are, as some have thought, to be left to the philosophers. This is true because the man who can duly sustain his character as a citizen, who is qualified for the management of public and private affairs, and who can govern communities by his counsels, settle them by means of laws, and improve them by judicial enactments, can
11   certainly be nothing else but an orator. Although I acknowledge, therefore, that I shall adopt some precepts which are contained in the writings of the philosophers, yet I shall maintain with justice and truth that they belong to my subject
12   and have a peculiar relation to the art of oratory. If we constantly have occasion to speak of justice, fortitude, temperance, and other similar topics, so that a cause can scarcely be found in which some such discussion does not occur, and if all such subjects are to be illustrated by invention and elocution, can it be doubted that, wherever power of intellect and copiousness of language are required, the art of the orator is to be there pre-eminently exerted?
13   These two accomplishments, as Cicero very plainly proves, were, as they are joined by nature, so also united in practice, so that the same persons were thought at once wise and eloquent. Subsequently, the study divided itself, and, through want of art, it came to pass that the arts were considered to be diverse [3]; for, as soon as the tongue became an instrument

[3] The basic premise of the whole *Institutio oratoria* is laid out in this key passage, which discusses the difference between the merely eloquent man and the merely wise man. Neither, for Quintilian, is complete. As Quintilian notes here, Cicero (*De oratore* III. 19, 72) had blamed Socrates for divorcing eloquence from philosophy. The passage might be compared with a famous one by Cicero: "Wisdom without eloquence does too little for the good of states, but that eloquence without wisdom is generally highly disadvantageous and is never helpful" (*De inventione* I. 1. 1).

of gain, and it was made a practice to abuse the gifts of eloquence, those who were esteemed as eloquent abandoned the
care of morals, which, when thus neglected, became, as it
were, the prize of the less robust intellects. Some, disliking the
toil of cultivating eloquence, afterward returned to the discipline of the mind and the establishment of rules of life, re-
taining themselves the better part, if it could be divided into
two—but assuming, at the same time, the most presumptuous
of titles, so as to be called the only cultivators of wisdom, a
distinction which neither the most eminent commanders nor
men who were engaged with the utmost distinction in the
direction of the greatest affairs and in the management of
whole commonwealths ever ventured to claim for themselves;
for they preferred rather to practice excellence of conduct
than to profess it. That many of the ancient professors of wisdom, indeed, both delivered virtuous precepts, and even lived
as they directed others to live, I will readily admit; but, in
our own times, the greatest vices have been hidden under this
name in many of the professors. They did not strive by virtue
and study to be esteemed philosophers, but adopted a pecu-
liarity of look, austerity or demeanor, and a dress different
from that of other men, as cloaks for the vilest immoralities.

But those topics, which are claimed as peculiar to philosophy, we all discuss everywhere. For what person (if he be not
an utterly corrupt character) does not sometimes speak of
justice, equity, and goodness? Who, even among rustics, does
not make some inquiries about the causes of the operations
of nature? As to the proper use and distinction of words, it
ought to be common to all who make their language an object of care. But it will be the orator who will understand and
express those matters best, and if he should ever arrive at
perfection, the precepts of virtue would not have to be sought
from the schools of the philosophers. At present it is necessary to have recourse, at times, to those authors who have,
as I said, adopted the deserted, but pre-eminently better, part
of philosophy, and to reclaim, as it were, what is our own,

14

15

16

17

not that we may appropriate their discoveries, but that we may show them that they have usurped what belonged to others.

18   Let the orator, therefore, be such a man as may be called truly wise, not blameless in morals only (for that, in my opinion, though some disagree with me, is not enough), but accomplished also in science, and in every qualification for

19   speaking—a character such as, perhaps, no man ever was. But we are not the less, for that reason, to aim at perfection, for which most of the ancients strove; though they thought that no wise man had yet been found, they nevertheless laid down

20   directions for gaining wisdom. For the perfection of eloquence is assuredly something, nor does the nature of the human mind forbid us to reach it; but if to reach it be not granted us, yet those who shall strive to gain the summit will make higher advances than those who, prematurely conceiving a despair of attaining the point at which they aim, shall at once sink down at the foot of the ascent.

21   Indulgence will so much the more then be granted me, if I shall not pass over those lesser matters which are necessary to the work which I have undertaken. The first book, therefore, will contain those particulars which are antecedent to the duties of the teacher of rhetoric. In the second book we shall consider the first elements of instruction under the hands of the professor of rhetoric and the questions which are asked

22   concerning the subject of rhetoric itself. The next five will be devoted to invention (for under this head will also be included arrangement); and the four following, to elocution, within the scope of which fall memory and pronunciation.[4]

4 These are the five ancient elements or "parts" of rhetoric. Invention deals with the discovery of materials for the speech; arrangement treats the sequence or order of their appearance in the speech; elocution, or style, deals with matters of wording, including such factors as vocal rhythm and rhetorical figures and tropes; memory deals with both natural and artificial means of recall; pronunciation, or delivery, with such external aspects as gesture, facial expression, and control of the voice. Taken together they form a complete textbook on the subject as it was taught in Roman times.

One will be added, in which the orator himself will be completely formed by us, since we shall consider, as far as our weakness shall be able, what his morals ought to be, what should be his practice in undertaking, studying, and pleading causes, what should be his style of eloquence, what termination there should be to his pleading, and what may be his employments after its termination.

Among all these discussions shall be introduced, as occasion shall require, the art of speaking, which will not only instruct students in the knowledge of those things to which alone some have given the name of art, and interpret (so to express myself) the law of rhetoric, but may serve to nourish the faculty of speech, and strengthen the power of eloquence; for, in general, those bare treatises on art,[5] through too much affectation of subtlety, break and cut down whatever is noble in eloquence, drink up, as it were, all the blood of thought, and lay bare the bones, which, while they ought to exist and be united by their ligaments, ought still to be covered with flesh. We, therefore, have not, like most authors, included in our books that small part merely, but whatever we thought useful for the education of the orator, explaining every point with brevity; for if we should say on every particular as much as might be said, no end would be found to our work. 23 24 25

It is to be stated, however, in the first place, that precepts and treatises on art are of no avail without the assistance of nature; and these instructions, therefore, are not written for him to whom talent is wanting, any more than treatises on agriculture, for barren ground. 26

There are also certain other natural aids, such as power of voice, a constitution capable of labor, health, courage, and gracefulness—qualities which, if they fall to our lot in a moderate degree, may be improved by practice, but which are 27

[5] Here Quintilian refers to the arid, highly schematized handbooks of rhetoric which were common in his day. Elsewhere (II. 13. 1–7) he derides writers who try to encompass the whole subject into "one short body of rules." This is one of the many times that Quintilian urges the cultivation of artistic discretion, rather than the mere learning of rules.

often so far wanting that their deficiency renders abortive the benefits of understanding and study. These very qualities, likewise, are of no profit in themselves without a skillful teacher, persevering study, and great and continued exercise in writing, reading, and speaking.

BOOK I

CHAPTER ONE

LET A FATHER, then, as soon as his son is born, conceive first of all the best possible hopes of him; he will thus grow the more solicitous about his improvement from the very beginning. It is a complaint without foundation that very few people are granted the faculty of comprehending what is imparted to them, and that most, through dullness of understanding, lose their labor and their time; on the contrary, you will find the greater number of men both ready in conceiving and quick in learning. Such quickness is natural to man; and as birds are born to fly, horses to run, and wild beasts to show fierceness, so to men peculiarly belong activity and sagacity of understanding—hence the origin of the mind is thought to be from heaven. But dull and unteachable persons are no more produced in the course of nature than are persons marked by monstrosity and deformities; such are certainly but few. It will be a proof of this assertion, that, among boys, good promise is shown in the far greater number; and, if it passes off in the progress of time, it is manifest that it was not natural ability, but care, that was wanting. But one surpasses another, you will say, in ability. I grant that this is true, but only so far as to accomplish more or less; there is no one who has not gained something by study. Let him who is convinced of this truth, bestow, as soon as he becomes a parent, the most vigilant possible care on cherishing the hopes of a future orator.

Before all things, let not the talk of the child's nurses be ungrammatical. Chrysippus [1] wished them, if possible, to be women of some knowledge; at any rate he would have the best

---

[1] The first of several references to the educational principles of Chrysippus (*ca.* 280–204 B.C.), a Greek Stoic philosopher.

chosen, as far as circumstances would allow. To their morals, doubtless, attention is first to be paid; but let them also speak
5 with propriety. It is they that the child will hear first; it is their words that he will try to form by imitation. We are by nature most tenacious of what we have imbibed in our infant years, as the flavor, with which you scent vessels when new, remains in them; nor can the colors of wool, for which its plain whiteness has been exchanged, be effaced. Those very habits, which are of a more objectionable nature, adhere with the greater tenacity; for good ones are easily changed for the worse, but when will you change bad ones into good? Let the child not be accustomed, therefore, even while he is yet an infant, to phraseology which must be unlearned.

6 In parents I should wish that there be as much learning as possible. Nor do I speak, indeed, merely of fathers; for we have heard that Cornelia, the mother of the Gracchi (whose very learned writing in her letters has come down to posterity), contributed greatly to their eloquence; the daughter of Laelius is said to have exhibited her father's elegance in her conversation; and the oration of the daughter of Quintus Hortensius, delivered before the Triumviri, is read not merely as an honor
7 to her sex. Nor let those parents, who have not had the fortune to get learning themselves, bestow the less care on the instruction of their children; but let them, on this very account, be more solicitous as to other particulars.

8 Of the boys, among whom he who is destined to this prospect is to be educated, the same may be said as concerning nurses.

Of *paedagogi* [2] this further may be said, that they should either be men of acknowledged learning, which I should wish to be the first object, or that they should be conscious of their want of learning; for none are more pernicious than those who, having gone some little beyond the first elements, clothe themselves in a mistaken persuasion of their own knowledge.

[2] There is no English equivalent of the term *paedagogus*, a servant or slave assigned to supervise the young boy and to escort him to such places as school. He was not usually, however, his teacher or tutor.

Since they disdain to yield to those who are skilled in teaching, and, growing imperious, and sometimes fierce, in a certain right, as it were, of exercising their authority (with which that sort of men are generally puffed up), they teach only their own folly. Nor is their misconduct less prejudicial to the manners of their pupils; for Leonides, the tutor of Alexander, as is related by Diogenes of Babylon, tinctured him with certain bad habits which adhered to him from his childish education, even when he was grown up and become the greatest of kings. 9

If I seem to my reader to require a great deal, let him consider that it is an orator that is to be educated—an arduous task, even when nothing is deficient for the formation of his character, and that more and more difficult labors yet remain; for there is need of constant study, the most excellent teachers, and a variety of mental exercises. The best of rules, therefore, are to be laid down; and if any one shall refuse to observe them, the fault will lie, not in the method, but in the man. 10 11

If, however, it should not be the good fortune of children to have such nurses as I should wish, let them at least have one attentive *paedagogus*, not unskilled in language, who, if anything is spoken incorrectly by the nurse in the presence of his pupil, may at once correct it, and not let it settle in his mind. But let it be understood that what I prescribed at first is the right course, and this only a remedy.

I prefer that a boy should begin with the Greek language, because he will acquire the Latin, which is in general use, even though we tried to prevent him; and because, at the same time, he ought first to be instructed in Greek learning, from which ours is derived. Yet I should not wish this rule to be so superstitiously observed that he should for a long time speak or learn only Greek, as is the custom with most people; for hence arise many faults of pronunciation, which are viciously adapted to foreign sounds, and also of language, in which, when Greek idioms have become inherent by constant usage, they keep their place most pertinaciously, even 12 13

14 when we speak a different tongue. The study of Latin ought, therefore, to follow at no long interval, and soon after to keep pace with the Greek; thus it will happen, that, when we have begun to attend to both tongues with equal care, neither will impede the other.

15   Some have thought that boys, as long as they are under seven years of age, should not be set to learn, because that is the earliest age that they can understand what is taught and endure the labor of learning. Of which opinion a great many writers say that Hesiod was, at least such writers as lived before Aristophanes the grammarian, for he was the first to deny that the *Hypothecae*,[3] in which this opinion is found, was the

16 work of that poet. But other writers likewise, among whom is Eratosthenes, have given the same advice. Those, however, advise better, who, like Chrysippus, think that no part of a child's life should be left uncared for; for Chrysippus, though he has allowed three years to the nurses, yet is of opinion that the minds of children may be imbued with excellent in-

17 struction even by them. And why should not that age, which is now confessedly subject to moral influence, be under the influence of learning? I am not, indeed, ignorant that during the whole time of which I am speaking, scarcely as much can be done as one year may afterwards accomplish; yet those who are of the opinion which I have mentioned, appear, with regard to this part of life, to have spared not so much the learn-

18 ers as the teachers. What else, after they are able to speak, will children do better, for they must do something? Or why should we despise the gain, how little soever it be, previous to the age of seven years? For certainly, small as may be the proficiency which an earlier age exhibits, the child will yet learn something greater during the very year in which he

19 would have been learning something less. This advancement, extended through each year, is a profit on the whole; and whatever is gained in infancy is an acquisition to youth. The same rule should be prescribed as to the following years, so that what every boy has to learn, he may not be too late in

3 *Admonitions,* a now lost didactic poem.

beginning to learn. Let us not then lose even the earliest period of life; so much the less, since the elements of learning
depend on the memory alone, which not only exists in children, but is even better at that time of life than it will ever
be again.

Yet I am not so unacquainted with differences of age as to 20
think that we should urge those of tender years severely or
exact a full complement of work from them. It will be necessary, above all things, to take care, lest the child should conceive a dislike to the application which he cannot yet love,
and continue to dread the bitterness which he has once tasted,
even beyond the years of infancy. Let his instruction be an
amusement to him; let him be questioned and praised; let
him never feel pleased that he does not know a thing; and
sometimes, if he is unwilling to learn, let another be taught
before him, of whom he may be envious. Let him strive for
victory now and then, and generally suppose that he gains it;
and let his powers be called forth by such rewards as that age
prizes.

We are giving small instructions, while professing to edu- 21
cate an orator. But even studies have their infancy; and as the
rearing of the very strongest bodies commenced with milk and
the cradle, so he, who was to be the most eloquent of men,
once uttered cries, tried to speak at first with a stuttering
voice, and hesitated at the shapes of the letters. Nor, if it is impossible to learn a thing completely, is it, therefore, unnecessary to learn it at all. If no one blames a father who thinks 22
that these matters are not to be neglected in regard to his son,
why should he be blamed who communicates to the public
what he would practice to advantage in his own house? And
this is so much the more the case, as younger minds more
easily take in small things; and as bodies cannot be formed
to certain flexures of the limbs except while they are tender,
so even strength itself makes our minds likewise more un-
yielding to most things. Would Philip, king of Macedonia, 23
have wished the first principles of learning to be communicated to his son Alexander by Aristotle, the greatest philos-

opher of that age, or would Aristotle have undertaken that office, if they had not both thought that the first rudiments of instruction are best treated by the most accomplished teacher, 24 and have an influence on the whole course? Let us suppose, then, that Alexander were committed to me, and laid in my lap, an infant worthy of so much solicitude (though every man thinks his son worthy of similar solicitude), should I be ashamed, even in teaching him his very letters, to point out some compendious methods of instruction?

In any case, that which I see practiced in regard to most children by no means pleases me, namely, that they learn the names and order of the letters before they learn their shapes. 25 This method hinders their recognition of them, as, while they follow their memory that takes the lead, they do not fix their attention on the forms of the letters. This is the reason why teachers, even when they appear to have fixed them sufficiently in the minds of children, in the straight order in which they are usually first written, make them go over them again the contrary way, and confuse them by variously changing the arrangement, until their pupils know them by their shape, not by their place. It will be best for children, therefore, to be taught the appearances and names of the letters at once, as 26 they are taught those of men. But that which is hurtful with regard to letters, will be no impediment with regard to syllables. I do not disapprove, however, the practice, which is well known, of giving children, for the sake of stimulating them to learn, ivory figures of letters to play with, or whatever else can be invented, in which that infantile age may take delight, and which may be pleasing to handle, look at, or name. 27 But as soon as the child shall have begun to trace the forms of the letters, it will not be improper that they should be cut for him, as exactly as possible, on a board, so that his stylus may be guided along them as along grooves, for he will then make no mistakes, as on wax (since he will be kept in by the edge on each side, and will be unable to stray beyond the boundary). By following these sure traces rapidly and frequently, he will form his hand, and not require the assistance

of a person to guide his hand with his own hand placed over
it. The accomplishment of writing well and expeditiously,   28
which is commonly disregarded by people of quality, is by
no means an indifferent matter. Writing itself is of the utmost
importance in our studies, and by it alone sure proficiency,
resting on the deepest roots, is secured. A too slow way of
writing retards thought, and a rude and confused hand cannot be read; hence, follows another task, that of reading off
what is to be copied from the writing. At all times, therefore, 29
and in all places, and especially in writing private and familiar letters, it will be a source of pleasure to us not to have
neglected even this accomplishment.

For learning syllables there is no short way; they must all   30
be learned throughout; nor are the most difficult of them, as
is the general practice, to be postponed, or else children may
be at a loss in writing words. Moreover, we must not even   31
trust to the first learning by heart; it will be better to have
syllables repeated, and to impress them long upon the memory; and in reading, too, not to hurry on, in order to make it
continuous or quick, until the clear and certain connection of
the letters becomes familiar, without any necessity to stop for
recollection. Let the pupil then begin to form words from
syllables, and to join phrases together from words. It is incred- 32
ible how much retardation to reading is caused by haste—for
hence arise hesitation, interruption, and repetition, as children attempt more than they can manage; and then, after
making mistakes, they become distrustful even of what they
know. Let reading, therefore, be at first sure, then continuous,   33
and for a long time slow, until by exercise a correct quickness
is gained. For to look to the right, as everybody teaches, and   34
to look forward, depends not merely on rule, but on habit,
since, while the child is looking to what follows, he has to
pronounce what goes before; and, what is very difficult, the direction of his thoughts must be divided, so that one duty may
be discharged with his voice, and another with his eyes.[4]

[4] The reference here is to the practice of teaching a student to direct
his eyes forward on the page even before he has finished pronouncing out

When the child shall have begun, as is the practice, to copy words, it will cause no regret if we take care that he may not waste his efforts on common words, and such as perpetually
35   occur. For he may readily learn the explanations of obscure terms, which the Greeks call *glosses,* while this other occupation is before him, and acquire, amid his first rudiments, a knowledge of that which would afterward demand a special time for it. Since, too, we are still attending to small matters, I would express a wish that even the lines which are set for him for his imitation in writing should not contain useless sen-
36   tences, but such as convey some moral instruction. The remembrance of such admonitions will attend him to old age, and will be of use even for the formation of his character. It is possible for him, also, to learn the sayings of eminent men, and select passages, chiefly from the poets (for the reading of poets is more pleasing to the young), in his playtime. Memory (as I shall show in its proper place) is most necessary to an orator, and is eminently strengthened and nourished by exercise; and, at the age of which we are now speaking, and which cannot, as yet, produce anything of itself, it is almost the only
37   faculty that can be improved by the aid of teachers. It will not be improper, however, to require of boys of this age (in order that their pronunciation may be fuller and their speech more distinct) to roll forth, as rapidly as possible, certain words and lines of studied difficulty, composed of several syllables, and those roughly clashing together, and, as it were, rugged-sounding; the Greeks call them "gags." This may seem a trifling matter to mention; but when it is neglected, many faults of pronunciation, unless they are removed in the years of youth, are fixed by incorrigible ill habit for the rest of life.

---

loud the words actually scanned by his eyes a split second earlier. The exercise is thus a double one, providing training in both word recognition and memory.

CHAPTER TWO

BUT LET us suppose that the child now gradually increases in 1
size, leaves the lap, and applies himself to learning in earnest.
In this place, accordingly, must be considered the question
whether it be more advantageous to confine the learner at
home, and within the walls of a private house, or to commit him
to the large numbers of a school, and, as it were, to public
teachers. The latter mode, I observe, has had the sanction of 2
those by whom the polity of the most eminent states was settled, as well as that of the most illustrious authors.

Yet it is not to be concealed that there are some who, from
certain notions of their own, disapprove of this almost public
mode of instruction. These persons appear to be swayed
chiefly by two reasons: one, that they take better precautions
for the morals of the young, by avoiding a concourse of human
beings of that age which is most prone to vice (indeed I wish
it were untrue that provocations to immoral conduct do arise);
the other, that whoever may be the teacher, he is likely to bestow his time more liberally on one pupil, than if he has to
divide it among several. The first reason indeed deserves great 3
considerations: for if it were certain that schools, though advantageous to studies, were pernicious to morals, a virtuous
course of life would seem to me preferable to one even of the
most distinguished eloquence. But in my opinion, the two
are combined and inseparable. For I am convinced that no
one can be an orator who is not a good man; and, even if
anyone could, I should be unwilling that he should be. On
this point, therefore, I shall speak first.

People think that morals are corrupted in schools; indeed 4
they are at times corrupted, but such may be the case even at
home. Many proofs of this fact may be adduced—proofs of
character having been vitiated, as well as preserved with the
utmost purity, under both modes of education. It is the dis-

position of the individual pupil, and the care taken of him, that make the whole difference. Suppose that his mind be prone to vice, suppose that there be neglect in forming and guarding his morals in early youth, then seclusion would afford no less opportunity for immorality than publicity. For the private tutor may be himself of bad character; nor is intercourse with vicious slaves at all safer than that with immodest

5 free-born youths. But if his disposition be good, and if there be not a blind and indolent negligence on the part of his parents, it will be possible for them to select a tutor of irreproachable character (a matter to which the utmost attention is paid by sensible parents), and to fix on a course of instruction of the very strictest kind. They may at the same time place at the elbow of their son some influential friend or faithful freedman, whose constant attendance may improve even those of whom apprehensions may be entertained.

6 The remedy for this object of fear is easy. Would that we ourselves did not corrupt the morals of our children! We enervate their very infancy with luxuries. That delicacy of education, which we call fondness, weakens all the powers, both of body and mind. What luxury will he not covet in his manhood, he who crawls about on purple! He cannot yet articulate his first words, when he already distinguishes scarlet, and

7 wants his purple. We form the palate of children before we form their pronunciation. They grow up in sedan chairs; if they touch the ground, they hang by the hands of attendants supporting them on each side. We are delighted if they utter anything immodest. Expressions which would not be tolerated even from the effeminate youths of Alexandria, we hear from them with a smile and a kiss. Nor is this wonderful; we have taught them—they have heard such language from ourselves.

8 They see our mistresses, our male objects of affection; every dining room rings with impure songs; things shameful to be told are objects of sight. From such practices springs habit, and afterward nature. The unfortunate children learn these vices before they know that they are vices; and hence, rendered effeminate and luxurious, they do not imbibe immorality from schools, but carry it themselves into schools.

But, it is said, one tutor will have more time for one pupil. ⁹
First of all, however, nothing prevents that one pupil, whoever he may be, from being the same with him who is taught
in the school. But if the two objects cannot be united, I should
still prefer the daylight of an honorable school to darkness
and solitude; for every eminent teacher delights in a large
concourse of pupils, and thinks himself worthy of a still more
numerous auditory. But inferior teachers, from a consciousness ¹⁰
of their inability, do not disdain to fasten on single pupils,
and to discharge the duty, as it were, of a mere *paedogogus*.
But supposing that either interest, or friendship, or money, ¹¹
should secure to any parent a domestic tutor of the highest
learning, and in every respect unrivaled, will he, however,
spend the whole day on one pupil? Or can the application of
any pupil be so constant as not to be sometimes wearied, like
the sight of the eyes, by continued direction to one object,
especially as study requires the far greater portion of time to
be solitary? For the tutor does not stand by the pupil while ¹²
he is writing, or learning by heart, or thinking; and when he
is engaged in any of those exercises, the company of any person whatsoever is a hindrance to him. Nor does every kind of
reading require at all times an oral reader or interpreter; for
when, if such were the case, would the knowledge of so many
authors be gained? The time, therefore, during which the
work, as it were, for the whole day may be laid out, is but
short. Thus, the instructions which are to be given to each, ¹³
may reach to many. Most of them, indeed, are of such a nature
that they may be communicated to all at once with the same
exertion of the voice. I say nothing of the topics and declamations of rhetoricians, at which, certainly, whatever be the
number of the audience, each will still carry off the whole.
For the voice of the teacher is not like a meal, which will not ¹⁴
suffice for more than a certain number, but like the sun, which
diffuses the same portion of light and heat to all. If a grammarian, too, discourses on the art of speaking, solves questions,
explains matters of history, or illustrates poems, as many as

15 shall hear him will profit by his instructions. But, it may be said, number is an obstacle to correction and explanation. Suppose that this be a disadvantage in a number (for what, in general, satisfies us in every respect?), we will soon compare that disadvantage with other advantages.

Yet I would not wish a boy to be sent to a place where he will be neglected. Nor should a good master encumber himself with a greater number of scholars than he can manage; and it is to be a chief object with us, also, that the master may be in every way our kind friend, and may have regard in his teaching, not so much to duty, as to affection. Thus we shall

16 never be confounded with the multitude. Nor will any master, who is in the slightest degree tinctured with literature, fail particularly to cherish that pupil in whom he shall observe application and genius, even for his own honor. But even if great schools ought to be avoided (a position to which I cannot assent, if numbers flock to a master on account of his merit), the rule is not to be carried so far that schools should be avoided altogether. It is one thing to shun schools entirely, another to choose from them.

17 If I have now refuted the objections which are made to schools, let me next state what opinions I myself entertain.

18 First of all, let him who is to be an orator, and who must live amid the greatest publicity, and in the full daylight of public affairs, accustom himself, from his boyhood, not to be abashed at the sight of men, nor pine in a solitary and, as it were, hermit-like way of life. The mind requires to be constantly excited and roused; while in such retirement, it either languishes, and contracts rust, as it were, in the shade, or, on the other hand, becomes swollen with empty conceit, since he who compares himself to no one else will necessarily attribute

19 too much to his own powers. Besides, when his acquirements are to be displayed in public, he is blinded at the light of the sun, and stumbles at every new object, as having learned

20 in solitude that which is to be done in public. I say nothing of friendships formed at school, which remain in full force even to old age, as if cemented with a certain religious obligation; for to have been initiated in the same studies is not a less

sacred bond than to have been initiated in the same sacred rites. That sense, too, which is called common sense—where shall a young man learn it when he has separated himself from society, which is natural not to men only, but even to dumb animals? Add to this, that at home he can learn only what is taught himself; at school, even what is taught others. He will daily hear many things commended, many things corrected; the idleness of a fellow student, when reproved, will be a warning to him; the industry of anyone, when commended, will be a stimulus; emulation will be excited by praise; and he will think it a disgrace to yield to his equals in age, and an honor to surpass his seniors. All these matters excite the mind; and though ambition itself be a vice, yet it is often the parent of virtues. 21 22

I remember a practice that was observed by my masters, not without advantage. Having divided the boys into classes, they assigned them their order in speaking in conformity to the abilities of each; and thus each stood in the higher place to declaim according as he appeared to excel in proficiency. Judgments were pronounced on the performances, and great was the strife among us for distinction; but to take the lead of the class was by far the greatest honor. Nor was sentence given on our merits only once; the thirtieth day brought the vanquished an opportunity of contending again. Thus, he who was most successful did not relax his efforts, while uneasiness incited the unsuccessful to retrieve his honor. I should be inclined to maintain, as far as I can form a judgment from what I conceive in my own mind, that this method furnished stronger incitements to the study of eloquence than the exhortations of preceptors, the watchfulness of *paedagogi,* or the wishes of parents. 23 24 25

But as emulation is of use to those who have made some advancement in learning, so, to those who are but beginning and are still of tender age, to imitate their schoolfellows is more pleasant than to imitate their master, for the very reason that it is more easy; for they who are learning the first rudiments will scarcely dare to exalt themselves to the hope of attaining that eloquence which they regard as the highest; 26

they will rather fix on what is nearest to them, as vines attached to trees gain the top by taking hold of the lower

27 branches first. This is an observation of such truth, that it is
the care even of the master himself, when he has to instruct
minds that are still unformed, not (if he prefer at least the
useful to the showy) to overburden the weakness of his scholars, but to moderate his strength, and to let himself down to

28 the capacity of the learner. For as narrow-necked vessels reject
a great quantity of the liquid that is poured into them, but
are filled by that which flows or is poured into them by degrees, so it is for us to ascertain how much for their grasp of
intellect will not enter their minds, as not being sufficiently

29 expanded to admit it. It is of advantage, therefore, for a boy
to have schoolfellows whom he may first imitate, and afterward try to surpass. Thus will he gradually conceive hope of
higher excellence.

To these observations I shall add, that masters themselves,
when they have but one pupil at a time with them, cannot
feel the same degree of energy and spirit in addressing him,

30 as when they are excited by a large number of hearers. Eloquence depends in a great degree on the state of the mind,
which must conceive images of objects, and transform itself,
so to speak, to the nature of the things of which we discourse.
Besides, the more noble and lofty a mind is, by the more
powerful springs, as it were, is it moved, and accordingly is

31 both strengthened by praise and enlarged by effort, and is
filled with joy at achieving something great. But a certain
secret disdain is felt at lowering the power of eloquence, acquired by so much labor, to one auditor; and the teacher is
ashamed to raise his style above the level of ordinary conversation. Let anyone imagine, indeed, the air of a man
haranguing, or the voice of one entreating, the gesture, the
pronunciation, the agitation of mind and body, the exertion,
and, to mention nothing else, the fatigue, while he has but
one auditor: Would not he seem to be affected with something like madness? There would be no eloquence in the
world, if we were to speak only with one person at a time.

CHAPTER THREE

LET HIM that is skilled in teaching ascertain first of all, when 1
a boy is entrusted to him, his ability and disposition. The
chief symptom of ability in children is memory, of which the
excellence is twofold: to receive with ease and to retain with
fidelity. The next symptom is imitation; for that is an indication of a teachable disposition, but with this provision, that
it express merely what it is taught, and not a person's manner
or walk, for instance, or whatever may be remarkable for
deformity. The boy who shall make it his aim to raise a laugh 2
by his love of mimicry will afford me no hope of good capacity; for he who is possessed of great talent will be well dis-
posed; else I should think it not at all worse to be of a dull,
than of a bad, disposition; but he who is honorably inclined
will be very different from the stupid or idle. Such a pupil as 3
I would have will easily learn what is taught him, and will
ask questions about some things, but will still rather follow
than run on before. That precocious sort of talent scarcely
ever comes to good fruit. Such are those who do little things 4
easily, and, impelled by impudence, show at once all that they
can accomplish in such matters. But they succeed only in
what is ready to their hand; they string words together, utter-
ing them with an intrepid countenance, not in the least dis-
couraged by bashfulness. They do little, but do it readily.
There is no real power behind, or any that rests on deeply 5
fixed roots, but they are like seeds which have been scattered
on the surface of the ground and shoot up prematurely, and
like grass that resembles corn, and grows yellow, with empty
ears, before the time of harvest. Their efforts give pleasure, as
compared with their years; but their progress comes to a
stand, and our wonder diminishes.

When a tutor has observed these indications, let him next 6

consider how the mind of his pupil is to be managed. Some boys are indolent, unless you stimulate them; some are indignant at being commanded; fear restrains some, and unnerves others; continued labor forms some; with others, hasty efforts

7   succeed better. Let the boy be given to me, whom praise stimulates, whom honor delights, who weeps when he is unsuccessful. His powers must be cultivated under the influence of ambition; reproach will sting him to the quick; honor will incite him; and in such a boy I shall never be apprehensive of indifference.

8   Yet some relaxation is to be allowed to all, not only because there is nothing that can bear perpetual labor (and even those things that are without sense and life are unbent by alternate rest, as it were, in order that they may preserve their vigor), but because application to learning depends on the will, which

9   cannot be forced. Boys, accordingly, when reinvigorated and refreshed, bring more sprightliness to their learning, and a more determined spirit, which for the most part spurns com-

10   pulsion. Nor will play in boys displease me: it is also a sign of vivacity, and I cannot expect that he who is always dull and spiritless will be of an eager disposition in his studies, when he is indifferent even to that excitement which is natural

11   to his age. There must, however, be bounds set to relaxation, lest the refusal of it beget an aversion to study, or too much indulgence in it a habit of idleness. There are some kinds of amusement, too, not unserviceable for sharpening the wits of boys, as when they contend with each other by proposing all

12   sorts of questions in turn. In their play, also, their moral dispositions show themselves more plainly, supposing that there is no age so tender that it may not readily learn what is right and wrong. The tender age may best be formed at a time when it is ignorant of dissimulation and most willingly submits to instructors; for you may break, sooner than mend,

13   that which has hardened into deformity. A child is to be admonished as early as possible, therefore, that he must do nothing too eagerly, nothing dishonestly, nothing without self-control; and we must always keep in mind the maxim of

Virgil, *adeo in teneris consuescere multum est,*[1] "of so much importance is the acquirement of habit in the young."

But that boys should suffer corporal punishment, though it be an accepted custom and Chrysippus makes no objection to it, I by no means approve; first, because it is a disgrace, and 14 a punishment for slaves, and in reality (as will be evident if you imagine the age changed), an affront; secondly, because, if a boy's disposition be so abject as not to be amended by reproof, he will be hardened, like the worst of slaves, even to stripes; and lastly, because, if one who regularly exacts his tasks be with him, there will not be the least need of any such chastisement. At present, the negligence of *paedagogi* seems 15 to be made amends for in such a way that boys are not obliged to do what is right, but are instead punished whenever they have not done it. Besides, after you have coerced a boy with stripes, how will you treat him when be becomes a young man, to whom such terror cannot be held out, and by whom more difficult studies must be pursued? Add to these considerations, 16 that many things unpleasant to be mentioned, and likely afterwards to cause shame, often happen to boys while being whipped, under the influence of pain or fear; and such shame enervates and depresses the mind, and makes them shun people's sight and feel a constant uneasiness. If, moreover, there 17 has been too little care in choosing governors and tutors of reputable character, I am ashamed to say how unworthy men may scandalously abuse their privilege of punishing, and what opportunity also the terror of the unhappy children may sometimes afford to others. I will not dwell upon this point; what is already understood is more than enough. It will be sufficient, therefore, to intimate that no man should be allowed too much authority over an age so weak and so unable to resist ill-treatment.

I will now proceed to show in what studies the boy must 18 be instructed who is to be so trained that he may become an orator, and which of them must be commenced at each particular period of youth.

[1] *Georgics* II. 272.

CHAPTER FOUR

1 IN REGARD to the boy who has attained facility in reading and writing, the next object is instruction from the grammarians. Nor is it of importance whether I speak of the Greek or Latin grammarian, though I am inclined to think that the Greek 2 should take the precedence. Both have the same method. This profession, then, distinguished as it is, most fittingly, into two parts, the art of speaking correctly, and the interpretation of the poets, carries more beneath than it shows on its surface.[1]

3 For not only is the art of writing combined with that of speaking, but correct reading also precedes illustration, and with all these is joined the exercise of judgment, which the old grammarians, indeed, used with such severity that they not only allowed themselves to distinguish certain verses with a particular mark of censure, and to remove from their sets, as spurious, certain books which had been inscribed with false titles, but even brought some authors within their canon, and 4 excluded others altogether from classification. Nor is it sufficient to have read the poets only; every class of writers must be studied, not simply for matter, but for words, which often receive their authority from writers. Nor can grammar be complete without a knowledge of music, since the grammarian has to speak of meter and rhythm; nor, if he is ignorant of astronomy, can he understand the poets, who, to say nothing of other matters, so often allude to the rising and setting of the stars in marking the seasons; nor must he be unacquainted with philosophy, both on account of numbers of passages, in almost all poems, drawn from the most abstruse subtleties of physical investigation, and also on account of Empedocles among the Greeks, and Varro and Lucretius among the Latins, 5 who have committed the precepts of philosophy to verse. The

1 This famous definition of the province of "grammar" includes both what today would be called "syntax" (the rules) and "literature."

grammarian has also need of no small portion of eloquence, that he may speak aptly and fluently on each of those subjects which are here mentioned. Those, therefore, are not to be heeded who deride this science as trifling and empty; for unless it lays a sure foundation for the future orator, whatever superstructure you raise will surely fall. It is an art which is necessary to the young, pleasing to the old, and an agreeable companion in retirement. Alone, of all departments of learning, it has in it more service than show.

Let no man, therefore, look down on the elements of gram- 6 mar as small matters; not because it requires great labor to distinguish consonants from vowels, and to divide them into the proper number of semivowels and mutes, but because, to those entering the recesses, as it were, of this temple, there will appear much subtlety on points, which may not only sharpen the wits of boys, but may exercise even the deepest erudition and knowledge. Is it in the power of every ear to distinguish 7 accurately the sounds of letters? No more, assuredly, than to distinguish the sounds of musical strings. But all grammarians will at least descend to the discussion of such curious points as these: whether any necessary letters be wanting to us, not indeed when we write Greek, for then we borrow two letters [2] from the Greeks, but, properly, in Latin: as in these words, 8 *seruus* and *uulgus,* the Aeolic digamma is required; and there is a certain sound of a letter between *u* and *i,* for we do not pronounce *optumum* like *optimum;* in *here,* too, neither *e* nor *i* is distinctly heard: whether, again, other letters are 9 redundant (besides the mark of aspiration, which, if it be necessary, requires also a contrary mark), as *k,* which is itself used to designate certain names, and *q* (similar to *k* in sound and shape, except that *q* is slightly slanted by our writers; *koppa* now remains among the Greeks, though only in the list of numbers), as well as *x,* the last of our letters, which indeed we might have done without, if we had not sought it. With regard to vowels, too, it is the business of the gram- 10 marian to see whether custom has taken any for consonants,

[2] *Y* and *Z*.

since *iam* is written as *ettam,* and *quos* as *tuos.* But vowels which
are joined, as vowels, make either one long vowel, as the ancients wrote, who used the doubling of them instead of the circumflex accent, or two; though perhaps someone may suppose
that a syllable may be formed even of three vowels; but this
cannot be the case, unless some of them do the duty of conso-
11 nants. The grammarian will also inquire how two vowels
only have the power of uniting with each other, when none
of the consonants can break any letter but another consonant.
But the letter *i* unites with itself, for *coniicit* is from *iacit;*
and so does *u,* as *uulgus* and *seruus* are now written. Let the
grammarian also know that Cicero was inclined to write *aiio*
and *Maiia* with a double *i;* and, if this be done, the one *i* will
12 be joined to the other as a consonant. Let the boy, therefore,
learn what is peculiar in letters, what is common, and what relationship each has to each, and let him wonder why *scabillum*
is formed from *scamnum,* or why *bipennis,* an axe with an
edge each way, is formed from *pinna,* which means something
sharp, that he may not follow the error of those, who, because
they think that this word is from two wings, would have the
wings of birds called *pinnae.*

13   Nor let him know only those changes which declension and
prepositions introduce, as *secat secuit, cadit excīdit, caedit
excīdit, calcat exculcat;* (so *lotus* from *lavare,* whence also
inlotus; and there are a thousand other similar derivations);
but also what alterations have taken place, even in nominative
cases, through lapse of time; for, as *Valesii* and *Fusii* have
passed into *Valerii* and *Furii,* so *arbos, labos, vapos,* as well
14 as *clamos* and *lases,* have had their day. This very letter *s,* too,
which has been excluded from these words, has itself, in some
other words, succeeded to the place of another letter; for instead of *mersare* and *pulsare,* they once said *mertare* and *pul-
tare.* They also said *fordeum* and *foedus,* using, instead of the
aspiration, a letter similar to *vau;* for the Greeks, on the other
hand, are accustomed to aspirate, whence Cicero, in his oration for Fundanius, laughs at a witness who could not sound
15 the first letter of that name. But we have also, at times, ad-

mitted *b* into the place of other letters, whence *Burrus,*
Bruges, and *Belena.* The same letter moreover has made *bel-*
lum out of *duellum,* whence some have ventured to call the
Duellii, Bellii. Why need I speak of *stlocus* and *stlites?* Why 16
need I mention that there is a certain relationship of the letter *t* to *d?* Hence, it is far from surprising if, on the old buildings of our city, and well-known temples, is read *Alexanter*
and *Cassantra.* Why should I specify that *o* and *u* are inter-
changed? *Hecoba* and *notrix, Culchides* and *Pulyxena,* were
used, and (that this may not be noticed in Greek words only),
dederont and *probaveront.* So *Odysseus,* whom the Aeolians
made *Ulysses,* was turned into *Ulixes.* Was not *e,* too, put in 17
the place of *i,* as *Menerva, leber, magester,* and *Diiove* and
Veiove for *Diiovi* and *Veiovi?* But it is enough for me to point
to the subject; for I do not teach but admonish those who are
to teach. The attention of the learner will then be transferred
to syllables, on which I shall make a few remarks under the
head of orthography.

He, whom this matter shall concern, will then understand
how many parts of speech there are, and what they are; though
as to their number, writers are by no means agreed.[3] For the 18
more ancient, among whom were Aristotle and Theodectes,
said that there were only *verbs, nouns,* and *convinctions,* because, that is to say, they judged that the force of language
was in verbs, and the matter of it in nouns (since the one is
what we speak, and the other that of which we speak), and

[3] This discussion of the "parts of speech" reflects the grammatical
situation in Quintilian's time. Controversy still swirled about this particular matter because there was not yet a widely accepted, authoritative
exposition of the subject; this was to come by the time of Aelius Donatus
(fl. A.D. 350), whose book *On the Parts of Speech* became a standard for
almost twelve hundred years. In the Middle Ages this little grammar
text (which helped to set the parts of speech at eight) was so widely
used that the term "Donat" or "Donet" became a synonym for "primer"
or "first book' in any subject. Its text is in Henry Keil (ed.), *Grammatici*
latini, 7 vols. (Lipsiae, 1864), IV, 355–366. For brief discussions of ancient
grammar, see Paul Abelson, *The Seven Liberal Arts* (New York, 1906),
p. 36; and R. H. Robins, *Ancient and Medieval Grammatical Theory in*
Europe (London: G. Bell and Sons Ltd., 1951), pp. 1–68.

that the union of words lay in convinctions, which, I know, are by most writers called conjunctions, but the other term

19 seems to be a more exact translation of συνδέσμῳ. By the philosophers, and chiefly the Stoics, the number was gradually increased; to the convinctions were first added articles, then prepositions; to nouns was added the appellation, next the pronoun, and afterward the participle, partaking of the nature of the verb; to verbs themselves were joined adverbs. Our language does not require articles, and they are therefore divided among other parts of speech. To the parts of speech al-

20 ready mentioned was added the interjection. Other writers, however, certainly of competent judgment, have made eight parts of speech, for instance, Aristarchus, and Palaemon in our own day, who have included the vocable, or appellation, under the name or noun as if a species of it. But those who make the noun one, and the vocable another, reckon nine. But there were some, nevertheless, who even distinguished the vocable from the appellation, so that the vocable should signify any substance manifest to the sight and touch, as a house, a bed; the appellation, that to which one or both of these properties should be wanting, as the wind, heaven, God, virtue. They added also the asseveration, as *heu*, "alas!" and the attrectation, as *fasceatim*, "in bundles"—distinctions which

21 are not approved by me. Whether προσηγορία should be translated by "vocable" or "appellation," and whether it should be comprehended under the noun or not, are questions on which, as being of little importance, I leave it free to others to form an opinion.

22 Let boys in the first place learn to decline nouns and conjugate verbs, for otherwise they will never arrive at the understanding of what is to follow. This admonition would be superfluous to give, were it not that most teachers, through ostentatious haste, begin where they ought to end, and, while they wish to show off their pupils in matters of greater display, retard their progress by attempting to shorten the road.

23 But if a teacher has sufficient learning, and (what is often

found not less wanting) be willing to teach what he has
learned, he will not be content with stating that there are
three genders in nouns, and specifying what nouns have two
or all three genders. Nor shall I hastily deem that tutor dili- 24
gent, who shall have shown that there are irregular nouns,
called *epicene,* in which both genders are implied under one,
or nouns which, under a feminine termination, signify males,
or, with a neuter termination, denote females (as *Muraena*
and *Glycerium*). A penetrating and acute teacher will search 25
into a thousand origins of names; derivations which have produced the names *Rufus,* "red," and *Longus,* "long," from personal peculiarities (among which will be some of rather obscure etymology, as *Sulla, Burrhus, Galba, Plancus, Pansa,
Scaurus,* and others of the same kind); some also from acci-
dents of birth, as *Agrippa, Opiter, Cordus, Posthumus;* some
from occurrences after birth, as *Vopiscus;* while others as
Cotta, Scipio, Laenas, Seranus, spring from various causes. We 26
may also find people, places, and many other things among
the origins of names. That sort of name among slaves, which
was taken from their masters, whence *Marcipores* and *Publi-
pores,* has fallen into disuse. Let the tutor consider, also,
whether there is not among the Greeks ground for a sixth
case, and among us even for a seventh; for when I say *hasta
percussi,* "I have struck with a spear," I do not express the
sense of an ablative case, nor, if I say the same thing in Greek,
that of a dative.

As to verbs, who is so ignorant as not to know their kinds, 27
qualities, persons, and numbers? Those things belong to the
reading school and to the lower departments of instruction.
But such points as are not determined by inflection will puz-
zle some people; for it may be doubted, as to certain words,
whether they are participles, or nouns formed from the verb,
as *lectus,*[4] *sapiens.* Some verbs look like nouns, as *freudator,* 28
nutritor. Is not the verb in *itur in antiquam silvam* [5] of a pe-

[4] Halm's text has *lectum;* Radermacher prints *tectum.*
[5] Virgil, *Aeneid* VI. 179.

culiar nature, for what beginning of it can you find? *Fletur* is similar to it. We understand the passive sometimes in one way, as,

> *panditur interea domus omnipotentis Olympi;* [6]

sometimes in another, as,

> *totis*
> *usque adeo turbatur agris.*[7]

There is also a third way, as *urbs habitatur,* whence likewise *campus curritur, mare navigatur. Pransus* also and *potus* have a different signification from that which their form indicates. I need hardly add that many verbs do not go through the whole course of conjugation. Some, too, undergo a change, as *fero* in the perfect; some are expressed only in the form of the third person, as *licet, piget;* and some bear a resemblance to nouns passing into adverbs; for, as we say *noctu* and *diu,* so we say *dictu* and *factu;* since these words are indeed participial, though not like *dicto* and *facto.*

6 *Ibid.,* X. 1.
7 Virgil, *Eclogues* I. 11.

CHAPTER FIVE

Since all language has three kinds of excellence, to be correct, perspicuous, and elegant (for to speak with propriety, which is its highest quality, most writers include under elegance), and the same number of faults, which are the opposites of the excellences just mentioned, let the grammarian consider well the rules for correctness which constitute the first part of grammar. These rules are required to be observed, *verbis aut singulis aut pluribus,* that is in regard to one word or to more than one word. The word *verbum* I wish to be here understood in a general sense, for it has two significations: the one, which includes all words of which language is composed, as in the verse of Horace,

verbaque provisam rem non invita sequentur.[1]

"And words, not unwilling, will follow provided matter"; the other, under which is comprehended only one part of speech, as *lego, scribo.* To avoid this ambiguity, some have preferred the terms *voces, dictiones,* or *locutiones.* Words, considered singly, are either our own, or foreign, simple or compound, proper or metaphorical, in common use or newly invented.

A word taken singly is more often objectionable than faultless; for however we may express anything with propriety, elegance, and sublimity, none of these qualities arise from anything but the connection and order of the discourse (since we commend single words merely as being well suited to the matter). The only good quality which can be remarked in them is their *vocalitas,* so to speak, called "euphony." This depends upon selection, when of two words which have the same signification and are of equal force, we make choice of the one that has the better sound.

First of all, let the offensiveness of barbarisms and solecisms

[1] *Ars poetica* 311.

be put away. But as these faults are sometimes excused, either from custom, or authority, or perhaps from their nearness to beauties (for it is often difficult to distinguish faults from figures of speech), let the grammarian, so that so uncertain a subject of observation may deceive no one, give his earnest attention to that nice discrimination of which we shall speak more fully in the part where we shall have to treat of figures of

6   speech.[2] Meanwhile, let an offence committed in regard to a single word be called a *barbarism*.

But someone may stop me with the remark, what is there here worthy of the promise of so great a work? Or who does not know that barbarisms are committed, some in writing, others in speaking? (Because what is written incorrectly must also be spoken incorrectly, though he who speaks incorrectly may not necessarily make mistakes in writing.) The first sort is caused by addition, curtailment, substitution, or transposition; the second, by separation or confusion of syllables, aspi-

7   ration, or other faults of sound. But though these may be small matters, boys are still to be taught, and we put grammarians in mind of their duty. If any one of these teachers, however, shall not be sufficiently accomplished, but shall have just entered the vestibule of the art, he will have to confine himself within those rules which are published in the little manuals of professors; the more learned will add many other instructions, the very first of which will be this, that we under-

8   stand barbarisms as being of several kinds. One, with reference to country, such as is committed when a person inserts an African or Spanish term in Latin composition; as when the iron ring, with which wheels are bound, is called *canthus* [i.e., *cantus*], though Persius uses this as a received word; as when Catullus got the word *ploxenum*, "a box," on the banks of the Po; and in the speech of Labienus (if it be not rather the speech of Cornelius Gallus), the word *casnar*, "a parasite," is brought from Gaul against Pollio; as to *mastruca*, "a shaggy

---

[2] Quintilian devotes a large part of Books VIII and IX to a detailed discussion of figures of speech, figures of thought, and the special figures of speech known as "tropes."

garment," which is a Sardinian word, Cicero has used it purposely in jest.

Another kind of barbarism is that which we regard as proceeding from the natural disposition, when he, by whom anything has been uttered insolently, or threateningly, or cruelly, is said to have spoken like a barbarian. The third kind of barbarism is that of which examples are everywhere abundant and which everyone can form for himself by adding a letter or syllable to any word he pleases, or taking one away, or substituting one for another, or putting one in a place where it is not right for it to be. But some grammarians, to make a show of learning, are accustomed, for the most part, to take examples of these from the poets, and find fault with the authors whom they interpret. A boy ought to know, however, that such forms of speech, in writers of poetry, are considered as deserving of excuse, or even of praise; and learners must be taught less common instances. Thus Tinca of Placentia (if we believe Hortensius, who finds fault with him) was guilty of two barbarisms in one word, saying *precula* instead of *pergula;* first, by the change of a letter, putting *c* for *g,* and secondly, by transposition, placing *r* before the preceeding *e.* But Ennius, when committing a like double fault, by saying *Metioeo Fufetioeo,* is defended on the ground of poetic licence. In prose, too, there are certain licenses; for Cicero speaks of an army of *Canopitae,* though the people of the city call it *Canobus;* and many writers have authorized *Trasumennum* for *Tarsumennum,* although there is a transposition in it. Other words suffer similar treatment; for if *assentior,* "I assent," be thought the proper way of spelling that word, Sisenna has said *assentio,* and many have followed him on grounds of analogy; or, if *assentio* be deemed the right method, the other form, *assentior,* is supported by common practice. Yet the prim and pedantic teacher will suppose that there is either curtailment in the one case, or addition in the other. I need hardly add that some forms, which, taken singly, are doubtless faulty, are used in composition without blame. For *dua, tre,* and *pondo,* are barbarisms of discordant gender; yet the compounds *duapondo,* "two pounds," and *trepondo,* "three pounds," have been used by everybody down to our own times; and Messala maintains that they are used with propriety. It may perhaps seem absurd to say that a barbarism, which is incorrectness in a single word, may be committed in number and gender, like a solecism; yet *scala,* "stairs," and *scopa,* "a broom," in the singular, and *hordea,* "barley," and *mulsa,* "mead," in the plural, as they are attended with no change, withdrawal, or addition of letters, are objectionable only because plurals are expressed in the singular, and singulars in the plural; and those who have used *gladia,* "swords," have committed a fault in gender. But this point, too, I am satisfied with merely mentioning, so that I myself may not appear to have added another question to a branch of study already perplexed through the fault of certain obstinate grammarians.[3]

Faults which are committed in speaking require more sagacity in criticizing them, because examples of them cannot be given from writing, except when they have occurred in verses, as the division of the diphthong in *Europai,* and the irregularity of the opposite kind, which the Greeks call *synaeresis* and *synalaepha,* and we call *conflexio,* "combination," as in the verse in Publius Varro,

> *tum te flagranti dejectum fulmine Phaethon.*[4]

For, if it were prose, it would be possible to enunciate those letters by their proper syllables. Those peculiarities, also, which occur in quantity, whether when a short syllable is made long, as in *Italiam fato profugus,*[5] or when a long one is made short, as in *Unius ob noxam et furias,*[6] you would not

16

17

18

---

[3] Here again, as he did earlier (I. 4. 17) in relation to letters. Quintilian has outlined an area of grammatical studies without claiming to solve the problems raised.

[4] The fault here is the use of *Phœthon* for *Phaëthon.* Publius Terentius Varro (82–35 B.C.), an obscure latin poet; only fragments of his work survive.

[5] *Aeneid* I. 2.

[6] *Ibid.,* I. 41.

remark except in verse; and even in verse they are not to be
regarded as faults. Those which are committed in sound are   19
judged only by the ear. As to the aspirate, however, whether
it be added or retrenched in variation from common practice,
it may be a question with us whether it be a fault in writing—
for example, whether *h* indeed be a letter, and not merely a
mark, as to which point opinion has often changed with time.
The ancients used it very sparingly even before vowels, as   20
they said *aedos* and *ircos;* and it was long afterward withheld
from conjunction with consonants, as in *Graccus* and *tri-*
umpus. But suddenly an excessive use of it became prevalent,
so that *choronae, chenturiones, praechones,* are still to be seen
in certain inscriptions; on which practice there is a well-
known epigram of Catullus.[7] Hence there remain, even to our   21
times, *vehementer, comprehendere,* and *mihi.* Among the ancient writers, also, especially those of tragedy, we find in old
copies *mehe* for *me.*

   Still more difficult is the marking of faults in respect to the   22
tenores, "tones" (which I find called by the old writers *tonores,*
as if the word were derived from the Greeks, who call them
τόνους), or accents, which the Greeks call προσῳδίας when the
acute is put for the grave, or the grave for the acute; as if, in
the word *Camíllus,* the first syllable should receive the acute
accent; or if the grave is put for the circumflex, as when the   23
first syllable of *Cethêgus* has the acute, for thus the quantity
of the middle syllable is altered; or if the circumflex is put
for the grave, as when the second syllable is circumflexed in
Appi, by contracting which, from two syllables into one, and
then circumflexing it, people commit two errors. But this   24
happens far more frequently in Greek words, as *Atreus,* which,
when I was young, the most learned old men used to pronounce with an acute on the first syllable, so that the second
was necessarily grave, as was also that of *Tereus* and *Nereus.*
Such have been the rules respecting accents. But I am quite   25
aware that certain learned men, and some grammarians also,
teach and speak in such a manner as to terminate a word at

7 Catullus LXXXI.

times with an acute sound for the sake of preserving certain distinctions in words, as in *circum* in these lines,

> *quae circum litora, circum*
> *piscosos scopulos,*[8]

lest, if they make the second syllable in *circum* grave, a *circus* might seem to be meant, not a *circuit. Quantum* and *quale,* also, when asking a question, they conclude with a grave accent; when making a comparison, with an acute; a practice, however, which they observe almost only in adverbs and pronouns; in other words, they follow the old custom. To me it appears to make a difference, that in these phrases we join the words; for when I say *circum litora,* I enunciate the words as one, without making any distinction between them; and, thus, one syllable only, as in a single word, is acute. The same is the case in this hemistich,

> *Trojae qui primus ab oris.*[9]

It sometimes happens, too, that the law of the meter alters the accent: as,

> *pecudes, pictaeque volucres.*[10]

For I shall pronounce *volucres* with an acute on the middle syllable because, though it be short by nature, it is long by position, that it may not form an iambus, which a heroic verse does not admit. But these words, taken separately, will not vary from the rule, or, if custom shall triumph, the old law of the language will be abolished; the observation of which law is more difficult among the Greeks (because they have several modes of speaking, which they call dialects, and because what is wrong in one is sometimes right in another). But among us the principle of accentuation is very simple. For in every word the acuted syllable is confined within the number of three syllables, whether those three be the only syllables

26
27
28
29
30

---

8 *Aeneid* IV. 254–255.
9 *Ibid.,* I. 1.
10 *Georgics* III. 243.

in the word, or the three last; and of these, the acuted syllable
is either the next, or the next but one, to the last. Of the
three syllables of which I am speaking, moreover, the middle
one will be long, or acute, or circumflex; a short syllable in
that position will, or course, have a grave sound, and will
accordingly acute the one that stands before it, that is, the
third from the end. But in every word there is an acute syllable, though never more than one; nor is that one ever the
last, and consequently in dissyllables it is the first. Besides
there is never in the same word one syllable circumflexed and
another acuted, for the same syllable that is circumflexed is
also acuted; neither of the two, therefore, will terminate a
Latin word. Those words, however, which consist of but one
syllable will be either acuted or circumflexed, so that there
may be no word without an acute.

In sounds also occur those faults of utterance and pronunciation of which specimens cannot be given in writing; the
Greeks, who are more happy in inventing names, call them
iotacisms, lambdacisms,[11] ἰσχνότητας, and πλατεασμούς: as also
κοιλοστομίαν, when the voice is heard, as it were, in the depths
of the throat. There are also certain peculiar and inexpres-
sible sounds for which we sometimes find fault with whole
nations. All the incorrectnesses, then, which we have mentioned above, being removed, there will result that which is
called ὀρθοέπεια, that is, a correct and clear utterance of words
with an agreeableness of sound; for so may a right pronunciation be termed.

All other faults arise out of more words than one—among
which faults is the *solecism*—though about this also there has
been controversy. For even those who admit that it lies in
the composition of words, yet contend that, because it may be
corrected by the amendment of a single word, it is the incorrectness of a word, and not a fault in composition; since,
whether *amarae corticis* or *medio cortice* constitutes a fault in
gender (to neither of which do I object, Virgil being the au-

31

32

33

34

35

---

[11] Iotacism is the doubling of the *i* sound; lambdacism is the doubling
of the *l*.

thor of both [12]; but let us suppose that one of the two is incorrect), the alteration of one word, in which the fault lay,
produces correctness of phraseology, so that we have *amari
corticis* or *media cortice*. This is a manifest misrepresentation;
for neither of the words is wrong, taken separately, but the
fault lies in them when put together, and it is a fault there-
36   fore of phrase. It is, however, a question of greater sagacity,
whether a solecism can be committed in a single word; as if a
man, calling one person to him, should say *venite,* or, sending
several away from him, should say *abi,* or *discede;* or, moreover, when an answer does not agree with the question, as if
to a person saying *quem video?* ("whom do I see?"), you
should reply *ego* ("I"). Some also think that the same fault is
committed in gesture, when one thing is signified by the
37   voice, and another by a nod or by the hand. With this opinion I do not altogether agree, nor do I altogether dissent from
it; for I allow that a solecism may occur in one word, but
not unless there be something having the force of another
word, to which the incorrect word may be referred; so that a
solecism arises from the union of things by which something
is signified or some intention manifested; and, that I may
38   avoid all cavilling, it sometimes occurs in one word, but never
in a word by itself.

   But under how many, and what forms, the solecism occurs,
is not sufficiently agreed. Those who speak of it most fully
make the nature of it fourfold, like that of the barbarism: so
that it may be committed by addition, as, *nam enim, de susum
in Alexandriam;* by retrenchment, as *ambulo viam, Aegypto*
39   *venio, ne hoc fecit;* by transposition, by which the order of
words is confused, as, *quoque ego, enim hoc voluit, autem non
habuit;* whether *igitur,* when placed at the beginning of a
phrase, ought to be included under this head, may be a matter
of dispute, because I see that eminent authors have been of
opposite opinions as to the practice, it being common among
40   some, while it is never found in others. These three sorts of

[12] *Eclogues* VI. 62–63 and *Georgics* II. 74.

irregularity some distinguish from the solecism, and call a fault of addition "a pleonasm," of retrenchment "an ellipsis," of inversion "an anastrophe," and allege that if these fall under the head of solecism, the "hyperbaton" may be included under the same title. Substitution is, without dispute, when 41 one thing is put for another; it is an irregularity which we find affecting all the parts of speech, but most frequently the verb, because it has most modifications. Accordingly, under the head of substitution, occur solecisms in gender, tense, persons, moods (or states, or qualities, if any one wish that they should be so called), being six, or, as some will have it, eight, in number (since into however many forms you distinguish each of the parts of speech of which mention has just been made, there will be so many sorts of errors liable to be committed), as well as in numbers, of which we have the singular and plural, the Greeks also the dual. There have, indeed, been some who assigned us also a dual, *scripsere, legere,* a termination which was merely a softening for the sake of avoiding roughness of sound, as, among the old writers, *male merere* for *male mereris.* Thus what they call the dual consists in that one sort of termination only, whereas among the Greeks it is found not only through almost the whole system of the verb, but also in nouns (though even so the use of it is very rare). But in no one of our authors is this distinction of 43 ending to be discovered; on the contrary, the phrases, *devenere locos,*[13] *conticuere omnes,*[14] *consedere duces,*[15] show us plainly that no one of them refers to two persons only; *dixere,* too, though Antonius Rufus gives it as an example of the contrary, the crier pronounces concerning more advocates than two.[16] Does not Livy, also, near the beginning of his first book, say, 44

[13] *Aeneid* I. 365.

[14] *Ibid.,* II. 1.

[15] Ovid, *Metamorphoses* XIII. 1.

[16] In trials it was the practice of the court crier to say *dixere,* "they have spoken," after the speeches of both sides were finished. Quintilian's point is that the expression could refer to several speakers, not always just two.

tenuere arcem Sabini, and a little afterwards, *in adversum Romani subiere?* [17] But whom shall I follow in preference to Cicero, who, in his *De oratore,* says, "I do not object to *scripsere,* though I consider *scripserunt* to be preferable?" [18]

45   In appellative and other nouns, likewise, the solecism shows itself in regard to gender, and to number, but especially to case. Whichsoever of those three shall be put in the place of another, the error may be placed under this head; as also incorrectnesses in the use of comparatives and superlatives, as well as cases in which the patronymic is put for the possessive, or the contrary. As to a fault committed in regard to

46   quantity, such as *magnum peculiolum* ("great little private property"), there will be some who will think it a solecism, because a diminution is used instead of the integral word. For my own part, though, I doubt whether I should not rather call it a misapplication of a word, for it is a departure from the signification: the impropriety of a solecism is not an error as to the sense of a word, but in the junction of words. In

47   respect to the participle, errors are committed in gender and case, as in the noun; in tense, as in the verb; and in number, as in both. The pronoun, also, has gender, number, and case, all of which admit mistakes of this kind. Solecisms are com-

48   mitted, too, and in great numbers, as to parts of speech, but it is not enough merely to remark this generally, lest the pupil should think a solecism committed only where one part of speech is put for another, as a verb where there ought to have been a noun, or an adverb where there ought to have been a

49   pronoun, and the like. For there are some nouns *cognate,* as they say, that is, of the same kind, in regard to which he who shall use another species than that which he ought to use, will be guilty of no less an error than if he were to use a word of

50   another genus. Thus *an* and *aut* are both conjunctions, yet you would be incorrect in asking, *hic, aut ille, sit? Ne* and *non* are both adverbs, yet he who should say *non feceris* for *ne feceris,* would fall into a similar error, since the one is an ad-

17 Livy, L. 12.
18 *De oratore* XLVII, 157.

verb of denying, the other of forbidding. I will add another example: *intro* and *intus* are both adverbs of place; yet *eo intus* and *intro sum* are solecisms. The same faults may be committed in regard to the different sorts of pronouns, interjections, and prepositions. The discordant collocation of preceding and following words, also, in a sentence of one clause, is a solecism.

There are expressions, however, which have the appearance of solecisms, and yet cannot be called faulty, as *tragoedia Thyestes, ludi Floralia,* and *Megalensia,*[19] for though these modes of expression have fallen into disuse in later times, there was never any variation from them among the ancients. They shall therefore be called *schemata* or *figures*—figures more common indeed among the poets, but allowable also to writers and speakers in prose. But a figure will generally have something right for its basis, as I shall show in that part of my work which I just before promised.[20] Yet what is now called a figure will not be free from the fault of solecism, if it be used by any one unknowingly. Of the same sort, though as I have already said they have nothing of figure, are names with a feminine termination which males have, and those with a masculine termination which females have. But of the solecism I shall say no more; for I have not undertaken to write a treatise on grammar, though, as grammar met me in my road, I was unwilling to pass it without paying my respects to it.

In continuation, that I may follow the course which I prescribed to myself, let me repeat that words are either Latin or foreign. Foreign words, like men and like many of our institutions, have come to us, I might almost say, from all nations. I say nothing of the Tuscans, Sabines, and Praenestines;

[19] These are examples of expressions in which common usage has normalized a technically incorrect form. *Tragoedia Thyestes* ("the tragedy Thyestes") should technically use the genitive case in the second word: *Tragoedia Thyestis* ("the tragedy of Thyestes"). Quintilian frequently expresses such awareness of the difference between formal rules and the standard of usage.

[20] That is, Books VIII and IX of the *Institutio oratoria.*

for though Lucilius attacks Vectius for using their dialect, since Pollio discovers Patavinity in Livy, I would consider

57 every part of Italy as Roman. Many Gallic words have prevailed among us, as *rheda,* "a chariot," and *petorritum,* "a four-wheeled carriage," of which, however, Cicero uses one, and Horace the other. *Mappa,* "a napkin," too, a term much used in the circus, the Carthaginians claim as theirs; and *gurdus,* a word which the common people use for "foolish,"

58 had, I have heard, its origin in Spain. But this division of mine is intended to refer chiefly to the Greek language, for it is from thence that the Roman language is in a very great degree derived. We use even pure Greek words where our own fail, as they also sometimes borrow from us. Hence arises the question whether it is proper that foreign words should be de-

59 clined with cases in the same way as our own. If you meet with a grammarian who is a lover of the ancients, he will say that there should be no departure from the Latin method; because, as there is in our language an ablative case, which the Greeks have not, it is by no means becoming for us to use one case

60 of our own, and five Greek cases. And he would also praise the merit of those who studied to increase the resources of the Latin language, and asserted that they need not introduce foreign practices; under the influence of which notion they said *Castorem,* with the middle syllable long, because such was the case with all our nouns whose nominative case ends in the same letters as *Castor;* and they retained the practice, moreover, of saying *Palaemo, Telamo,* and *Plato* (for so Cicero also called him), because they found no Latin word that termi-

61 nated with the letters *o* and *n.* Nor did they willingly allow masculine Greek nouns to end in -*as* in the nominative case, and accordingly, we read in Caelius, *Pelia cincinnatus;* in Messala, *bene fecit Euthia;* in Cicero, *Hermagora;* so that we

62 need not wonder that the forms *Aenea* and *Anchisa* were used by most of the old writers: for, said they, if those words were written as *Maecenas, Suffenas, Asprenas,* they would end in the genitive case, not with the letter -*e,* but with the syllable -*tis.* Hence, to *Olympus* and *tyrannus* they gave an acuted middle syllable, because our language does not permit the

first syllable of a word, if short, to have an acute accent when two long syllables follow. Thus the genitive had the forms *Achilli* and *Ulixi,* as did many others similar. The modern grammarians have now made it a practice rather to give Greek declensions to Greek nouns; a practice which cannot, however, always be observed. For myself, I prefer following the Latin method, as far as propriety allows; for I would not now say *Calypsonem,* like *Junonem,* though Caius Caesar, following the older writers, uses this mode of declining. But custom has prevailed over authority. In using other words, which may be declined without impropriety in either way, he who shall prefer to use the Greek form will speak, not indeed like a Roman, but without incurring blame.

Simple words are what they are in their first position, that is, in their own nature. Compound words are either formed by subjoining words to prepositions, as *innocens* (care being taken that there be not two prepositions inconsistent with each other, as *imperterritus,* otherwise two may be at times joined together, as *incompositus, reconditus,* and, a word which Cicero uses, *subabsurdum*); or they coalesce, as it were, from two bodies into one, as *maleficus.* For to form words out of three constituent parts I should certainly not grant to our language; though Cicero says that *capsis* is compounded of *cape si vis;* [21] and some are found to maintain that *Lupercalia* also consists of three parts of speech, *luere per caprum.* As to *solitaurilia,* it is now believed that it is for *suovetaurilia,* and such indeed is the sacrifice, as it is described also in Homer.[22] But these words are constructed, not so much of three words, as of parts of three words. Pacuvius however appears to have formed compounds, most inelegantly of a preposition and two other words:

Nerei repandirostrum, incurvicervicum pecus,

"The broad-nosed, crook-necked flock of Nereus." Compounds, however, are formed either of two entire Latin words, as *superfui, subterfugi* (though it is a question whether these

63

64

65

66

67

68

21 *De oratore* XLV. 154.
22 *Odyssey* XI. 130.

are indeed formed of entire words); or of an entire and incomplete word, as *malevolus;* of an incomplete and entire word, as *noctivagus;* of two incomplete words, as *pedissequus;* of a Latin and a foreign word, as *biclinium;* of a foreign and a Latin word, as *epitogium* and *Anticato;* or of two foreign words, as *epirhedium,* for though the preposition is Greek, and *rheda* Gallic, and though neither the Greek nor the Gaul uses the compound, yet the Romans have formed their word

69 of the two foreign words. Frequently, too, the union causes a change in the prepositions, as *abstulit, aufugit, amisit,* though the preposition is merely *ab,* and *coit,* the preposition being *con;* and so *ignavi, erepublica,* and similar compounds.

70 But the composition of words in general is better suited to the Greeks; with us it is less successful; though I do not think that this results from the nature of the language; but we look with more favour on foreign compounds; and, accordingly, while we admire κυρταύχενα, we hardly defend *incurvicervicum* from derision.

71 Words are proper when they signify that to which they were first applied; metaphorical, when they have one signification by nature, and another in the place in which they are used. Common words we use with greater safety; new ones we do not form without some danger; for if they are well received, they add but little merit to our style, and, if rejected, they

72 turn to jokes against us. Yet we must make attempts, for, as Cicero says, even words which have seemed harsh at first, become softened by use.[23]

As to the *onomatopoeia,* it is by no means granted to our language; for, if we should venture to produce anything like those justly admired expressions λίγξε βιός, "the bow twanged," and σίζεν ὀφθαλμός, "the eye hissed," who would endure it?[24] We should not even dare to say *balare,* "to bleat," or *hinnire,* "to neigh," unless those words were supported by the sanction of antiquity.

23 *De natura deorum* I. 34. 95.
24 *Iliad* IV. 125 and *Odyssey* IX. 394.

CHAPTER SIX

BY SPEAKERS, as well as writers, there are certain rules to be 1
observed. Language is based on reason, antiquity, authority,
and custom. It is analogy, and sometimes etymology, that
affords the chief support to reason. A certain majesty, and, if
I may so express myself, religion, graces the antique. Au- 2
thority is commonly sought in orators or historians. As to the
poets, the obligation of the meter excuses their phraseology,
except in those cases when the measure of the feet offers no
impediment to the choice of either of two expressions, but
they fancifully prefer one to the other, as in the following
phrases: *imo de stirpe recisum, aeeriae quo congessere palum-
bos, silice in nuda,*[1] and the like. Since the judgment of men
eminent in eloquence stands in place of reason, then even
error is without dishonor in following illustrious guides. Cus- 3
tom, however, is the surest preceptor in speaking: we must
use phraseology, like money, which has the public stamp.

But all these particulars require great judgment, especially
analogy, which, translating it closely from Greek into Latin,
people have called *proportion*. It requires that a writer or 4
speaker compare whatever is at all doubtful with something
similar concerning which there is no doubt, so as to prove
the uncertain by the certain. This is done in two ways: by a
comparison of similar words, in respect chiefly to their last
syllables (for which reason the words that have but one syllable are said not to be accountable to analogy), and by looking
to diminutives. Comparison in nouns shows either their gen- 5
der or their declension; their gender, as, when it is inquired
whether *funis* be masculine or feminine, *panis* may be an object of comparison with it; their declension, as, if it should
be a subject of doubt whether we should say *hac domu* or
hac domo, and *domuum* or *domorum*, then *domus, anus,*

[1] *Aeneid* XII. 208; *Eclogues* III. 69; *Eclogues* I. 15.

6   *manus* may be compared with each other. The formation of diminutives shows only the gender of words, as (that I may take the same word for an example) *funiculus* proves that *funis* is masculine.

7   There is also similar reason for comparison in verbs; as if any one, following the old writers, should pronounce *fervere* with the middle syllable short, he would be convicted of speaking incorrectly, since all verbs which end with the letters *e* and *o* in the indicative mood, when they have assumed the letter *e* in the middle syllables in the infinitive, have it necessarily long, as *prandeo, pendeo, spondeo,*

8   *prandēre, pendēre, spondēre*. But those which have *o* only in the indicative, when they end with the same letter *e* in the infinitive, shorten it, as *lego, dico, curro, legĕre, dicĕre, currĕre;* although there occurs in Lucilius,

> *Fervit aqua et fervet; fervit nunc, fervet ad annum*

"The water boils and will boil; it boils now, and will boil

9   for a year." [2] But with all respect to a man of such eminent learning, if he thinks *fervit* similar to *currit* and *legit, fervo* will be a word like *curro* and *lego,* a word which has never been heard by me. But this is not a just comparison; for *servit* is like *fervit,* and he that follows this analogy must say

10   *fervire* as well as *servire*. The present indicative also is sometimes discovered from the other moods and tenses; for I remember that some people who had blamed me for using the word *pepigi,* were convinced by me of their error; they had allowed, indeed, that the best authors had used *pepigi,* but denied that analogy permitted its use, since the present indicative *paciscor,* as it had the form of a passive verb, made in

11   the perfect tense *pactus sum*. But I, besides adducing the authority of orators and historians, maintained that *pepigi* was also supported by analogy; for, as we read in the Twelve Tables, *ni ita pagunt,*[3] I found *cadunt* similar to *pagunt,* whence the present indicative, though it had fallen into disuse through time, was evidently *pago,* like *cado;* and it was

12   therefore certain that we say *pepigi* like *cecidi*. But we must

---

2 Lucilius, IX. 5, 357.

3 The Halm text has *ni ita pacunt.*

remember that the course of analogy cannot be traced through all the parts of speech, as it is in many cases at variance with itself. Learned men, indeed, endeavor to justify some departures from it, as, when it is remarked how much *lepus* and *lupus,* though of similar terminations in the nominative, differ in their cases and numbers, they reply that they are not of the same sort, since *lepus* is epicene, and *lupus* masculine; although Varro, in the book in which he relates the origin of the city of Rome, uses *lupus* as feminine, following Ennius and Fabius Pictor. But those same grammarians, when they 13 are asked why *aper* makes *apri,* and *pater, patris,* assert that the first is declined absolutely, and the second with reference to something; and, besides, as both are derived from the Greek, they recur to the rule that πατρός gives *patris,* and κάπρου *apri.* But how will they escape from the fact that nouns, 14 which end with the letters *u* and *s* in the nominative singular, never, even though feminine, end with the syllable *-ris* in the genitive, yet that *Venus* makes *Veneris;* and that, though nouns ending in *-es* have various endings in the genitive, yet their genitive never ends in that same syllable *-ris,* when, nevertheless, *Ceres* obliges us to say *Cereris?* And what shall 15 I say of those parts of speech, which, though all of similar commencement, proceed with different inflections, as *Alba* makes *Albani* and *Albenses, volo, volui* and *volavi?* For analogy itself admits that verbs, which end with the letter *o* in the first person singular, are variously formed in the perfect, as *cado* makes *cecidi; spondeo, spopondi; pingo, pinxi; lego, legi; pono, posui; frango, fregi; laudo, laudavi.*

Analogy was not sent down from heaven when men were first 16 made to give them rules for speaking, but was discovered after men had begun to speak, and after it was observed how each word in speaking terminated. It is not therefore founded on reason, but on example; nor is it a law for speaking, but the mere result of observation, so that nothing but custom has been the origin of analogy. Yet some people adhere to it with a most 17 unpleasantly perverse attachment to exactness; so that they will say *audaciter* in preference to *audacter,* though all ora-

tors adopt the latter, and *emicavit* instead of *emicuit,* or *con-
ire* instead of *coire.* Such persons we may allow to say *audi-
visse,* and *scivisse, tribunale,* and *faciliter;* let them also have
their *frugalis,* instead of *frugi,* for how else can *frugalitas* be
18 formed? Let them also prove that *centum millia nummum*
and *fidem deum* are two solecisms, since they err in both case
and number; for we were ignorant of this, and were not
merely complying with custom and convenience, as in most
cases, of which Cicero treats nobly, as of everything else, in
19 his *De oratore.*[4] Augustus, too, in his letters written to Caius
Caesar, corrects him for preferring to say *calidum* rather than
caldum, not because *calidum* is not Latin, but because it is
unpleasing, and, as he has himself expressed it by a Greek
word, περίεργον.

20 All this, indeed, they consider as mere ὀρθοέπειαν, "orthoepy,"
which I by no means set aside, for what is so necessary as
correctness of speech? I think that we ought to adhere to it
as far as possible, and to make persevering resistance against
innovators—but to retain words that are obsolete and disused
is a species of impertinence, and of puerile ostentation in
21 little things. Let the extremely learned man, who has saluted
you without an aspirate, and with the second syllable length-
ened (for the verb, he will say, is *avere*), say also *calefacere*
and *conservavisse* rather than what we say; and with these let
22 him join *face, dice,* and the like. His way is the right way;
who will deny it? But a smoother and more beaten road is
close by the side of it. There is nothing, however, with which
I am more offended, than that these men, led away by oblique
cases, permit themselves, I do not say not to find, but even to
alter nominative cases, as when *ebur* and *robur,* so spoken and
written by the greatest authors, are made to change the vowel
of the second syllable into *o,* because their genitives are *roboris* and *eboris,* and because *sulpur* and *guttur* preserve the
vowel *u* in the genitive. For which reason also *jecur* and *femur*

4 *De oratore* XLVI. 155. Quintilian's sarcasm in these passages is directed against those who cling blindly to rigid rules of analogy, regard-
less of usage.

have raised disputes. This change of theirs is not less auda- 23
cious than if they were to substitute the letter *o* for *u* in the
genitive case of *sulpur* and *guttur*, because *eboris* and *roboris*
are formed with *o*. Note the example of Antonius Gnipho,
who acknowledges that *robur* and *ebur* are proper words, and
even *marmur*, but would have the plurals of them to be *ro-
bura, ebura, marmura*. But if they had paid attention to the 24
affinity of letters, they would have understood that *roboris* is
as fairly formed from *robur* as *militis, limitis*, from *miles,
limes*, or *judicis, vindicis*, from *judex, vindex*, and would have
observed some other forms to which I have adverted above. Do 25
not similar nominative cases, as I remarked, diverge into very
dissimilar forms in the oblique cases, as *Virgo, Juno; fusus,
lusus; cuspis, puppis;* and a thousand others? It happens, too,
that some nouns are not used in the plural, others not in the
singular; some are indeclinable; some depart altogether from
the form of their nominatives, as *Jupiter*. The same peculiar- 26
ity happens in verbs, as *fero, tuli*, of which the perfect is
found, and nothing more. Nor is it of much importance,
whether those unused parts are actually not in existence, or
whether they are too harsh to be used; for what, for example,
will *progenies* make in the genitive singular, or what will *spes*
make in the genitive plural? Or how will *quire* and *ruere*,
form themselves in the perfect passive, or in the passive participles? It is needless to advert to other words, when it is even 27
uncertain whether *senatus* makes *senatus senatui* or *senati
senato*. It appears to me, therefore, to have been not unhap-
pily remarked that it is one thing to speak Latin, and another
to speak grammar. Of analogy I have now said enough, and
more than enough.

Etymology, which inquires into the origin of words, is called 28
by Cicero notation, because its designation in Aristotle is
σύμβολον, that is, *nota*[5]; for to a literal rendering of "word for
word," which would be *veriloquium*, Cicero himself, who
formed that word, is averse. There are some, who, looking
rather to the meaning of the word, call it "origination." This 29

[5] *Topics* VIII. 35.

part of grammar is sometimes of the utmost use; as often, indeed, as the matter, concerning which there is any dispute, stands in need of interpretation; as when Marcus Caelius would prove that he was a *homo frugi,* "a frugal man," not because he was temperate (for on that point he could not speak falsely), but because he was profitable to many, that is *fructuosus,* from whence, he said, was derived *frugality.* A place is accordingly assigned to etymology in definitions. Sometimes, also, it endeavors to distinguish barbarous from polite words; as when a question arises whether Sicily should be called *Triquetra* or *Triquedra,* and whether we should say *meridies* or *medidies;* and similar questions concerning other words which yield to custom. But it carries with it much learning, whether we employ it in treating of words sprung from the Greek, which are very numerous (especially those inflected according to the Aeolic dialect to which our language has most similitude), or in inquiring from our knowledge of ancient history, into the names of men, places, nations, cities. Whence come the names of the *Bruti, Publicolae, Pici;* why do we say *Latium, Italia, Beneventum;* what is our reason for using the terms *Capitol, Quirinal* hill, and *Argiletum?*

I would now allude also to those minuter points on which the greatest lovers of etymology weary themselves: men who bring back to their true derivation, by various and manifold arts, words that have become a little distorted, by shortening or lengthening, adding, taking away, or interchanging letters or syllables. In this pursuit, through weakness of judgment, they run into the most contemptible absurdities. Let *consul* be (I make no objection) from "consulting" or from "judging," for the ancients called *consulere* "judicare," whence still remains the phrase *rogat boni consulas,* that is, *bonum judices.* Let it be old age that has given a name to the senate, for the senators are fathers; let *rex, rector,* and abundance of other words, be indisputably from *rego;* nor would I dispute the ordinary derivation of *tegula, regula,* and other words similar to them; let *classis,* also, be from *calare,* "to call together," and let *lepus* be for *levipes,* and *vulpes* for *volipes.* But shall we

30

31

32

33

34

also allow words to be derived from contraries, as *lucus,* "a grove," from *luceo,* "to shine," because, being thick with shade, *parum lucet,* it does not shine? As *ludus,* "a school," from *ludo,* "to play," because it is as far as possible from play? As *Ditis,* "Pluto," from *dives,* "rich," because he is by no means rich? Or shall we allow *homo,* "man," to be from *humus,* "the ground," because he was sprung from the ground, as if all animals had not the same origin, or as if the first men had given a name to the ground before they gave one to themselves? Shall we allow *verba,* "words," to be from *aer verberatus,* "beaten air"? Let us go on, and we shall get so far that *stella,* "a star," will be believed to be *luminis stilla,* "a drop of light," the author of which derivation, an eminent man in literature, it would be ungenerous for me to name in regard to a point on which he is censured by me. But those who have recorded such etymologies in books have themselves set their names to them; and Caius Granius thought himself extremely clever for saying that *caelibes,* "bachelors," was the same as *caelites,* "inhabitants of heaven," because they are alike free from a most heavy burden, resting his derivation, too, on an argument from the Greek, for he affirmed that ἠθέους was used in the same sense. Nor does Modestus yield to him in imagination, for he says that because Saturn cut off the genitalia of *Caelus,* men who have no wives are, therefore, called *caelibes.* Lucius Aelius declares that *pituita,* "phlegm," is so called *quia petat vitam,* because "it aims at life." But who may not be pardoned after Varro,[6] who wished to persuade Cicero (for it was to him that he wrote this), that *ager,* "a field," is so called because *in eo agatur aliquid,* "something is done in it," and that *graculos,* "jackdaws," are so named because they fly *gregatim,* "in flocks," though it is evident that the one is derived from the Greek, and the other from the cries of the birds themselves? But of such importance was it to Varro to make derivations that *merula,* "a blackbird," he declared, was so named because it flies alone, as if *mera volans.* Some have not hesitated to apply to etymology for the origin of every

35

36

37

38

---

[6] *De lingua latina* V. 34 and 76.

name or word; deducing *Longus* and *Rufus*, as I remarked, from personal peculiarities; *strepere* and *murmurare* from particular sounds; with which they join, also, certain derivatives, as *velox*, "swift," deduced from *velocitas*, "swiftness," and the greater number of compounds (as being similar to them), which, doubtless, have their origin from something, but demand no exercise of ingenuity, for which indeed except on doubtful points there is no opportunity in these investigations.

39   Words derived from *antiquity* have not only illustrious patrons, but also confer on style a certain majesty, not unattended with pleasure; for they have the authority of age, and, as they have been disused for a time, bring with them a charm similar to that of novelty. But there is need of moderation in
40   the use of them, in order that they may not occur too frequently, nor show themselves too manifestly, since nothing is more detestable than affectation; nor should they be taken from a remote and already forgotten age, as are *topper*, "quickly," *antegerio*, "very much," *exanclare*, "to draw out," *prosapia*, "a race," and the verses of the Salii, which are
41   scarcely understood by the priests themselves. Those verses, however, religion forbids to be changed, and we must use what has been consecrated; but how faulty is speech, of which the greatest virtue is perspicuity, if it needs an interpreter! Consequently, as the oldest of new words will be the best, so the newest of old words will be the best.

42   The case is similar with regard to *authority*, for though he may seem to commit no fault who uses those words which the greatest writers have handed down to him, yet it is of much importance for him to consider, not only what words they used, but how far they gave a sanction to them. No one would now tolerate from us *tuburchinabundus*, "devouring," or *lurchinabundus*, "voracious," though Cato was the father of them; nor would people endure *lodices*, "blankets," in the masculine gender, though that gender pleases Pollio; nor *gladiola* for "little swords," though Messala has used it; nor *parricidatus*, "parricide," which was thought scarcely endurable in Caelius; nor would Calvus induce me to use *collos*, "necks";

all which words, indeed, those authors themselves would not now use.

There remains, therefore, *custom,* for it would be almost ridiculous to prefer the language which men have spoken rather than that which they now speak. What else, indeed, is old language, but the old manner of speaking? But even for following custom, judgment is necessary; we must settle, in the first place, what that is which we call custom; for if custom be merely termed that which the greater number do, it will furnish a most dangerous rule, not only for language, but, what is of greater importance, for life. For where is there so much virtue that what is right can please the majority? Therefore, to pluck out hairs, to cut the hair of the head in a succession of rings, and to drink to excess in the bath—whatever country those practices may have invaded—will not become the proper custom, because no one of them is undeserving of censure. So just as we do bathe and clip our hair, and take our meals together according to custom, so, in speaking, it is not whatever has become a vicious practice with many that is to be received as a rule of language. For, not to mention how the ignorant commonly speak, we know that whole theatres, and all the crowd of the circus, have frequently uttered barbarous exclamations. Custom in speaking, therefore, I shall call the agreement of the educated, just as I call custom in living the agreement of the good.

43

44

45

CHAPTER SEVEN

1   SINCE WE have mentioned what rules are to be followed in speaking, we must now specify what are to be observed by writers. What the Greeks call *orthography,* we may call the art of writing correctly. This art does not consist in knowing of what letters every syllable is composed (for this study is beneath the profession even of the grammarian), but exercises 2   its whole subtlety, in my opinion, on dubious points. As it is the greatest of folly to place a mark on all long syllables, since most of them are apparent from the very nature of the word that is written, yet it is at times necessary to mark them, as when the same letter gives sometimes one sense and sometimes another, according as it is short or long; thus *malus* is distinguished by a mark, to show whether it means "a tree" 3   or "a bad man"; *palus,* too, signifies one thing when its first syllable is long, and another when its second is long; and when the same letter is short in the nominative and long in the ablative, we have generally to be informed by this mark which quantity we are to adopt.

4   Grammarians have in like manner thought that the following distinction should be observed: namely, that we should write the preposition *ex,* if the word *specto* was compounded with it, with the addition of *s* in the second syllable, *exspecto;* 5   if *pecto,* without the *s.* It has been a distinction, also, observed by many, that *ad,* when it was a preposition, should take the letter *d,* but when a conjunction, the letter *t;* and that *cum,* if it signified time, should be written with a *q* and two *u*'s 6   following, but if it meant accompaniment, with a *c.* Some other things were even more trifling than these, as that *quicquid* should have a *c* for the fourth letter, lest we should seem to ask a double question, and that we should write *quotidie,* not *cotidie,* to show that it was for *quot diebus.* But these notions have already passed away among other puerilities.

It is however a question, in writing prepositions, whether it   7
is proper to observe the sound which they make when joined
to another word, or that which they make when separate, as,
for instance, when I pronounce the word *obtinuit;* for our
method of writing requires that the second letter should be
b, while the ear catches rather the sound of *p*; or when I say   8
immunis, for the letter *n*, which the composition of the word
requires, is influenced by the sound of the following syllable,
and changed into another *m*. It is also to be observed, in   9
dividing compound words, whether you ought to attach the
middle consonant to the first or to the second syllable; for
aruspex, as its latter part is from *spectare*, will assign the
letter *s* to the third syllable, while *abstemius*, as it is formed
of *abstinentia temeti*, "abstinence from wine," will leave the
s to the first syllable. As to *k*, I think it should not be used in   10
any words, except those which it denotes of itself, so that it
may be put alone. This remark I have not omitted to make,
because there are some who think *k* necessary when *a* follows,
even though there is the letter *c*, which suits itself to all
vowels.

But orthography submits to custom, and has therefore fre-   11
quently been altered. I say nothing of those ancient times
when there were fewer letters, and when their shapes were
different from these of ours, and their natures also different, as
that of *o* among the Greeks, which was sometimes long and
sometimes short, and, as among us, was sometimes put for the
syllable which it expresses by its mere name. I say nothing also   12
of *d*, among the ancient Latins, being added as the last letter
to a great number of words, as is apparent from the rostral
pillar erected to Caius Duellius in the forum; nor do I speak
of *g* being used in the same manner, as, on the *pulvinar* of
the Sun, which is worshipped near the temple of Romulus, is
read *vesperug*, which we take for *vesperugo*. Nor is it necessary   13
to say anything here of the interchange of letters of which I
have spoken above,[1] for perhaps as they wrote they also spoke.

It was for a long time a very common custom not to double   14

[1] I. 4, 12–17 (p. 31).

the semivowels; while, on the other hand, even down to the
time of Accius and later, they wrote, as I have remarked, long
15 syllables with two vowels. Still longer continued the practice
of using *e* and *i* together, joining them in the same manner
as the Greeks in the diphthong ει. This practice was adopted
for a distinction in cases and numbers, as Lucilius admonishes
us:

> *jam pueri venere: E postremum facito, atque I,*
> *ut puerei plures fiant;*

and afterward,

> *mendaci furique addes E, quum dare furei*
> *jusseris.*[2]

16 However this addition of *e* is both superfluous, since *i* has the
nature of a long as well as of a short letter, and also sometimes
is inconvenient; for in those words which have *e* immediately
before the last syllable, and end with *i* long, we should use,
if we adopted that method, a double *e*, as *aurecí, argenteei,*
17 and the like; and this would be extremely embarrassing to
those who are being taught to read; as happens also among
the Greeks by the addition of the letter *i*, which they not only
write at the end of dative cases, but sometimes even in the
middle of a word, as ΛΗΙΣΤΗΙ, because etymology, in making
a division of the word into three syllables, requires that letter.
18 The diphthong *æ*, for the second letter of which we now
substitute *e*, our ancestors expressed, with a varied pronunciation, by *a* and *i*, some using it in all cases like the Greeks,
others only in the singular, when they had to form a genitive
or dative case, whence Virgil, a great lover of antiquity, has
inserted in his verses *pictai vestis,* and *auqai*[3]; but in the
19 plural number of such nouns they use *e*, as *Syllae, Galbae.*
There is on this point also a precept of Lucilius, which, as it

---

2 *Sermones* IX. 5, 364 ff. "Now the boys are come: make the conclusion
e and *i*, so that the boys (*puerei*) may be made plural." And again, "To
a liar and a slave you shall add *e*." In other words, make the ending
fur-ei to indicate the dative case.

3 *Aeneid* IX. 26 and VII. 464.

is expressed in a great number of verses, whoever is incredulous about it may seek in his ninth book.

I may mention, too, that in the time of Cicero, and somewhat later, the letter *s*, as often as it occurred between two long vowels, or followed a long vowel, was doubled, as *caussae, cassus, divissiones;* for that both he and Virgil wrote in this way, their own hands show. But those of a somewhat earlier period wrote the word *jussi,* which we now express with two *s*'s, with only one. That *optimus, maximus,* should take *i* as their middle letter, which among the ancients was *u*, is said to have been brought about by an inscription to Caius Caesar. The word *here* we now end with the letter *e;* but I still find in the books of the old comic writers *Heri ad me venit*[4]; the same mode of spelling is found in the letters of Augustus, which he wrote or corrected with his own hand. Did not Cato the Censor, also, for *dicam* and *faciam,* write *dicem* and *faciem?* And did he not observe the same method in other verbs which terminate in a similar way? This is indeed manifest from his old writings, and is remarked by Messala in his book on the letter *s. Sibe* and *quase* occur in the writings of many authors; but whether the authors themselves intended them to be written thus, I do not know; that Livy spelled them in that way, I learn from Pedianus, who himself imitated Livy; we end those words with the letter *i*.

Why need I allude to *vortices* and *vorsus* and other similar words, in which Scipio Africanus is said to have first changed the second letter into *e?* Our tutors wrote *ceruum* and *seruum* with the letters *u* and *o, ceruom, seruom,* in order that the same two vowels, following each other, might not coalesce and be confounded in the same sound; they are now written with two *u*'s, on the principle which I have stated, though in neither way is the word which we conceive exactly expressed. Nor was it without advantage that Claudius introduced the Aeolic letter for such cases. It is an improvement of the present day that we spell *cui* with the three letters which I have just written; for in this word, when we were boys, they used,

4 Terence, *Phormio* 36.

Marginal reference numbers: 20, 21, 22, 23, 24, 25, 26, 27

making a very offensive sound, *qu* and *oi*, only that it might
be distinguished from *qui*.

28   What shall I say, too, of words that are written otherwise
than they are pronounced? *Gaius* is spelled with the letter *c*,
which, inverted, means a woman; for that women were called
Caiae, as well as men *Caii*, appears even from our nuptial
29   ceremonies.[5] Nor does *Gneius* assume that letter, in designat-
ing a praenomen, with which it is sounded. We read, too,
columna and *consules* with the letter *n* omitted; and *Subura*,
when it is designated by three letters, takes *c* as the third.[6]
There are many other peculiarities of this kind; but I fear
that those which I have noticed have exceeded the limits of
so unimportant a subject.

30   On all such points let the grammarian use his own judgment, for in this department it ought to be of the greatest
authority. For myself, I think that all words (unless custom
has ordered otherwise) should be written in conformity with
31   their sound. For this is the use of letters—to preserve words,
and to restore them, like a deposit, to readers; and they ought,
therefore, to express exactly what we are to say.

32   These are the most important points as to speaking and
writing correctly. The other two departments, those of speaking with significancy and elegance, I do not indeed take away
from the grammarians, but, as the duties of the rhetorician remain for me to explain, I will reserve them for a more important part of my work.

33   Yet the reflection recurs to me, that some will regard those
matters of which I have just treated as extremely trifling, and
even as impediments to the accomplishment of anything
greater. Nor do I myself think that we ought to descend to
extreme solicitude and puerile disputations about them; I
even consider that the mind may be weakened and contracted
34   by being fixed upon them. But no part of grammar will be
hurtful, except what is superfluous. Was Cicero the less of an

[5] In which the woman said, *Ubi tu Caius, ibi ego Caia.*
[6] Apparently *Sucusa* was its original form, the *c* changing into a *b* and
the *-sa* ending being transformed into *-rra*.

orator because he was most attentive to the study of grammar, and because, as appears from his letters, he was a rigid exactor, on all occasions, of correct language from his son? Did the writings of Julius Caesar on analogy diminish the vigor of his intellect? Or was Messala less elegant as a writer, because he devoted whole books, not merely to single words, but even to single letters? These studies are injurious, not to those who pass through them, but only to those who dwell immoderately upon them.

35

CHAPTER EIGHT

1 READING REMAINS to be considered. Only practice can teach how a boy may know when to take breath, where to divide a verse, where the sense is concluded, where it begins, when the voice is to be raised or lowered, what is to be uttered with any particular inflection of sound, or what is to be pronounced with greater slowness or rapidity, with greater animation or

2 gentleness than other passages. There is but one direction, therefore, which I have to give in this part of my work—namely, so that he may be able to do all this successfully, let him understand what he reads.

Let his mode of reading aloud, however, be manly above all, uniting gravity with a certain degree of sweetness. Let not his reading of the poets be like that of prose, for it is verse, and the poets say that they sing. Yet let it not degenerate into sing-song, or be rendered effeminate with unnatural softness, as is now the practice among most readers; on which sort of reading we hear that Caius Caesar, while he was still under age, observed happily to some one that was practicing it, "If you are singing, you sing badly; if you pretend to read, you

3 nevertheless sing." Nor would I have *prosopopeiae* [1] pronounced, as some would wish them, after the manner of actors; though I think there should be a certain alteration of the voice by which they may be distinguished from those passages in which the poet speaks in his own person.

4 Other points demand much admonition to be given on them. Care is to be taken, above all things, that tender minds, which will imbibe deeply whatever has entered them while rude and ignorant of everything, may learn not only what is

[1] *Prosopopeia* was an exercise in which students read passages or speeches indicative of the character of another person. Thus Quintilian is advising that the student should not actually "act out" a part, even though he should indicate by his voice the nature of the passage read.

eloquent, but, still more, what is morally good. It has accordingly been an excellent custom, that reading should com-   5
mence with Homer and Virgil, even though to understand
their merits there is need of maturer judgment; but for the
acquisition of judgment there is abundance of time; for they
will not be read once only. In the meantime, let the mind of
the pupil be exalted with the sublimity of the heroic verse,
conceive ardor from the magnitude of the subjects, and be
imbued with the noblest sentiments. The reading of tragedies   6
is beneficial; the lyric poets nourish the mind, provided that
you select from them, not merely authors, but portions of their
works—for the Greeks are licentious in many of their writings,
and I should be loath to interpret Horace in certain passages.
As to elegy, at least that which treats of love, and hendecasyl-
lables, and poems in which there are portions of Sotadic verses
(for concerning Sotadic verses [2] themselves no precept need
even be mentioned)—let them be altogether kept away, if it be
possible; if not, let them at least be reserved for the greater
strength of mature age. Of comedy, which may contribute   7
very much to eloquence, as it extends to all sorts of characters and passions, I will state a little further on, in the
proper place, the good which I think it may do to boys; when
their morals are out of danger, it will be among the subjects
to be chiefly read. It is of Menander that I speak, though I
would not set aside other comic writers; for the Latin authors,   8
too, will confer some benefit. Both those writings should be
the subjects of lectures for boys, which may best nourish the
mind and enlarge the thinking powers; for the reading of
other books, which relate merely to erudition, advanced life
will afford sufficient time.

The old Latin authors, however, will be of great use,
though most of them, indeed, were stronger in genius than in
art. Above all they will supply a *copia verborum*, a "fulness of
vocabulary," while in their tragedies may be found a weightiness of thought, and in their comedies elegance, and some-   9

2 Sotades *(fl.* 300 B.C.) was a writer of coarse satires. Both the Sotadean
and hendecasyllabic meters were used frequently for indecent satires.

thing as it were of Atticism. There will be seen in them, too,
a more careful regard to regularity of structure than in most
of the moderns, who have considered that the merit of every
kind of composition lies solely in the thoughts. Purity, certainly, and—that I may so express myself—manliness, is to be
gained from them, especially since we ourselves have fallen
into all the vices of refinement, even in our manner of speaking. Let us, moreover, trust to the practice of the greatest
¹⁰ orators, who have recourse to the poems of the ancients, both
for the support of their arguments, and for the adornment of
their eloquence. For in Cicero most of all, and frequently also
¹¹ in Asinius, and others nearest to his times, we see verses of
Ennius, Accius, Pacuvius, Lucilius, Terence, Caecilius, and
other poets, introduced, with the best effect, not only for showing the learning of the speakers, but for giving pleasure to
the hearers, whose ears find in the charms of poetry a relief
from the want of elegance in forensic pleading. To this is to
be added the no mean advantage that the speakers confirm
¹² what they have stated by the sentiments of the poets, as by
so many testimonies. But those first observations of mine have
reference rather to boys, the latter to more advanced students,
for the love of letters, and the benefit of reading, are bounded,
not by the time spent at school, but by the extent of life.

In lecturing on the poets, the grammarian must attend also
¹³ to minor points.[3] Thus, after taking a verse to pieces, he may
require the parts of speech to be specified, and the peculiarities of the feet, which are necessary to be known, not merely
for writing poetry, but even for prose composition. He may
also distinguish what words are barbarous, or misapplied,* or

[3] The extremely detailed method of grammatical analysis described in
this passage appears also in the grammatical works of Priscian (*fl.* A.D.
500), who reveals the same concern for close examination of written texts.
One of Priscian's works, *Partitiones duodecim versum aeneides* (text in
Keil, III, 459–515), devotes fifty-seven printed pages to only the first
twelve lines of Virgil's *Aeneid*. The method evidently became a tradition
among Latin grammarians, and must surely have had a great effect on
such later developments as Christian exegesis of the language of Holy
Scripture.

used contrary to the rules of the language; not that the poets   14
may thus be disparaged (to whom, as they are commonly
forced to obey the meter, so much indulgence is granted, that
even solecisms are designated by other names in poetry, for
we call them, as I have remarked, metaplasms, schematisms,
and schemata, and give to necessity the praise of merit), but
that the tutor may instruct the pupil in figurative terms, and
exercise his memory. It is likewise useful, among the first
rudiments of instruction, to show in how many senses each   15
word may be understood. As regards *glossemata*, too, that is,
words not in general use, no small attention is requisite in the
grammatical profession. With still greater care, however, let
him teach all kinds of tropes, from which not only poetry,   16
but even prose, receives the greatest ornament, as well as the
two sorts of schemata or figures, called figures of speech and
figures of thought. My observations on these figures, as well as
those on tropes, I put off to that portion of my work in which
I shall have to speak of the embellishments of composition.[4]   17
But let the tutor, above all things, impress upon the minds of
his pupils what merit there is in a just disposition of parts,
and a becoming treatment of subjects; what is well suited to
each character; what is to be commended in the thoughts, and
what in the words; where diffuseness is appropriate, and where
contraction.

To these duties will be added explanations of historical   18
points, which must be sufficiently minute, but not carried into
superfluous disquisitions; for it will suffice to lecture on facts
which are generally admitted, or which are at least related by
eminent authors. To examine, indeed, what all writers, even
the most contemptible, have ever related, is a proof either of

[4] That is, Books VIII and IX. Quintilian defines a trope as "the conversion of a word or phrase from its proper signification to another, in
order to increase its force" (VIII. 6. 1). Typical examples are metaphor,
allegory, and hyperbole. He defines a figure as "a form of speech artfully varied from common usage" (IX. 1. 14). Ancient doctrine divided
the figures into two types: figures of thought, depending upon mental
conceptions, and figures of speech, depending upon the form of words
or combination of words.

extravagant laboriousness, or of useless ostentation; it chains and overloads the mind, which might give its attention to
19 other things with more advantage. For he who makes researches into all sorts of writings, even such as are unworthy to be read, is capable of giving his time even to the very men
20 who wrote them. Since it is known to have happened to Didymus, than whom no man wrote more books, that, when he denied a certain story, as unworthy of belief, his own book
21 containing it was laid before him. This occurs chiefly in fabulous stories, descending even to what is ridiculous, and sometimes licentious; whence every unprincipled grammarian has the liberty of inventing many of his comments, so that he may lie with safety concerning whole books and authors, as it may occur to him, for writers that never existed cannot be produced against him. In the better known class of authors they are often exposed by the curious. Hence it shall be accounted by me among the merits of a grammarian to be ignorant of some things.

CHAPTER NINE

WE HAVE now concluded two of the departments which this 1
profession undertakes: the art of speaking correctly and the
explanation of authors. They call the one *methodicē* and the
other *historicē.* Let us add, however, to the business of the
grammarian, some rudiments of the art of speaking, in which
they may initiate their pupils who are still too young for the
teacher of rhetoric. Let boys learn, then, to relate orally the 2
fables of Aesop, which follow next after the nurse's stories, in
plain language, not rising at all above mediocrity, and afterward to express the same simplicity in writing. Let them
learn, too, to take to pieces the verses of the poets, and then
to express them in different words; and afterward to represent them, somewhat boldly, in a paraphrase, in which it is
allowable to abbreviate or embellish certain parts, provided
that the sense of the poet be preserved. He who shall success- 3
fully perform this exercise, which is difficult even for accomplished professors, will be able to learn anything.

Let *sentences,* also, and *chriae* and *ethologies,*[1] be written
by the learner, with the occasions of the sayings added according to the grammarians, because these depend upon reading.
The nature of all these is similar, but their form different;
because a sentence is a general proposition; ethology is confined to certain persons. Of *chriae* several sorts are specified: 4
one similar to a sentence, which is introduced with a simple

---

[1] A sentence (*sententia*) or aphorism is a pithy enunciation of some
general proposition, usually exhorting something or showing what something is. It is the root of the modern English "sententious," meaning
terse but weighty expression. There is no satisfactory English synonym
for *chria,* which is the relation of some saying or action, showing its intention clearly, and usually having some moral instruction in view. Butler translated the term as "moral essay." The *ethologia* is a description
or illustration of the character or morals of a person (from the root word,
ethos, referring to character).

statement, "He said," or "He was accustomed to say"; another, which includes its subject in an answer: "He, being
asked," or, "When this remark was made to him, replied"; a
third, not unlike the second, commences, "When some one
5 had not said, but done, something." Even in the acts of people
some think that there is a *chria,* as, "Crates, having met with
an ignorant boy, beat the boy's tutor"; and there is another
sort, almost like this, which, however, they do not venture to
call by the same name, but term it a χρειῶδες; as, "Milo, having
been accustomed to carry the same calf every day, ended by
carrying a bull." In all these forms the declension is conducted
through the same cases, and a reason may be given as well for
6 acts as for sayings. Stories told by the poets should, I think,
be treated by boys, not with a view to eloquence, but for the
purpose of increasing their knowledge. Other exercises of
greater toil and ardor, which the Latin teachers of rhetoric
have abandoned, have thus been rendered the necessary work
of teachers of grammar. The Greek rhetoricians have better
understood the weight and measure of their duties.

CHAPTER TEN

THESE REMARKS I have made, as briefly as I could, upon gram- 1
mar, not so as to examine and speak of everything, which
would be an infinite task, but merely of the most essential
points. I shall now add some concise observations on the other
departments of study, in which I think that boys should be
initiated before they are committed to the teacher of rhetoric,
in order that that circle of instruction, which the Greeks call
ἐγκύκλιον παιδείαν, may be completed.

For about the same age the study of other accomplishments 2
must be commenced; concerning which, as they are themselves
arts, and cannot be complete without the art of oratory, but
are nevertheless insufficient of themselves to form an orator,
it is made a question whether they are necessary to this art.
Of what service is it, say some people, for pleading a cause, or 3
pronouncing a legal opinion, to know how equilateral triangles may be erected upon a given line? Or how will he who
has marked the sounds of the lyre by their names and intervals
be better able to defend an accused person, or direct consulta-
tions, on that account? They may perhaps recall, also, the 4
many speakers, effective in every way in the forum, who have
never attended a geometrician, and who know nothing of
musicians except by the common pleasure of listening to
them. To these observers I answer in the first place (what
Cicero also frequently remarks in his book *De oratore*, addressed to Brutus),[1] that it is not such an orator as is or has
been, that is to be formed by us, but that we have conceived
in our mind an idea of the perfect orator, an orator deficient
in no point whatever. For when the philosophers would form 5
their wise man, who is to be perfect in every respect—as
they say, a kind of mortal god—they not only believe that he

[1] For instance, *De oratore* XXVIII. 100–XXXVI. 125, in which Cicero
describes the broad education required by the consummate orator.

should be instructed in a general knowledge of divine and human things, but conduct him through a course of questions which are certainly petty if you consider them merely in themselves (as, sometimes, through studied subtleties of argument), not because questions about horns or crocodiles [2] can form a wise man, but because a wise man ought never to be in error

6 even in the least matters. In like manner, it is not the geometrician, or the musician, or the other studies which I shall add to theirs, that will make the perfect orator (who ought to be a wise man), yet these accomplishments will contribute to his perfection. We see an antidote, for example, and other medicines to heal diseases and wounds, compounded of many and sometimes opposite ingredients, from the various qualities of which results that single compound which resembles none of them, yet takes its peculiar virtues from them all.

7 Mute insects, too, compose the exquisite flavor of honey, inimitable by human reason, of various sorts of flowers and juices. Shall we wonder that eloquence, than which the providence of the gods has given nothing more excellent to men, requires the aid of many arts, which, even though they may not appear, or put themselves forward, in the course of a speech, yet contribute to it a secret power, and are silently felt?

8 "People have been eloquent," someone may say, "without these arts"; but I want a perfect orator. "They contribute little assistance," another may observe; but that, to which even little shall be wanting, will not be a whole; and it will be agreed that perfection is a whole, of which though the hope may be on a distant height, as it were, yet it is for us to suggest every means of attaining it, that something more, at least, may thus be done. But why should our courage fail us? Nature does not forbid the formation of a perfect orator—and it is disgraceful to despair of what is possible.

2 These are examples of puzzling questions. The first is a syllogism: "You have whatever you have not lost. You have not lost horns. Therefore you have horns." The second poses a question: "A crocodile, having seized a woman's son, said he would restore him to her if she would tell him the truth. She replied, 'You will not restore my son.' Ought the crocodile to restore her son?"

For myself, I could be quite satisfied with the judgment of the ancients; for who is ignorant that music (to speak of that science first) enjoyed, in the days of antiquity, so much, not only of cultivation, but of reverence, that those who were musicians were deemed also prophets and sages. Not to mention others, there were Orpheus and Linus, both of whom are transmitted to the memory of posterity as having been descended from the gods, and the one, because he soothed the rude and barbarous minds of men by the wonderful effect of his strains, as having drawn after him not only wild beasts, but even rocks and woods. Timagenes declares that music was the most ancient of sciences connected with literature—an opinion to which the most celebrated poets give their support, according to whom the praises of gods and heroes used to be sung to the lyre at royal banquets. Does not Virgil's Iopas, too, sing *errantem lunam solisque labores,* "the wandering moon, and labors of the sun"[3]; the illustrious poet thus plainly asserting that music is united with the knowledge of divine things? If this position be granted, music will be necessary also for the orator. As I observed, this part of learning, which, after being neglected by orators has been taken up by the philosophers, was a portion of our business; without the knowledge of such subjects there can be no perfect eloquence.

Nor can anyone doubt that men eminently renowned for wisdom have been cultivators of music, when Pythagoras and those who followed him spread abroad the notion, which they doubtless received from antiquity, that the world itself was constructed in conformity with the laws of music, which the lyre afterward imitated. Nor were they content, moreover, with that concord of discordant elements which they call "harmony," but attributed even sound to the celestial motions[4]; for Plato, not only in certain other passages, but especially in his *Timaeus,* cannot even be understood except by those who have thoroughly imbibed the principles of this part of learning. What shall I say, too, of the philosophers in

9

10

11

12

13

3 *Aeneid* I. 742.
4 I.e., the music of the spheres.

general, whose founder, Socrates himself, was not ashamed, even in his old age, to learn to play on the lyre? It is related that the greatest generals used to play on the harp and flute, and that the troops of the Lacedaemonians were excited with musical notes. What other effect, indeed, do horns and trumpets produce in our legions, since the louder is the concert of their sounds, so much greater is the glory of the Romans than that of other nations in war? It was not without reason, therefore, that Plato thought music necessary for a man who would be qualified for engaging in government, and whom the Greeks call "statesman." Even the chiefs of that sect which appears to some extremely austere, and to others extremely harsh, were inclined to think that some of the wise might bestow a portion of their attention on this study.[5] Lycurgus, also, the maker of most severe laws for the Spartans, approved of the study of music. Nature herself, indeed, seems to have given music to us as a benefit, to enable us to endure labors with greater facility, for musical sounds cheer even the rower; and it is not only in those works in which the efforts of many, while some pleasing voice leads them, conspire together, that music is of avail, but the toil even of people at work by themselves finds itself soothed by song, however rude.

I appear, however, to be making a eulogy on this finest of arts, rather than connecting it with the orator. Let us pass lightly over the fact, then, that grammar and music were once united; since Archytas and Aristoxenus, indeed, thought grammar comprehended under music. That they themselves were teachers of both arts, not only Sophron shows (a writer, it is true, only of mimes, but one whom Plato so highly valued that he is said to have had his books under his head when he was dying), but also Eupolis, whose Prodamus teaches both music and grammar, and Maricas, that is to say, Hyperbolus, confesses that he knows nothing of music but letters. Aristophanes,[6] also, in more than one of his comedies, shows that boys were accustomed to be thus instructed in times of old. In the

---

[5] Quintilian apparently refers here to the Stoics.

[6] *Knights*, line 188.

Hypobolimaeus of Menander, an old man, laying before a
father, who is claiming a son from him, an account, as it were,
of the expense that he had bestowed upon his education, says
that he has paid a great deal to musicians and geometers.
Hence, too, it was customary at banquets that the lyre should 19
be handed round after the meal; and Themistocles on con-
fessing that he knew not how to play, "was accounted," to use
the words of Cicero, "but imperfectly educated." [7] Among the 20
Romans, likewise, it was usual to introduce lyres and flutes at
feasts. The verses of the Salii also have their tunes; and these
customs, as they were all established by Numa, prove that not
even by those who seem to have been rude and given to war,
was the cultivation of music neglected, as far as that age admitted it. It passed at length, indeed, into a proverb among 21
the Greeks that the uneducated had no commerce either with
the Muses or the Graces.

But let us consider what peculiar advantage he who is to 22
be an orator may expect from music. Music has two kinds of
measures, the one in the sounds of the voice, the other in
the motions of the body; for in both a certain due regulation
is required. Aristoxenus the musician divides all that belongs
to the voice into "rhythm," and "melody in measure"; of
which the one consists in modulation, the other in singing and
tunes. Are not all these qualifications, then, necessary to the
orator, the one of which relates to gesture, the second to the
collocation of words, and the third to the inflections of the
voice, which in speaking are extremely numerous? Such is 23
undoubtedly the case, unless we suppose, perchance, that a
regular structure and smooth combination of words is requisite only in poems and songs, and is superfluous in making a
speech; or that composition and modulation are not to be
varied in speaking, as in music, according to the nature of the
subject. Music, however, by means of the tone and modulation 24
of the voice, expresses sublime thoughts with grandeur, pleasant ones with sweetness, and ordinary ones with calmness, and
sympathizes in its whole art with the feelings attendant on

[7] *Tusculan Disputations* I. 2. 4.

25 what is expressed. In oratory, accordingly, the raising, lowering, or other inflection of the voice tends to move the feelings
of the hearers. Thus we try to excite the indignation of the
judges in one modulation of phrase and voice (that I may
again use the same term), and their pity in another; for we
see that minds are affected in different ways even by musical
instruments, though no words can be uttered by them.

26   A graceful and becoming motion of the body, also, which
the Greeks call *eurythmic,* is necessary, and cannot be sought
from any other art than music; a qualification on which no
small part of oratory depends, and for treating which a special
27 portion of our work is set apart.[8] If an orator shall pay extreme attention to his voice, what is so properly the business
of music? But neither is this department of my work to be
anticipated, so that we must confine ourselves in the meantime to the single example of Caius Gracchus, the most eminent orator of his time, behind whom, when he spoke in public, a musician used to stand and to give with a pitchpipe,
which the Greeks call *tonarion,* the tones in which his voice
28 was to be exerted. To this he attended even in his most tur-
bulent harangues, both when he frightened the patricians,
and after he began to fear them.

    For the sake of the less learned, and those, as they say, "of
a duller muse," I would wish to remove all doubt of the utility
29 of music. They will allow, assuredly, that the poets should be
read by him who would be an orator; but are they, then, to
be read without a knowledge of music? If any one is so blind
of intellect, however, as to hesitate about the reading of other
poets, he will doubtless admit that those should be read who
30 have written poems for the lyre. On these matters I should
have to enlarge more fully, if I recommended this as a new
study; but since it has been perpetuated from the most ancient times, even from those of Chiron and Achilles to our
own (among all, at least, who have not been averse to a regular
course of mental discipline), I must not proceed to make the
31 point doubtful by anxiety to defend it. Though I consider it

    [8] That is, *Institutio oratoria* XI. 3 which discusses delivery.

sufficiently apparent, however, from the very examples which I have now given, what music pleases me, and to what extent, yet I think that I ought to declare more expressly, that that sort of music is not recommended by me, which, prevailing at present in the theater, and being of an effeminate character, languishing with lascivious notes, has in a great degree destroyed whatever manliness was left among us. Rather I prefer those strains in which the praises of heroes were sung, and which heroes themselves sung—not the sounds of psalteries and languishing lutes, which ought to be shunned even by modest females—but the knowledge of the principles of the art, which is of the highest efficacy in exciting and allaying the passions. For Pythagoras, as we have heard, calmed a party of young men, when urged by their passions to offer violence to a respectable family, by requesting the female musician who was playing to them, to change her strain to a spondaic measure. Chrysippus assigns a special tune for the lullaby of nurses, which is used with children. There is also a subject for declamation in the schools, not unartfully invented, in which it is supposed that a flute player, who had played a Phrygian tune to a priest while he was sacrificing, is accused, after the priest has been driven to madness and has thrown himself over a precipice, of having been the cause of his death; if such causes have to be pleaded by an orator, and cannot be pleaded without a knowledge of music, how can even the most prejudiced forbear to admit that this art is necessary to our profession?

As to geometry,[9] people admit that some attention to it is of advantage in tender years, for they allow that the thinking powers are excited, and the intellect sharpened by it, and that a quickness of perception is thence produced; but they fancy that it is not, like other sciences, profitable after it has been acquired, but only while it is being studied. Such is the common opinion respecting it. But it is not without reason that the greatest men have bestowed extreme attention on this science, for as geometry is divided between numbers and fig-

[9] It is evident from his later remarks that he includes all mathematics under the term "geometry."

ures, the knowledge of numbers, assuredly, is necessary not only to an orator, but to everyone who has been initiated even in the rudiments of learning. In pleading causes, it is very often in request; when the speaker, if he hesitates, I do not say about the amount of a calculation, but if he even betray, by any uncertain or awkward movement of his fingers, a want of confidence in his calculations, is thought to be but im-

36   perfectly accomplished in his art. The knowledge of linear figures, too, is frequently required in causes, for lawsuits occur concerning boundaries and measures. But geometry has a still greater connection with the art of oratory.

37   Order, in the first place, is necessary in geometry, and is it not also necessary in eloquence? Geometry proves what follows from what precedes, what is unknown from what is known, and do we not draw similar conclusions in speaking? Does not the well-known mode of deduction from a number of proposed questions consist almost wholly in syllogisms? Accordingly, you may find more persons to say that geometry is allied

38   to logic than that it is allied to rhetoric. But even an orator, though rarely, will yet at times prove his points logically, for he will use syllogisms if his subject shall require them, and will of necessity use the enthymeme, which is a rhetorical syllogism. Besides, of all proofs, the strongest are what are called geometrical demonstrations—and what does oratory make its object more indisputably than proof?

39   Geometry often, moreover, by demonstration, proves what is apparently true to be false. This is also done with respect to numbers, by means of certain figures which they call *pseudographs,* and at which we were accustomed to play when we were boys. But there are other questions of a higher nature. For who would not believe the asserter of the following proposition: "Of whatever places the boundary lines measure the same length, of those places the areas also, which are con-

40   tained by those lines, must necessarily be equal"? But this proposition is fallacious, for it makes a vast difference what figure the boundary lines may form: Therefore, historians, who have thought that the dimensions of islands are suffi-

ciently indicated by the space traversed in sailing round them, have been justly censured by geometricians. For the nearer to perfection any figure is, the greater is its capacity; and if the boundary line, accordingly, shall form a circle, which of all plane figures is the most perfect, it will embrace a larger area than if it shall form a square of equal circumference. Squares, again, contain more than triangles of equal circuit, and triangles themselves contain more when their sides are equal than when they are unequal. Some other examples may perhaps be too obscure, but let us take an instance most easy of comprehension, even to the ignorant. There is scarcely any man who does not know that the dimensions of an acre extend two hundred and forty feet in length, and the half of that number in breadth; and it is easy to calculate what its circumference is, and how much ground it contains. A figure of a hundred and eighty feet on each side, however, has the same periphery, but a much larger area contained within its four sides. If any one thinks it too much trouble to make the calculation, he may learn the same truth by means of smaller numbers. Ten feet, on each side of a square, will give forty for the circumference, and a hundred for the area; but if there were fifteen feet on each side, and five at each end, they would, with the same circuit, deduct a fourth part from the area enclosed. If, again, nineteen feet be extended in parallel lines, only one foot apart, they will contain no more squares than those along which the parallels shall be drawn; and yet the periphery will be of the same extent as that which encloses a hundred. Thus, the further you depart from the form of a square, the greater will be the loss to the area. It may, therefore, happen even that a smaller area may be enclosed by a greater periphery than a larger one. Such is the case in plane figures; on hills, and in valleys, it is evident even to the untaught that there is more ground than sky.

Need I add that geometry raises itself still higher, so as even to ascertain the system of the world? When it demonstrates, by calculations, the regular and appointed movements of the celestial bodies, we learn that, in that system, there is nothing unordained or fortuitous: a branch of knowledge which may

47 be sometimes of use to the orator. When Pericles freed the Athenians from fear, at the time that they were alarmed by an eclipse of the sun, by explaining to them the causes of the phenomenon; or when Sulpicius Gallus, in the army of Paulus Aemilius, made a speech on an eclipse of the moon, that the minds of the soldiers might not be terrified as by a supernatural prodigy—do they not, respectively, appear to have dis-

48 charged the duty of an orator? Had Nicias been possessed of such knowledge in Sicily, he would not have been confounded with similar terror, and have given over to destruction the finest of the Athenian armies. Dion, we know, when he went to overthrow the tyranny of Dionysius, was not deterred by a

49 similar phenomenon. Though the utility of geometry in war, however, be put out of the question, though we do not dwell upon the fact that Archimedes alone protracted the siege of Syracuse to a great extent, it is sufficient, assuredly, to establish what I assert, that numbers of questions, which it is difficult to solve by any other method—as those about the mode of dividing, about division to infinity, and about the rate of progressions—are accustomed to be solved by those geometrical demonstrations. If an orator has to speak (as the next book will show) on all subjects, no man, assuredly, can become a perfect orator without a knowledge of geometry.

CHAPTER ELEVEN

SOME TIME is also to be devoted to the actor, but only so far 1
as the future orator requires the art of delivery. I do not wish
the boy whom I educate for this pursuit, either to be broken
to the shrillness of a woman's voice, or to repeat the tremulous
tones of an old man's. Neither let him imitate the vices of the 2
drunkard, nor adapt himself to the baseness of the slave; nor
let him learn to display the feelings of love, or avarice, or fear:
acquirements which are not at all necessary to the orator, and
which corrupt the mind, especially while it is yet tender and
uninformed in the early youth; for frequent imitation settles 3
into habit. It is not even every gesture or motion that is to be
adopted from the actor; for though the orator ought to regulate both to a certain degree, yet he will be far from appear-
ing in a theatrical character, and will exhibit nothing extravagant either in his looks, or the movements of his hands, or his
walk. If there is any art used by speakers in these points, after
all, the first object of it should be that it may not appear to
be art.

What is then the duty of the teacher as to these particulars? 4
Let him, in the first place, correct faults of pronunciation, if
there be any, so that the words of the learner may be fully
expressed, and that every letter may be uttered with its proper
sound. For we find inconvenience from the too great weakness
or too great fulness of the sound of some letters. Some, as if
too harsh for us, we utter but imperfectly, or change them for
others not altogether dissimilar, but, as it were, smoother.
Thus *lambda* takes the place of *rho,* in which even Demos- 5
thenes found difficulty (the nature of both letters is the same
also with us); and when *c,* and similarly *g,* are wanting in full
force, they are softened down into *t* and *d.* Those niceties 6
about the letter *s,* such a master will not even tolerate; nor
will he allow his pupil's words to sound in his throat, or to

rumble as from emptiness of the mouth; nor will he (what is utterly at variance with purity of speaking) permit him to overlay the simple sound of a word with a fuller sort of pro-

7 nunciation, which the Greeks call καταπεπλασμένον: a term by which the sound of flutes is also designated, when, after the holes are stopped through which they sound the shrill notes, they give forth a bass sound through the direct outlet only.

8 The teacher will be cautious, likewise, that concluding syllables be not lost; that his pupil's speech be all of a similar character; that whenever he has to raise his voice, the effort

9 may be that of his lungs, and not of his head; that his gesture may be suited to his voice, and his looks to his gesture. He will have to take care, also, that the face of his pupil, while speaking, look straight forward; that his lips be not distorted; that no opening of the mouth immoderately distend his jaws; that his face be not turned up, or his eyes cast down too much, or

10 his head inclined to either side. The face offends in various ways: I have seen many speakers, whose eyebrows were raised at every effort of the voice; those of others I have seen contracted; and those of some even disagreeing, as they turned up one toward the top of the head, while with the other, the eye

11 itself was almost concealed. To all these matters, as we shall hereafter show, a vast deal of importance is to be attached, for nothing can please which is unbecoming.

12 The actor will also be required to teach how a narrative should be delivered; with what authority persuasion should be forced; with what force anger may show itself; and what tone of voice is adapted to excite pity. This instruction he will give with the best effect, if he select particular passages from plays, such as are most adapted for this object, that is,

13 such as most resemble pleadings. The repetition of these passages will not only be most beneficial to pronunciation, but

14 also highly efficient in fostering eloquence. Such may be the pupil's studies while immaturity of age will not admit of anything higher. As soon as it shall be proper for him to read orations, however, and when he shall be able to perceive their beauties, then, I would say, let some attentive and skillful

tutor attend him, who may not only form his style by reading, but oblige him to learn select portions of speeches by heart, and to deliver them standing, with a loud voice, and exactly as he will have to plead. He may, in this way, exercise by pronunciation both his voice and his memory.

Nor do I think that those orators are to be blamed who 15
have devoted some time even to the masters of gymnastic in the *palaestra*.[1] I do not speak of those by whom part of life is spent rubbing themselves with oil, and the rest in drinking wine, and who have oppressed the powers of the mind by excessive attention to the body. (Such characters I should wish to be as far off as possible from the pupil that I am training.) Nevertheless the same name is given to those by whom gesture 16
and motion are formed; so that the arms may be properly extended; that the action of the hands may not be ungraceful or unseemly; that the attitude may not be unbecoming; that there may be no awkwardness in advancing the feet; and that the head and eyes may not be at variance with the turn of the rest of the body. For no one will deny that all such particulars 17
form a part of delivery, or will separate delivery itself from oratory. Assuredly, the orator must not disdain to learn what he must practice, especially when this *chironomia*, which is, as is expressed by the word itself, "the law of gesture," had its origin even in the heroic ages, and was approved by the most eminent men of Greece, even by Socrates himself. It was also regarded by Plato as a part of the qualifications of a public man, and was not omitted by Chrysippus in the directions which he wrote concerning the education of children. The 18
Spartans, we have heard, had among their exercises a certain kind of dance, as contributing to qualify men for war. Nor was dancing thought a disgrace to the ancient Romans, as the dance which continues to the present day, under the sanction and in the religious rites of the priests, is a proof; as is also

1 In other words, Quintilian is suggesting that a wise orator can learn something useful even from those who study bodily movements for a different purpose. Self-control in gymnastic movements, he would say, is similar to the bodily self-control needed by the speaker. Thus, he also sees some virtue in dancing as a means of learning bodily movement.

the remark of Crassus in the third book of Cicero's *De oratore*,[2] where he recommends that an orator should adopt a bold and manly action of body, not learned from the theater and the player, but from the camp, or even from the *palaestra*. The observation of this discipline has descended without censure even to our time. By me, however, it will not be continued beyond the years of boyhood, nor for long in them; for I do not wish the gesture of an orator to be formed to resemble that of a dancer, but I would have some influence from such juvenile exercises left, so that the gracefulness communicated to us while we were learning may secretly attend us when we are not thinking of our movements.

19

---

2 *De oratore* III. 59. 220.

CHAPTER TWELVE

It is a common question whether, supposing all these things 1
are to be learned, they can all be taught and acquired at the
same time. Some deny that this is possible, as the mind must
be confused and wearied by so many studies of different tendency for which neither the understanding, nor the body, nor
time itself, can suffice. Even though mature age may endure
such labor, they say, yet that of childhood ought not to be
thus burdened.

But these reasoners do not understand how great the power 2
of the human mind is—that mind which is so busy and active,
and which directs its attention, so to speak, to every quarter,
so that it cannot even confine itself to do only one thing, but
bestows its force upon several, not merely in the same day,
but at the same moment. Do not players on the harp, for ex- 3
ample, exert their memory, and attend to the sound of their
voice, and the various inflections of it, while, at the same
time, they strike part of the strings with their right hand, and
pull, stop, or let loose others with their left, while not even
their foot is idle, but beats time to their playing, all these acts
being done simultaneously? Do not we advocates, when sur- 4
prised by a sudden necessity to plead, say one thing while we
are thinking of what is to follow, while at the very same
moment the invention of arguments, the choice of words, the
arrangement of matter, gesture, delivery, look, and attitude,
are necessarily objects of our attention? If all these considerations of so varied a nature are forced, as by a single effort,
before our mental vision, why may we not divide the hours
of the day among different kinds of study, especially as variety
itself refreshes and recruits the mind, while, on the contrary,
nothing is more annoying than to continue at one uniform
labor? Accordingly writing is relieved by reading, and the
tedium of reading itself is relieved by changes of subject. How- 5

ever many things we may have done, we are yet to a certain degree fresh for that which we are going to begin. Who, on the contrary, would not be stupified, if he were to listen to the same teacher of any art, whatever it might be, through the whole day? But by change a person will be refreshed, as is the case with respect to food, by varieties of which the stomach is reinvigorated, and is fed with several sorts less unsatisfac-
6   torily than with one. Or let those objectors tell me what other mode there is of learning. Ought we to attend to the teacher of grammar only, and then to the teacher of geometry only, and cease to think, during the second course, of what we learned in the first? Should we then transfer ourselves to the musician, our previous studies being still allowed to escape us? Or while we are studying Latin, ought we to pay no attention to Greek? Or, to make an end of my questions at once,
7   ought we do nothing but what comes last before us? Why, then, do we not give similar counsel to husbandmen, that they should not cultivate at the same time their fields and their vineyards, their olives and other trees, and that they should not bestow attention at once on their meadows, their cattle, their gardens, and their beehives? Why do we ourselves devote some portion of our time to our public business, some to the wants of our friends, some to our domestic accounts, some to the care of our persons, and some to our pleasures, any one of which occupations would weary us, if we pursued it without intermission? So much more easy is it to do many things one after the other, than to do one thing for a long time.

8   That boys will be unable to bear the fatigue of many studies is by no means to be feared, for no age suffers less from fatigue. This may perhaps appear strange, but we may prove
9   it by experience. For minds, before they are hardened, are more ready to learn. This is proved by the fact that children, within two years after they can fairly pronounce words, speak almost the whole language, though no one incites them to learn; but for how many years does the Latin tongue resist the efforts of our purchased slaves! You may well understand, if you attempt to teach a grown-up person to read, that those

who do everything in their own art with excellence, are not without reason called "instructed from boyhood." The temper of boys is better able to bear labor than that of men. As neither the falls of children, with which they are so often thrown on the ground, nor their crawling on hands and knees, nor, soon after, constant play and running all day hither and thither, inconvenience their bodies so much as those of adults, because they are of little weight and no burden to themselves, so their minds likewise, I conceive, suffer less from fatigue, because they exert themselves with less effort, and do not apply to study by putting any force upon themselves, but merely yield themselves to others to be formed. Moreover, in addition to the other pliancy of that age, they follow their teachers, as it were, with greater confidence, and do not see themselves to measure what they have already done. Consideration about labor is as yet unknown to them; moreover, as we ourselves have frequently experienced, toil has less effect upon the powers than thought.

Nor will they ever, indeed, have more disposable time, because all improvement at this age is from hearing. When the pupil shall retire by himself to write, when he shall produce and compose from his own mind, he will then either not have leisure, or will want inclination, to commence such exercises as I have specified. Since the teacher of grammar, therefore, cannot occupy the whole day, and indeed ought not to do so, lest he should disgust the mind of his pupil, to what studies can we better devote his fragmentary intervals (so to term them) of time? For I would not wish the pupil to be worn out in these exercises; nor do I desire that he should sing, or accompany songs with musical notes, or descend to the minutest investigations of geometry. Nor would I make him like an actor in delivery, nor like a dancing master in gesture. Even if I did require all such qualifications, there would still be abundance of time, for the immature part of life, which is devoted to learning, is long, and I am not speaking of slow intellects. Why did Plato, let me ask, excel in all these branches of knowledge which I think necessary to be acquired by him who would be an orator? He did so, because, not being satisfied with the instruction which Athens could afford, or with the science of the Pythagoreans, to whom he had sailed in Italy, he went also to the priests of Egypt and learned their mysteries.

16   We shroud our own indolence under the pretext of difficulty, for we have no real love of our work; nor is eloquence ever sought by us because it is the most honorable and noble of attainments, or for its own sake; but we apply ourselves 17 to labor only with mean views and for sordid gain. Plenty of orators may speak in the forum, with my permission, and acquire riches also, without such accomplishments as I recommend—only may every trader in contemptible merchandise be richer than they, and may the public crier make greater profit by his voice! I would not wish to have even for a reader of this work a man who would compute what returns his studies 18 will bring him. But he who shall have conceived, as with a divine power of imagination, the very idea itself of genuine oratory, and who shall keep before his eyes true eloquence— the queen, as an eminent poet calls her, of the world [1]—and shall seek his gain, not from the pay that he receives for his pleadings, but from his own mind, and from contemplation and knowledge, a gain which is enduring and independent of fortune, will easily prevail upon himself to devote the time, which others spend at shows, in the Campus Martius, at dice, or in idle talk (to say nothing of sleep and the prolongation of banquets) to the studies of geometry and music. How much more pleasure will he secure from such pursuits than from 19 unintellectual gratifications! For divine providence has granted this favor to mankind, that the more honorable occupations are also the more pleasing. But the very pleasure of these reflections has carried me too far. Let what I have said, therefore, suffice concerning the studies in which a boy is to be instructed before he enters on more important occupations; the next book will commence, as it were, a new subject, and enter on the duties of the teacher of rhetoric.

1 Pacuvius (220–130 B.C.), a famous tragic poet.

BOOK II

CHAPTER ONE

IT HAS been a prevalent custom (which daily gains more and 1
more ground) for pupils to be sent to the teachers of eloquence—to the Latin teachers always, and to the Greeks sometimes—at a more advanced age than reason requires. Of this
practice there are two causes: first, that the rhetoricians, especially our own, have relinquished a part of their duties; and
second, that the grammarians have appropriated what does
not belong to them. The rhetoricians think it their business 2
merely to declaim, and to teach the art and practice of declaiming, confining themselves, too, to deliberative and judicial subjects (for others they despise as beneath their profession). The grammarians, on their part, do not deem it
sufficient to have taken what has been left them (on which account also gratitude should be accorded them), but encroach
even upon *prosopopeiae* and suasory speeches, in which even
the very greatest efforts of eloquence are displayed. Hence, 3
accordingly, it has happened, that what was the first business
of the one art has become the last of the other, and that boys
of an age to be employed in higher departments of study remain sunk in the lower school, and practice rhetoric under the
grammarian. Thus—what is eminently ridiculous—a youth
seems unfit to be sent to a teacher of declamation until he already knows how to declaim.

Let us assign each of these professions its due limits. Let 4
grammar (which, turning it into a Latin word, they have
called *literatura*, "literature") know its own boundaries, especially as it is so far advanced beyond the humility indicated
by its name, to which humility the early grammarians re-
stricted themselves. This subject, though but weak at its
source, yet, having gained strength from the poets and his-

torians, now flows on in a full channel; since, besides the art of speaking correctly, which would otherwise be far from a comprehensive art, it has engrossed the study of almost all the highest departments of learning. But let not rhetoric, to which the power of eloquence has given its name, decline its own duties, or rejoice that the task belonging to itself is appropriated by another; for while it neglects its duties, it is almost expelled from its proper domain. I would not deny, indeed, that some of those who profess grammar may make such progress in knowledge as to be able to teach the principles of oratory; when they do so, however, they will be discharging the duties of a rhetorician, and not their own.

We make it also a subject of inquiry, when a boy may be considered ripe for learning what rhetoric teaches. In which inquiry it is not to be considered of what age a boy is, but what progress he has already made in his studies. That I may not make a long discussion, I think that the question of when a boy ought to be sent to the teacher of rhetoric is best decided by the answer, "When he shall be qualified." But this very point depends upon the preceding subject of consideration; for if the office of the grammarian is extended even to suasory speeches, the necessity for the rhetorician will come later. If the rhetorician, however, does not shrink from the earliest duties of his profession, his attention is required even from the time when the pupil begins narrations, and produces his little exercises in praising and blaming. Do we not know that it was a kind of exercise among the ancients, suitable for improvement in eloquence, for pupils to speak on *theses*,[1] *commonplaces*,[2] and other questions (without embracing particu-

[1] A *thesis* is a *quaestio infinita*: a general question unlimited by time, place, or persons. A famous ancient example was, "Should a man marry?" Cicero (*De inventione* I. 6. 8) ascribes to Hermagoras the distinction between the general question and the *causa*, or "special question," involving individual times, places, and persons. Quintilian discusses the *thesis* later as a school exercise (II. 4. 24).

[2] A *commonplace* (*communus locus*) is for Quintilian a general statement on a point of morality or law. While he does not in this passage supply an example, he discusses the classroom use of commonplaces later (II. 4. 22).

lar circumstances or persons), on which all causes, both real
and imaginary, depend? Hence it is evident how dishonorably
the profession of rhetoric has abandoned that department
which it held originally, and for a long time solely. But what   10
is there among those exercises, of which I have just now
spoken, that does not relate both to other matters peculiar to
rhetoricians, and, indisputably, to the sort of causes pleaded
in courts of justice? Have we not to make statements of facts
in the forum? I know not whether that department of rhetoric
is not most of all in demand there. Are not eulogy and invec-   11
tive often introduced in those disputations? Do not commonplaces, both those which are leveled against vice (such as were
composed, we read, by Cicero), and those in which questions
are discussed generally (such as were published by Quintus
Hortensius, as, "Ought we to trust to light proofs?" and "For
witnesses and against witnesses"), mix themselves with the
inmost substance of causes? These weapons are in some de-   12
gree to be prepared, so that we may use them whenever circumstances require. He who shall suppose that these matters
do not concern the orator, will think that a statue is not
begun when its limbs are cast.

Nor let anyone blame this haste of mine (as some will consider it) on the supposition that I think the pupil who is to
be commited to the professor of rhetoric is to be altogether
withdrawn from the teachers of grammar. To these also their   13
proper time shall be allowed, nor need there be any fear that
the boy will be overburdened with the lessons of two masters.
His labor will not be increased, but that which was mixed together under one master will be divided. Each tutor will thus
be more efficient in his own province. This method, to which
the Greeks still adhere, has been disregarded by the Latin
rhetoricians, and, indeed, with some appearance of excuse, as
there have been others to take over their duty.

CHAPTER TWO

1 As soon therefore as a boy shall have attained such proficiency in his studies as to be able to comprehend what we have called the first precepts of the teachers of rhetoric, he must be put under the professors of that art.

2 Of these professors the morals must first be ascertained. I proceed to treat this point in this part of my work, not because I do not think that the same examination is to be made, and with the utmost care, in regard also to other teachers (as indeed I have shown in the preceding book), but because the very age of the pupils makes attention to the matter still more

3 necessary. For boys are consigned to these professors when almost grown up, and continue their studies under them even after they are become men; and greater care must in consequence be adopted with regard to them, in order that the purity of the master may secure their more tender years from corruption, and his authority deter their bolder age from li-

4 centiousness. Nor is it enough that he give in himself an example of the strictest morality, unless he regulate also, by severity of discipline, the conduct of those who come to receive his instructions.

Let him adopt, then, above all things, the feelings of a parent toward his pupils, and consider that he succeeds to the place of those by whom the children were entrusted to him.

5 Let him neither have vices in himself, nor tolerate them in others. Let his austerity not be stern, nor his affability too easy, lest dislike arise from the one, or contempt from the other. Let him discourse frequently on what is honorable and good, for the oftener he admonishes, the more seldom will he have to chastise. Let him not be of an angry temper, and yet not a conniver at what ought to be corrected. Let him be plain in his mode of teaching, and patient of labor, but rather diligent in exacting tasks than fond of giving them of excessive

length. Let him reply readily to those who put questions to 6
him, and question of his own accord those who do not. In
commending the exercises of his pupils, let him be neither
niggardly nor lavish; for the one quality begets dislike of
labor, and the other self-complacency. In amending what re- 7
quires correction, let him not be harsh, and, least of all, not
reproachful; for that very circumstance, that some tutors
blame students as if they hated them, deters many young men
from their proposed course of study. Let him speak much 8
every day himself, for the edification of his pupils. Although
he may point out to them, in their course of reading, plenty
of examples for their imitation, yet the living voice, as it is
called, feeds the mind more nutritiously—especially the voice
of the teacher, whom his pupils, if they are but rightly instructed, both love and reverence. How much more readily we
imitate those whom we like can scarcely be expressed.

The liberty of standing up and showing exultation by giv- 9
ing applause, as is done under most teachers, is by no means
to be allowed to boys; for the approbation even of young
men, when they listen to others, ought to be but temperate.
Hence it will result that the pupil will depend on the judgment of the master, and will think that he has expressed properly whatever shall have been approved by him. But that most 10
mischievous politeness, as it is now termed, which is shown
by students in their praise of each other's compositions, whatever be their merits, is not only unbecoming and theatrical,
and foreign to strictly regulated schools, but even a most de-
structive enemy to study, for care and toil may well appear
superfluous, when praise is ready for whatever the pupils have
produced. Those therefore who listen, as well as he who 11
speaks, ought to watch the countenance of the master, for they
will thus discern what is to be approved and what to be condemned. Thus, power will be gained from composition, and
judgment from being heard. But now, eager and ready, they 12
not only start up at every period, but dart forward, and cry
out with indecorous transports. The compliment is repaid in
kind, and upon such applause depends the fortune of a dec-

lamation; and hence result vanity and self-conceit, insomuch
that, being elated with the tumultuous approbation of their
class-fellows, they are inclined, if they receive but little praise
13 from the master, to form an ill opinion of him. But let masters, also, desire to be heard themselves with attention and
modesty; for the master ought not to speak to suit the taste of
his pupils, but the pupils to suit that of the master. If possible,
moreover, his attention should be directed to observe what
each pupil commends in his speeches, and for what reason;
and he may then rejoice that what he says will give pleasure,
not more on his own account than on that of his pupils who
judge with correctness.

14 That mere boys should sit mixed with young men, I do not
approve. Though such a man as ought to preside over their
studies and conduct may keep even the eldest of his pupils
under control, yet the more tender ought to be separate from
the more mature, and they should all be kept free, not merely
from the guilt of licentiousness, but even from the suspicion
15 of it. This point I thought proper briefly to notice (that the
master and his school should be clear of gross vice, I do not
suppose it necessary even to intimate). And if there is any
father who would not shrink from flagrant vice in choosing
a tutor for his son, let him be assured that all other rules
which I am endeavoring to lay down for the benefit of youth
are, when this consideration is disregarded, useless to him.

CHAPTER THREE

Nor is the opinion of those to be passed in silence, who, even when they think boys fit for the professor of rhetoric, imagine that they are not at once to be consigned to the most eminent, but detain them for some time under inferior teachers. Their notion is that moderate ability in a master is not only better adapted for beginning instruction in art, but easier for comprehension and imitation, as well as less disdainful of undertaking the trouble of the elements. On this head I think no longer labor necessary to show how much better it is to be imbued with the best instructions, and how much difficulty is attendant on eradicating faults which have once gained ground, since double duty falls on succeeding masters, and the task of teaching is, indeed, heavier and more important than that of teaching at first. Accordingly, they say that Timotheus, a famous instructor in playing the flute, was accustomed to ask twice as much pay from those whom another had taught, as from those who presented themselves to him in a state of ignorance. The mistakes committed in the matter, however, are two: one, that people think inferior teachers sufficient for a time, and, from having an easily satisfied appetite, are content with their instructions. (Such supineness, though deserving of reprehension, would yet be in some degree endurable if teachers of that class taught only worse, and not less.) The other mistake which is even more common, is that people imagine that those who have attained eminent qualifications for speaking will not descend to inferior matters, and that this is sometimes the case because they disdain to bestow attention on minuter points, and sometimes because they cannot give instruction in them. For my part, I do not consider a man a real teacher if he is unwilling to teach little things. But I argue that the ablest teachers can teach little things best, if

95

they will: first, because it is likely that he who excels others in eloquence, has gained the most accurate knowledge of the
6   means by which men attain eloquence; second, because method, which, with the best qualified instructors, is always plainest, is of great efficacy in teaching; and lastly, because no man rises to such a height in greater things that the lesser fade entirely from his view. Unless indeed we believe that though Phidias made a Jupiter well, another might have wrought, in better style than he, the accessories to the decoration of the work; or that an orator may not know how to speak; or that an eminent physician may be unable to cure trifling ailments.

7   Is there not then, it may be asked, a certain height of eloquence too elevated for the immaturity of boyhood to comprehend it? I readily confess that there is; but the eloquent professor must also be a man of sense, not ignorant of teaching, and capable of lowering himself to the capacity of the learner; as any fast walker, if he should happen to walk with a child, would give him his hand, relax his pace, and not go on
8   quicker than his companion could follow. What shall be said, too, if it generally happens that instructions given by the most learned are far more easy to be understood, and more lucid than those of others? For clarity is the chief virtue of eloquence, and the less ability a man has, the more he tries to raise and swell himself out, as those of short stature exalt
9   themselves on tiptoe, and the weak use most threats. As to those whose style is inflated, displaying a vitiated taste, and who are fond of resounding words, or are faulty from any other mode of vicious affectation, I am convinced that they labor under the fault, not of strength, but of weakness, as bodies are swollen, not with health, but with disease, and as men who have tired of the straight road generally wander from it. Accordingly, the less able a teacher is, the more obscure will he be.

10   It has not escaped my memory that I said in the preceding book (when I observed that education in schools was preferable to that at home), that pupils commencing their studies, or

but little advanced in them, devote themselves more readily
to imitate their schoolfellows than their master, such imitation being more easy to them. This remark may be understood
by some in such a sense that the opinion which I now advocate may appear inconsistent with that which I advanced before. But such inconsistency will be far from me, for what 11
I then said is the very best of reasons why a boy should be
consigned to the best possible instructor—because even the
pupils under him, being better taught than those under inferior masters, will either speak in such a manner as it may
not be objectionable to imitate, or, if they commit any faults,
will be immediately corrected, whereas the less learned teacher
will perhaps praise even what is wrong, and cause it, by his
judgment, to recommend itself to those who listen to it. Let 12
a master therefore be excellent in morals as well as in eloquence; one who, like Homer's Phoenix, may teach his pupil
at once to speak and to act.[1]

1 *Iliad* IX. 432.

CHAPTER FOUR

1 I SHALL now proceed to state what I conceive to be the first duties of rhetoricians in giving instruction to their pupils, putting off for a while the consideration of what is called, in common language, the "art of rhetoric" itself.[1] For to me it appears most eligible to commence with that to which the pupil has learned something similar under the grammarians.

2 Of narrations (besides that which we use in pleadings),[2] we understand that there are three kinds; the *fable,* which is the subject of tragedies and poems, and which is remote, not merely from truth, but from the appearance of truth; the *argumentum,* which comedies represent, and which, though false, has a resemblance to truth; and the *history,* in which is contained a relation of facts. Since we have consigned poetic narratives to the grammarians, let the historical type form the commencement of study under the rhetorician; this is a kind of narrative which, as it has more of truth, has also more of 3 substance. What appears to me the best method of narrating, I will show when I treat of the judicial part of pleading. In the meantime it will suffice to intimate that it ought not to be dry and insipid (for what necessity would there be to bestow

1 At the end of his discussion of the early education of the citizen-orator, Quintilian begins (II. 11. 1) an elaborate treatment of the five canons of *ars rhetorica.* This occupies most of the remainder of the *Institutio oratoria.* (For the author's own outline of this plan, see Preface, 21–22, pp. 8–9.) Quintilian's point here, as before, is that other writers have regarded the art of rhetoric too narrowly, leaping at once into technical discussions of the *ars* without first considering the student's educational needs.

2 In the six-part speech arrangement system popularized by Cicero (exordium, narration, partition, confirmation, refutation, and peroration), the second step is the *narratio:* an exposition of events that the speaker presents as the facts of the case. See Cicero, *De inventione* I. 19–21. Quintilian (IV. 2. 2) refers to it as "the statement of facts."

so much pains upon study, if it were thought sufficient to state facts without dress or decoration?), nor ought it to be erratic, and wantonly adorned with far-fetched descriptions, in which many speakers indulge with an emulation of poetic license. Both these kinds of narrative are faulty, yet that 4 which springs from poverty of mind is worse than that which comes from exuberance.

From boys, perfection of style can neither be required nor expected. But the fertile genius, fond of noble efforts, and conceiving at times a more than reasonable degree of ardor, is greatly to be preferred. Nor, if there be something of ex- 5 uberance in a pupil of that age, would it at all displease me. I would even have it an object with teachers themselves to nourish minds that are still tender with more indulgence, and to allow them to be satiated, as it were, with the milk of more liberal studies. The body, which mature age may afterward nerve, may for a time be somewhat plumper than seems desirable. Hence there is hope of strength, while a child that has 6 the outline of all his limbs exact commonly portends weakness in subsequent years. Let that age be daring, invent much, and delight in what it invents, though it be often not sufficiently severe and correct. The remedy for exuberance is easy, but barrenness is incurable by any labor. That temper in boys 7 will afford me little hope in which mental effort is prematurely restrained by judgment. I like what is produced to be extremely copious, profuse even beyond the limits of propriety. Years will greatly reduce superfluity; judgment will smooth away much of it; something will be worn off, as it were, by use, if there be but metal from which something may be hewn and polished off, and such metal there will be, if we do not make the plate too thin at first, so that deep cutting may break it. That I hold such opinions concerning this age, 8 he will be less likely to wonder who shall have read what Cicero says: "I wish fecundity in a young man to give itself full scope." [3]

Above all, therefore, and especially for boys, a dry master

[3] *De oratore* II. 21. 88.

is to be avoided, not less than a dry soil, void of all moisture, for plants that are still tender. Under the influence of such a tutor, they at once become dwarfish, looking as it were toward the ground, and daring to aspire to nothing above everyday

9   talk. To them, leanness is in place of health, and weakness instead of judgment; and, while they think it sufficient to be free from fault, they fall into the fault of being free from all merit. Let not even maturity itself, therefore, come too fast; let not the grape juice, while yet in the vat, become too mellow, for properly vinted wine will bear years, and will be improved by age.

10   Nor is it improper for me, moreover, to offer this admonition; that the powers of boys sometimes sink under too great severity in correction; for they despond, and grieve, and at last hate their work, and, what is most prejudicial, while they

11   fear everything, they cease to attempt anything. There is a similar conviction in the minds of the cultivators of trees in the country who think that the knife must not be applied to tender shoots, as they appear to shrink from the steel, and to

12   be unable as yet to bear an incision. A teacher ought, therefore, to be as agreeable as possible, that remedies, which are rough in their own nature, may be rendered soothing by gentleness of hand; he ought to praise some parts of his pupils' performances, to tolerate some, and to alter others, giving his reasons why the alterations are made; and also to make some passages clearer by adding something of his own. It will also be of service at times for the master himself to dictate whole subjects, which the pupil may imitate and admire for the

13   present as his own. But if a boy's composition were so faulty as not to admit of correction, I have found him benefited whenever I told him to write on the same subject again, after it had received fresh treatment from me, observing that "he could do still better," since study is cheered by nothing more

14   than hope. Different ages, however, are to be corrected in different ways, and work is to be required and amended according to the degree of the pupil's abilities. I used to say to boys when they attempted anything extravagant or verbose,

that "I was satisfied with it for the present, but that a time would come when I should not allow them to produce compositions of such a character." Thus they were satisfied with their abilities, and yet not led to form a wrong judgment.

But that I may return to the point from which I digressed, I should wish narrations to be composed with the utmost possible care. It is of service to boys at an early age, when their speech is but just commenced, to repeat what they have heard in order to improve their faculty of speaking. Let them accordingly be made, and with very good reason, to go over their stories again, and to pursue them from the middle, either backward or forward; but let this be done only while they are still at the knees of their teachers, and, as they can do nothing else, are beginning to connect words and things, that they may thus strengthen their memories. But when they are striving to attain the command of pure and correct language, extemporary garrulity, without waiting for thought, or scarcely taking time to rise, is the offspring of mere ostentatious boastfulness. Hence arises empty exultation in ignorant parents, and in their children contempt of application, want of all modesty, a habit of speaking in the worst style, the practice of all kinds of faults, and—what has often been fatal even to great proficiency—an arrogant conceit of their own abilities. There will be a proper time for acquiring facility of speech, nor will that part of my subject be lightly passed over by me; but in the meantime it will be sufficient if a boy with all his care, and with the utmost application of which that age is capable, can write something tolerable. To this practice let him accustom himself, and make it natural to him. He only will succeed in attaining the eminence at which we aim, or the point next below it, who shall learn to speak correctly before he learns to speak rapidly.

To narrations is added, not without advantage, the task of refuting and confirming them, which is called ἀνασκευή and κατασκευή. This may be done, not only with regard to fabulous subjects, and such as are related in poetry, but with regard even to records in our annals. It might be inquired whether

15

16

17

18

it is credible that a crow settled upon the head of Valerius
when he was fighting, to annoy the face and eyes of his Gallic
enemy with his beak and wings: there will be ample matter
for discussion on both sides of the question. So there will be
also concerning the serpent, of which Scipio is said to have
been born, as well as about the wolf of Romulus, and the
Egeria of Numa. As to the histories of the Greeks, there is generally license in them similar to that of the poets. Questions
are often wont to arise, too, concerning the time or place at
which a thing is said to have been done, sometimes even about
a person; as Livy, for instance, is frequently in doubt, and
other historians differ one from another.

20   The pupil will then proceed by degrees to higher efforts, to
praise illustrious characters and censure the immoral—an exercise of manifold advantage—for the mind is thus employed
about a multiplicity and variety of matters, while the understanding is formed by the contemplation of good and evil.
Hence is acquired, too, an extensive knowledge of things in
general; and the pupil is soon furnished with examples, which
are of great weight in every kind of causes, and which he will
use as occasion requires. Next succeeds exercise in comparison, which of two characters is the better or the worse; this,
though it is managed in a similar way, yet both doubles the
topics, and treats not only of the nature, but of the degrees of
virtues and of vices. But on the management of praise and
the contrary, since it is the third part of rhetoric, I shall give
directions in the proper place.[4]

22   *Commonplaces* (I speak of those in which, without specifying persons, it is usual to declaim against vices themselves,
as against those of the adulterer, the gamester, the licentious
person), are of the very nature of speeches on trials. If you
add the name of an accused party, they are real accusations.
These, however, are usually altered from their treatment as

---

[4] *Institutio oratoria* III. 7. Ancient doctrine identified three types of
speeches: judicial or legal; political or deliberative; and epedeictic. This
third type, the epedeictic, to which Quintilian refers here, deals with
praise and blame. For the basic statement of the three types see Aristotle,
Rhetoric I. 3.

general subjects to something specific, as when the subjects of a declamation is a blind adulterer, a poor gamester, a licentious old man. Sometimes also they have their use in a defense; 23 for we occasionally speak in favor of luxury or licentiousness; and a procurer or parasite is sometimes defended in such a way that we advocate, not the person, but the vice.

Theses, which are drawn from the comparison of things, 24 as whether a country or city life is more desirable, and whether the merit of a lawyer or a soldier is the greater, are eminently proper and copious subjects for exercise in speaking, and contribute greatly to improvement, both in the province of persuasion and in discussions on trials. The latter of the two subjects just mentioned is handled with great copiousness by Cicero in his pleading for Muraena.[5] Such *theses* as 25 whether a man ought to marry; and whether political offices should be sought, belong almost wholly to the deliberative species, for, if persons be but added, they will be suasory.

My teachers were accustomed to prepare us for conjectural 26 causes by a kind of exercise far from useless, and very pleasant to us, in which they desired us to investigate and show why among the Lacedaemonians Venus was represented armed; why Cupid was thought to be a boy, and winged, and armed with arrows and a torch; and questions of a similar nature, in which we endeavored to ascertain the intention, or object about which there is so often a question in controversies. This may be regarded as a sort of *chria.*

Such questions as those about witnesses (whether we ought 27 always to believe them) and concerning arguments (whether we ought to put any trust in trifling ones) belong to forensic pleading; this is so manifest that some speakers, not undistinguished in civil offices, have kept them ready in writing, and have carefully committed them to memory, that, whenever opportunity should offer, their extemporaneous speeches might be decorated with them, as with ornaments fitted into them. By which practice (for I cannot delay to express my 28 judgment on the point), they appeared to me to confess great

[5] *Pro Muraena* IX,21 ff.

weakness in themselves. For what can such men produce appropriate to particular causes, of which the aspect is perpetually varied and new? How can they reply to questions propounded by the opposite party? How can they at once meet objections, or interrogate a witness, when, even on topics of the commonest kind, such as are handled in most causes, they are unable to pursue the most ordinary thoughts in any words

29 but those which they have long before prepared? When they say the same things in various pleadings, their cold meat—as it were, served up over and over again—must create loathing in the speakers themselves. Or their unhappy household furniture, which, as among the ambitious poor, is worn out by being used for several different purposes, must, when detected so often by the memory of their hearers, cause a feeling of

30 shame in them. Indeed, there is scarcely any commonplace so common, which can incorporate well with any pleading, unless it be bound by some link to the peculiar question under

31 consideration; otherwise, it will show that it is not so much inserted as attached, either because it is unlike the rest, or because it is very frequently borrowed without reason—not because it is wanted, but because it is ready. Some speakers, for the sake of sentiment, introduce the most verbose commonplaces, whereas it is from the subject itself that sentiments

32 ought to arise. Such remarks are ornamental and useful if they spring from the question, but every remark, however beautiful, unless it tends to gain the cause, is certainly superfluous, and sometimes even noxious. But this digression has been sufficiently prolonged.

33   The praise or censure of laws requires more mature powers, such as may almost suffice for the very highest efforts. Whether this exercise partakes more of the nature of deliberative or controversial oratory is a point that varies according to the custom and right of particular nations. Among the Greeks the proposer of laws was called to plead before the judge; among the Romans it was customary to recommend or disparage a law before the public assembly. In either case, however, few arguments, and those of a certain type, are advanced; for there

are but three kinds of laws: sacred, public, and private. This ³⁴
division has regard chiefly to the commendation of a law, as
when the speaker extols it by a kind of gradation: because it
is a law, because it is public, because it is made to promote
the worship of the gods. Points about which questions usu- ³⁵
ally arise are common to all laws. For a doubt may arise,
either concerning the right of him who proposes the law (as
concerning that of Publius Clodius who was accused of not
having been properly created tribune); or concerning the va-
lidity of the proposal itself, a doubt which may refer to a variety of matters, as for instance, whether the proposal has been
published on three market days, or whether the law may be
said to have been proposed, or to be proposed, on an improper
day, or contrary to protests, or to the auspices, or in any other
way at variance with legitimate proceedings; or whether it be
opposed to any law still in force. But such considerations do ³⁶
not enter into these student exercises, which are without any
allusion to persons, times, or particular causes.

Other points, whether treated in real or fictitious discus- ³⁷
sions, are much the same, for the fault of any law must be
either in words or in matter. As to words, it is questioned
whether they be sufficiently expressive; or whether there is any
ambiguity in them; as to matter, whether the law is consistent
with itself; whether it ought to have reference to past time
or to individuals. But the most common inquiry is whether it
be proper or expedient. Nor am I ignorant that of this inquiry ³⁸
many divisions are made by most professors; but I, under the
term "proper," include consistency with justice, piety, religion, and other similar virtues. The consideration of justice,
however, is usually discussed with reference to more than one
point; for a question may either be raised about the subject
of the law, as whether it be deserving of punishment or reward, or about the measure of reward or punishment, to
which an objection may be taken as well for being too great ³⁹
as little. Expediency, also, is sometimes determined by the
nature of the measure, sometimes by the circumstances of the
time. As to some laws, it becomes a question whether they can

be enforced. Nor ought students to be ignorant that laws are sometimes censured wholly, sometimes partly, as examples of
40 both are afforded us in highly celebrated orations. Nor does it escape my recollection that there are laws which are not proposed for perpetuity, but with regard to temporary honors or commands, such as the *lex Manilia,* about which there is an oration of Cicero. But concerning these, no directions can be given in this place, for they depend upon the peculiar nature of the subjects on which the discussion is raised, and not on any general consideration.

41   On such subjects did the ancients, for the most part, exercise the faculty of eloquence, borrowing their mode of argument, however, from the logicians. To speak on fictitious cases, in imitation of pleadings in the forum or in public councils, is generally agreed to have become a practice among the
42 Greeks about the time of Demetrius Phalereus. Whether that sort of exercise was invented by him, I (as I have acknowledged also in another book) [6] have not succeeded in discovering; nor do those who affirm most positively that he did invent it, rest their opinion on any writer of good authority. Cicero tells us that the Latin teachers of eloquence commenced this practice toward the end of the life of Lucius Crassus [7]; of these teachers the most eminent was Plotius.

---

[6] Presumably Quintilian's lost work, *De causis corruptae eloquentiae* (*Concerning the Causes of the Corruption of Eloquence*), to which he also refers in VI. Preface 3, and in VIII. 6. 76.

[7] Crassus, the spokesman for Cicero, discusses Latin professors of rhetoric in *De oratore* III. 24. 93.

CHAPTER FIVE

But of the proper mode of declaiming I shall speak a little [1] further on. Meanwhile, as we are treating of the first rudiments of rhetoric, I should not omit, I think, to observe how much the professor would contribute to the advancement of his pupils, if, just as the explanation of the poets is required from teachers of grammar, so he, in like manner, would exercise the pupils under his care in the reading of history, and even still more in that of speeches. This is a practice which I myself have adopted in the case of a few pupils whose age required it, and whose parents thought it would be serviceable to them. But though I then deemed it an excellent method, [2] two circumstances were obstructions to the practice of it: first, that long custom had established a different mode of teaching and second, that they were mostly fullgrown youths, who did not require that exercise, who were forming themselves on my model. But though I should make a new discovery ever so [3] late, I should not be ashamed to recommend it for the future. I know, however, that this is now done among the Greeks, but chiefly by assistant masters, since the time would seem hardly sufficient if the professors were always to lecture to each pupil as he read. Such lecturing, indeed, as is given, so that boys [4] may follow the writing of an author easily and distinctly with their eyes, and such even as explains the meaning of every uncommon word that occurs—this is to be regarded as far below the profession of a teacher of rhetoric.

But to point out the beauties of authors, and, if occasion [5] ever present itself, their faults, is eminently consistent with that profession and engagement, by which he offers himself to the public as a master of eloquence. I do not require such toil from teachers, however, that they should call their pupils to their laps, and labor at the reading of whatever book each [6] of them may fancy. For to me it seems easier, as well as far more advantageous, that the master, after calling for silence, should appoint some one pupil to read (and it will be best that this duty should be imposed on them by turns), so that they may thus accustom themselves to clear pronunciation.

7   Then, after explaining the cause for which the oration was composed (so that what is said will be better understood), he should leave nothing unnoticed which is important to be remarked, either in the thought or the language: he should observe what method is adopted in the exordium for conciliating the judge; what clearness, brevity, and apparent sincerity is displayed in the statement of facts; what design there is in certain passages, and what well-concealed artifice (for that is the only true art in pleading which cannot be per-

8   ceived except by a skilful pleader); what judgment appears in the division of the matter; how subtle and urgent is the argumentation; with what force the speaker excites, with what amenity he soothes; what severity is shown in his invectives, what urbanity in his jests; how he commands the feelings, forces a way into the understanding, and makes the opinions

9   of the judges coincide with what he asserts. In regard to the style, too, he should notice any expression that is peculiarly appropriate, elegant, or sublime; when the amplification deserves praise, what quality is opposed to it; what phrases are happily metaphorical, what figures of speech are used; what part of the composition is smooth and polished, and yet manly and vigorous.

10   Nor is it without advantage, indeed, that inelegant and faulty speeches—yet such as many, from depravity of taste, would admire—should be read before boys, and that it should be shown how many expressions in them are inappropriate, obscure, timid, low, mean, affected, or effeminate. Such expressions, however, are not only extolled by many readers, but, what is worse, are extolled for the very reason that they are

11   vicious. Straightforward language, naturally expressed, seems to some of us to have nothing of genius; but whatever departs, in any way, from the common course, we admire as something exquisite; as, with some persons, more regard is shown for fig-

ures that are distorted and in any respect monstrous, than for such as have lost none of the advantages of ordinary conformation. Some, too, who are attracted by appearance, think that 12 there is more beauty in men who are depilated and smooth, who dress their locks (hot from the curling irons) with pins, and who are radiant with a complexion not their own, than unsophisticated nature can give: as if beauty of person could be thought to spring from corruption of manners.

Nor will the preceptor be under the obligation merely to 13 teach these things, but frequently to ask questions upon them, and try the judgment of his pupils. Thus carelessness will not come upon them while they listen, nor will the instructions that shall be given fail to enter their ears. Thus, they will at the same time be conducted to the end which is sought in this exercise, namely that they themselves may conceive and understand. For what object have we in teaching them, but that they may not always require to be taught?

I will venture to say that this sort of diligent exercise will 14 contribute more to the improvement of students than all the treatises of all the rhetoricians that ever wrote. Doubtless, however, they are of considerable use, but their scope is more general, and how indeed can they go into all kinds of questions that arise almost every day? Likewise, though certain 15 general precepts are given in the military art, it will yet be of far more advantage to know what plan any leader has adopted wisely or imprudently, and in what place or at what time—for in almost every art precepts are of much less avail than practical experiments. Shall a teacher declaim so that 16 he may be a model to his hearers, and will not Cicero and Demosthenes, if read, profit them even more? Shall a pupil, if he commits faults in declaiming, be corrected before the rest, and will it not be more serviceable to him to correct the speech of another? Indisputably. And even more agreeable, for every person prefers that others' faults should be blamed rather than his own. Nor are there wanting more arguments 17 for me to offer; but the advantage of this plan can escape the observation of no one, and I wish that there may not be so much unwillingness to adopt it as there will be pleasure in having adopted it.

18   If this method be followed, there will remain a question not very difficult to answer, which is, what authors ought to be read by beginners? Some have recommended inferior writers, as they thought them easier of comprehension; others have advocated the more florid kind of writers, as being better 19 adapted to nourish the minds of the young. For my part, I would have the best authors commenced at once, and read always; but I would choose the clearest in style, and most intelligible. I recommend Livy rather than Sallust, for instance, to be read by boys. He is the greater historian, but to 20 understand him there is need of some proficiency. Cicero, as it seems to me, is agreeable even to beginners and sufficiently intelligible, and may not only profit but even be loved; and next to Cicero (as Livy advises), such authors as most resemble Cicero.

21   There are two points in style on which I think that the greatest caution should be used in respect to boys: one is that no master, from being too much an admirer of antiquity, should allow them to harden, as it were, in the reading of the Gracchi, Cato, and other like authors. They would thus become uncouth and dry; since they cannot as yet understand their force of thought, and, content with adopting their style, which at the time it was written was doubtless excellent, but is quite unsuitable to our day, they will appear to themselves 22 to resemble those eminent men. The other point, which is the opposite of the former, is to avoid being captivated with the flowers of modern affectation, lest they should be so seduced by a corrupt kind of pleasure, as to love that luscious manner of writing which is the more agreeable to the minds of youth 23 in proportion as it has more affinity with them. When their taste is formed, however, and out of danger of being corrupted, I should recommend them to read not only the ancients (from whom, if a solid and manly force of thought be adopted, while the rust of a rude age is cleared off, our present style will receive additional grace), but also the writers of the

present day, in whom there is much merit. For nature has not   24
condemned us to stupidity, but we ourselves have changed our
mode of speaking, and have indulged our fancies more than
we ought; and thus the ancients did not excel us so much in
genius as in severity of manner. It will be possible, therefore,
to select from the moderns many qualities for imitation, but
care must be taken that they be not contaminated with other
qualities with which they are mixed. Yet that there have been   25
recently, and are now, many writers whom we may imitate
entirely, I would not only agree (for why should I not?) but
even affirm. But who they are it is not for everybody to decide.   26
We may even err with greater safety in regard to the ancients;
and I would therefore postpone the reading of the moderns,
so that imitation may not go before judgment.

CHAPTER SIX

1 THERE HAS been also a diversity of practice among teachers in the following respect. Some of them, not confining themselves to giving directions as to the division of any subject which they assigned their pupils for declamation, developed it more fully by speaking on it themselves, and amplified it not only 2 with proofs but with appeals to the feelings. Others, giving merely the first outlines, spoke after the declamations on whatever points each pupil had omitted, and polished some passages with no less care than they would have used if they had themselves been rising to speak in public.

Both methods are beneficial, and therefore for my own part I give no distinction to either of them above the other. If it should be necessary to follow only one of the two, however, it will be of greater service to point out the right way at first, than to recall those who have gone astray from their errors: 3 first, because to the subsequent emendation they merely listen, but the preliminary division they carry to their meditation and their composition; and, secondly, because they more willingly attend to one who gives directions than to one who finds faults. Whatever pupils, too, are of a high spirit, are apt, especially in the present state of manners, to be angry at 4 admonition and to offer silent resistance to it. Not that faults are therefore to be less openly corrected, for regard is to be had to the other pupils, who will think that whatever the master has not amended is right. But both methods should be 5 united and used as occasion may require. To beginners should be given matter designed, as it were, beforehand, in proportion to the abilities of each. But when they shall appear to have formed themselves sufficiently on their model, a few brief directions may be given them, following which they may 6 advance by their own strength without any support. It is proper that they should sometimes be left to themselves, lest from the bad habit of being always led by the efforts of others, they should lose all capacity of attempting and producing anything for themselves. But when they seem to judge pretty accurately of what ought to be said, the labor of the teacher is almost at an end; though, should they still commit errors, they must be again put under a guide. Something of this kind 7 we see birds practice when they divide food, collected in their beaks, among their tender and helpless young ones; but, when they seem sufficiently grown, teach them, by degrees, to venture out of the nest, and flutter round their place of abode, themselves leading the way; and at last leave their strength, when properly tried, to the open sky and their own self-confidence.

CHAPTER SEVEN

1 ONE CHANGE, I think, should certainly be made in what is customary with regard to the age of which we are speaking. Pupils should not be obliged to learn by heart what they have composed, and to repeat it, as is usual, on a certain day. This is a task which fathers are particularly fond of exacting, thinking that their children study only when they repeat frequent declamations. Actually, proficiency depends chiefly on

2 the diligent cultivation of style. For though I would wish boys to compose, and to spend much time in that employment, yet, as to learning by heart, I would rather recommend for that purpose select passages from orations or histories, or any other

3 sort of writings deserving of such attention. The memory will thus be more efficiently exercised in mastering what is another's than what is its own; and those who shall have been practiced in this more difficult kind of labor, will fix in their minds, without trouble, what they themselves have composed,

4 as being more familiar to them. They will also accustom themselves to the best compositions, and they will always have in their memories something which they may imitate, and will, even without being aware, reproduce that fashion of style which they have deeply impressed upon their minds. They will have at command, moreover, an abundance of the best words, phrases, and figures, not sought for the occasion, but offering themselves spontaneously, as it were, from a store treasured within them. To this is added the power of quoting the happy expressions of any author, which is agreeable in common conversation, and useful in pleading; for phrases which are not coined for the sake of the cause in hand have the greater weight, and often gain us more applause than if they were our own.

5 Yet pupils should sometimes be permitted to recite what they themselves have written, that they may reap the full re-

ward of their labor from that kind of applause which is most desired. This permission will most properly be granted when they have produced something more polished than ordinary, that they may thus be presented with some return for their study, and rejoice that they have deserved to recite their composition.

CHAPTER EIGHT

1 IT IS generally, and not without reason, regarded as an excellent quality in a master to observe accurately the differences of ability in those whom he has undertaken to instruct, and to ascertain in what direction the nature of each particularly inclines him—for there is in talent an incredible variety, nor

2 are the forms of the mind fewer than those of the body. This may be understood even from orators themselves, who differ so much from each other in their style of speaking, that no one is like another, though most of them have set themselves to

3 imitate those whom they admired. It has also been thought advantageous by most teachers to instruct each pupil in such a manner as to foster by learning the good qualities inherited from nature, so that the powers may be assisted in their progress toward the object to which they chiefly direct themselves. Thus, a master of palaestric exercises, when he enters a gymnasium full of boys, is able, after trying their strength and comprehension in every possible way, to decide for what kind

4 of exercise each ought to be trained. In the same way a teacher of eloquence, they say, when he has clearly observed which boy's genius delights most in a concise and polished manner of speaking, and which in a spirited, or grave, or smooth, or rough, or brilliant, or elegant one, will so accommodate his instructions to each, that he will be advanced in that depart-

5 ment in which he shows most ability. Nature, after all, attains far greater power when seconded by culture, and he that is led contrary to nature cannot make due progress in the studies for which he is unfit; he makes those talents, for the exercise of which he seemed born, weaker by neglecting to cultivate them.

6 This opinion seems to me only partly true (for to him that follows reason there is free exercise of judgment even in opposition to received persuasions). To distinguish peculiarities

of talent is absolutely necessary; and to make choice of particular studies to suit them is what no man would discountenance. For one youth will be fitter for the study of history [7] than another; one will be qualified for writing poetry, another for the study of law, and some perhaps fit only to be sent into the fields. The teacher of rhetoric will decide in accordance with these peculiarities, just as the master of the *palaestra* will make one of his pupils a runner, another a boxer, another a wrestler, or fit him for any other of the exercises that are practiced at the sacred games.

But he who is destined for the public forum must strive to [8] excel, not merely in one accomplishment, but in all the accomplishments that are requisite for that art. This is true even though some of them may seem too difficult for him when he is learning them, for instruction would be altogether superfluous if the natural state of the mind were sufficient. If a [9] pupil that is vitiated in taste, and turgid in his style, as many are, is put under our care, shall we allow him to go on in his own way? Him that is dry and jejune in his manner, shall we not nourish, and, as it were, clothe? For if it be necessary to prune something away from certain pupils,[1] why should it [10] not be allowable to add something to others? Yet I would not fight against nature, for I do not think that any good quality, which is innate, should be detracted, but that whatever is [11] inactive or deficient should be invigorated or supplied. What was the true meaning of that famous teacher Isocrates, whose writings are as strong a proof that he spoke well as his scholars are what he taught well, when he formed such an opinion of Ephorus and Theopompus as to say that "the one wanted the rein and the other the spur"? Did he think that the slowness in the duller and the ardor in the more impetuous were to be fostered by education? On the contrary, he thought that the

---

1 A reference to the proverbial expression echoed in Cicero: "It is easier to prune a tree than to grow one." Earlier, it will be recalled, Quintilian has advocated (II. 4. 5–8) using the exuberance of youth to encourage copious invention in their speeches; these are the boys to be "pruned" as they mature. Here, then, he is speaking of those others to whom something must be added rather than taken away.

qualities of each ought to be mixed with those of the other.
12 We must so far accommodate ourselves, however, to feeble intellects, that they may be trained only to that to which nature invites them; thus they will do with more success the only thing which they can do. But if richer material fall into our hands, from which we justly conceive hopes of a true
13 orator, no rhetorical excellence must be left unstudied. For though such a genius be more inclined, as indeed it must be, to the exercise of certain powers, yet it will not be averse to that of others, and will render them, by study, equal to those in which it naturally excelled. Likewise the skilful trainer in bodily exercise (that I may adhere to my former illustration), will not, if he undertakes to form a pancratiast,[2] teach him to strike with his fist or his heel only, or instruct him merely in wrestling, or only in certain artifices of wrestling, but will train him in everything pertaining to the pancratiastic art.

There may perhaps be some pupil unequal to some of these exercises. He must then apply chiefly to that in which he can
14 succeed. For two things are especially to be avoided: one, to attempt what cannot be accomplished; and the other, to divert a pupil from what he does well to something for which he is less qualified. But if he be capable of instruction, the tutor, like Nicostratus whom we when young knew at an advanced age, will bring to bear upon him every art of instruction alike, and render him invincible, as Nicostratus was in wrestling and boxing (for success in both of which contests he was crowned
15 on the same day). How much more must such training, indeed, be pursued by the teacher of the future orator! For it is not enough that he should speak concisely, or artfully, or vehemently, any more than for a singing master to excel in acute, or middle, or grave tones only, or even in particular subdivisions of them. Eloquence is like a harp, not perfect unless with all its strings stretched, it be in unison from the highest to the lowest note.

2 The *pancratium* was an athletic event involving both wrestling and boxing.

CHAPTER NINE

HAVING SPOKEN thus fully concerning the duties of teachers, I 1
give pupils, for the present, only this one admonition—that
they are to love their tutors not less than their studies, and to
regard them as parents, not indeed of their bodies, but of
their minds. Such affection contributes greatly to improve- 2
ment, for pupils, under its influence, will not only listen with
pleasure, but will believe what is taught them, and will desire
to resemble their instructors. They will come together, in as-
sembling for school, with pleasure and cheerfulness; they will
not be angry when corrected, and will be delighted when
praised; and they will strive, by their devotion to study, to
become as dear as possible to the master. For as it is the duty 3
of preceptors to teach, so it is that of pupils to show themselves teachable; neither of these duties, otherwise, will be of
avail without the other. And just as the generation of man
is effected by both parents, and as you will in vain scatter seed,
unless the furrowed ground, previously softened, cherish it, so
neither can eloquence come to its growth unless by mutual
agreement between him who communicates and him who
receives.

CHAPTER TEN

1 WHEN THE pupil has been well instructed and sufficiently exercised in these preliminary studies, which are not in themselves inconsiderable but are members and portions, as it were, of higher branches of learning, the time will have nearly arrived for entering on deliberative and judicial subjects. But before I proceed to speak of those matters, I must say a few words on the art of declamation, which, though the most recently invented of all exercises, is indeed by far the most use-

2 ful. For it comprehends within itself all those exercises of which I have been treating, and presents us with a very close resemblance to reality. It has been so much adopted, accordingly, that it is thought by many to be sufficient of itself to form oratory, since no excellence in actual speaking can be

3 specified which is not found in this prelude to speaking. The practice however has so degenerated through the fault of the teachers, that the license and ignorance of declaimers have been among the chief causes that have corrupted eloquence.[1] But of that which is good by nature we may surely make a

4 good use. Let, therefore, the subjects themselves, which shall be imagined, be as like as possible to truth; and let declamations to the utmost extent that is practicable, imitate those pleadings for which they were introduced as a preparation.

5 For as to magicians, and the pestilence, and oracles, and stepmothers more cruel than those of tragedy, and other subjects

---

1 Quintilian in this prophetic passage warns of the dangers inherent in a system which produces skilled declaimers for an Imperial society which no longer affords a safe public forum for the speaker. Historians of rhetoric usually apply the term "Second Sophistic" to the oratorical excesses occurring from about A.D. 100 to A.D. 400. A useful short treatment of this phenomenon may be found in Charles S. Baldwin, *Medieval Rhetoric and Poetic* (New York: The Macmillan Co., 1928), pp. 2–50. For a translation of some typical declamations, including some of the fanciful type mentioned by Quintilian, cf. William A. Edward, *The Suasoriae of the Elder Seneca* (Cambridge: Cambridge University Press, 1927).

more imaginary than these, we shall in vain seek them among the sponsions and interdicts of the courts. What, then, it may be said—shall we never suffer students to handle such topics as are above belief and (to say the truth) poetical, so that they may expatiate and exult in their subject, and swell forth, as it were, into full body? It would indeed be best not to suffer them; but at least let not the subjects, if grand and turgid, appear also, to him who regards them with severe judgment, foolish and ridiculous. If we must grant the use of such topics, let the declaimer swell himself occasionally to the full, provided he understands that, as four-footed animals, when they have been blown with green fodder, are cured by losing blood, and thus return to food suited to maintain their strength, so must his turgidity be diminished, and whatever corrupt humors he has contracted be discharged, if he wishes to be healthy and strong. Otherwise his empty swelling will be hampered at the first attempt at any real pleading. 6 7

Those, assuredly, who think that the whole exercise of declaiming is altogether different from forensic pleading, do not see even the reason for which that exercise was instituted. For, if it is no preparation for the forum, it is merely like theatrical ostentation, or insane raving. To what purpose is it to instruct a judge who has no existence? To state a case that all know to be fictitious? To bring proofs of a point on which no man will pronounce sentence? This indeed is nothing more than trifling; but how ridiculous is it to excite our feelings, and to work upon an audience with eager and sorrow, unless we are indeed preparing ourselves, by imitations of battle, for serious contests and a regular field? Will there then be no difference, it may be asked, between the mode of speaking at the bar, and mere exercise in declamation? I answer that if we speak in classrooms for the sake of improvement, there will be no difference. I wish, too, that it were made a part of the exercise to use names; that causes more complicated, and requiring longer pleadings, were invented; that we were less afraid of words in daily use; and that we were in the habit of mingling jests with our declamation. In all these points, how- 8 9 ever much we may have been trained in the schools in other respects, we are novices at the bar.

10

11 But even if a declamation be composed merely for display, we ought surely to exert our voice in some degree to please the audience. For even in those oratorical compositions which are doubtless based in some degree upon truth but are adapted to please the multitude (such as are the panegyrics which we read, and all that epideictic kind of eloquence), it is allowable to use great elegance, and not only to acknowledge the efforts of art (which ought generally to be concealed in forensic pleadings), but to display it to those who are called together for the purpose of witnessing it. Declamation, therefore, as it is an imitation of real pleadings and deliberations, ought closely to resemble reality; insofar as it carries with it something of ostentation, however, it ought to clothe itself in a certain elegance. Such is the practice of actors, who do not pronounce exactly as we speak in common conversation, for such pronunciation would be devoid of art; nor do they depart far from nature, since by such a fault imitation would be destroyed; but they exalt the simplicity of familiar discourse with a certain scenic grace.

12

13

14 However, some inconveniences will attend us from the nature of the subjects which we have imagined, especially since many particulars in them are left uncertain, which we settle as suits our purpose, such as age, fortune, children, parents, strength, laws, and manners of cities; and other matters of a similar kind. Sometimes, too, we draw arguments from the very faults of the imaginary causes. But on each of these points we shall speak in its proper place. For though the whole object of the work intended by us has regard to the formation of an orator, yet, lest students may think anything wanting, we shall not omit in passing whatever may occur that fairly relates to the teaching of the schools.

15

[In Chapter Eleven Quintilian turns to a formal discussion of the art of rhetoric, which occupies most of the remainder of the *Institutio oratoria.*]

ON THE ADULT EDUCATION
OF THE CITIZEN-ORATOR

BOOK TEN
OF THE *INSTITUTIO ORATORIA*

BOOK X

CHAPTER ONE

But these precepts of being eloquent, though necessary to 1
be known, are not sufficient to produce the full power of eloquence unless there be united to them a certain Facility,
which among the Greeks is called *Hexis,* "habit." I know that
it is often asked whether more is contributed by writing, by
reading, or by speaking. This question we should have to examine with careful attention if in fact we could confine ourselves to any one of these activities; but in truth they are all 2
so connected, so inseparably linked with one another, that it
any one of them is neglected, we labor in vain in the other
two—for our speech will never become forcible and energetic
unless it acquires strength from great practice in writing; and
the labor of writing, if left destitute of models from reading,
passes away without effect, as having no director; while he
who knows how everything ought to be said, will, if he has
not his eloquence in readiness and prepared for all emergencies, merely brood, as it were, over locked-up treasure.

Though some one element, again, may be requisite above 3
others, it will not necessarily, for that purpoes, be chief in
importance for forming the orator. For since the business of
the orator lies in speaking, *to speak* is doubtless necessary to
him before anything else; and it is evident that from speaking the commencement of the art arose; also that the next
thing in order is *imitation;*[1] and, last of all, diligent exercise 4
in writing. But as we cannot arrive at the highest excellence
otherwise than by initial efforts, so, as our work proceeds,

1 That is, careful reading and listening for the purpose of identifying
and then imitating the best qualities of good models. It is also an important method in the instruction of the young, as Quintilian points out in
Books I and II. See the Introduction, pp. 30–31.

those things which are of the greatest importance begin to appear of the least.

But I am not here saying how the orator is to be trained—for that has been told already, if not satisfactorily, at least as well as I could—but by what kind of discipline an athlete, who has already learned all his exercises from his master, is to be prepared for real contests. Let me, therefore, instruct the student, who knows how to invent and arrange his matter, and who has also acquired the art of selecting and disposing his words, by what means he may be able to practice, in the best and easiest possible manner, that which he has learned.

5   Can it then be doubted, that he must secure certain resources, which he may use whenever it shall be necessary? Those resources will consist in *supplies of matter and of*
6   *words.* But every cause has its own peculiar matter, or matter common to it with but few others; words are to be prepared for all kinds of causes. If there were a single word for every single thing, words would require less care, for all would then at once present themselves with the things to be expressed. As some, however, are more appropriate, or more elegant, or more significant, or more euphonious, than others, they ought all, not only to be known, but to be kept in readiness, and, if I may so express myself, in sight, so that, when they present themselves to the judgment of the speaker, the choice of the
7   best of them may be easily made. I know that some make a practice of learning by heart such words as have the same signification, in order that one word out of several may the more readily occur to them, and that, when they have used one of the number, they may, if it should be wanted again within a short space of time, substitute for it, for the sake of avoiding repetition, another from which the same thing may be understood. But this is a childish practice, attended with miserable labor, and productive of very little profit; for the learner merely musters a crowd of words, to snatch from it without distinction whichsoever first presents itself.

8   By us, on the contrary, our stock of words must be prepared with judgment, as we have a view to the proper force

of oratory and not to the volubility of the charlatan. But this
object we shall effect by reading and listening to the best language; for, by such exercise, we shall not only learn words
expressive of things, but shall learn for what place each word
is best adapted. Almost all words, indeed, except a few that   9
are of indecent character, find a place in oratorical composition; and the writers of iambics and of the old comedy are
often commended for the use of words of that description;
but it is sufficient for us at present to look to our own work.
All sorts of words, then, except those to which I have alluded,
may be excellently employed in some place or other; for we
have sometimes occasion for low and coarse words; and such
as would seem mean in the more elegant parts of a speech,
are, when the subject requires them, adopted with propriety.²

To understand words thoroughly, and to learn not only the   10
signification of them, but their forms and measures, and to be
able to judge whether they are adapted to the places to which
they are assigned, are branches of knowledge that we cannot
acquire but by assiduous reading and hearing, since we receive all language first of all by the ear. Hence infants brought
up, at the command of princes, by dumb nurses and in solitude, were destitute of the faculty of speech, though they are
said to have uttered some unconnected words.³

There are, however, some words of such a nature that they   11
express the same thing by different sounds, so exactly that it
makes no difference to the sense which we use in preference to
another; for instance *ensis* and *gladius*. There are others,
again, which, though properly belonging to distinct objects,
are yet by a trope, as it were, used for conveying the same
idea; as *ferrum* and *mucro*.⁴ Thus, too, by a catachresis, we   12
call all assassins *sicarii*,⁵ whatever be the weapon with which

2 See also Quintilian's discussion of "custom" in I.vi.43–45.
3 Quintilian speaks as if this experiment had been conducted several
times, though the only well-known instance is that of Psametichus, King
of Egypt, as recorded in Herodotus II.2.
4 *Ferrum* means any steel weapon, *mucro* the point of such a weapon.
5 From *sica*, a dagger or poniard.

they have committed slaughter. Some things, moreover, we indicate by a circumlocution, as *pressi copia lactis.*⁶ Many things
also, by change of words, we express figuratively, as, for *I
know,* we say *I am not ignorant,* or *It does not escape me,* or
It does not fail to attract my attention, or *Who is not aware?*
13 or *No man doubts.* We may likewise profit by the near import
of words, for *I understand, I perceive, I see,* have often just
the same meaning as *I know.* Of such synonyms reading will
furnish us with copious supplies, so that we may use them not
only as they present themselves, but as they ought to be
14 adopted. For such terms do not always express exactly the
same things; and though I may properly say "I see" in reference to the perception of the mind, I cannot say "I understand" in reference to the sight of the eyes; nor, though *mucro*
15 indicates *gladius,* does *gladius* indicate *mucro.* But though a
copious stock of words be thus acquired, we are not to read or
hear merely for the sake of words; for in all that we teach
examples are more powerful even than the rules which are
taught—I mean when the learner is so far advanced that he
can enter into the subjects without a guide, and pursue them
with his own unassisted efforts—inasmuch as what the master
teaches, the orator exhibits.
16   Some speeches contribute more to our improvement when
we hear them delivered, others when we peruse them. He who
speaks to us rouses us by his animation, and excites us, not by
an artificial representation and account of things, but by the
things themselves. Everything seems to live and move before
us, and we catch the new ideas, as it were at their birth, with
partiality and affection. We feel interested, not only in the
event of the cause, but in the perilous efforts of those who
17 plead it. In addition to this, a becoming tone and action, a
mode of delivery adapted to what particular passages require,
(which is perhaps the most powerful element in oratory),
and, in a word, all excellent qualities in combination teach us
at the same time. In reading, on the other hand, the judgment is applied with more certainty, for, when a person is

⁶ "Plenty of pressed milk" for "cheese." Virgil, *Eclogues* I.81.

listening to speeches, his own partiality for any particular
speaker, or the ordinary applause of approving auditors,
often deprives him of the free exercise of his judgment. Some- 18
times we are ashamed to express dissent from others, and are
prevented, by a sort of secret modesty, from trusting too much
to ourselves, though what is faulty sometimes please the majority, and even what does not please is applauded by those
who are engaged to applaud. On the contrary, too, it some- 19
times happens that the bad taste of the audience does not
do justice to the finest passages. But reading is free, and does
not escape us with the rapidity of oral delivery, but allows us
to go over the same passages more than once, whether we have
any doubt of their meaning, or are desirous to fix them in our
memory. Let us review, then, and reconsider the subject of
our reading, and as we consign our food to our stomach only
when it is masticated and almost dissolved, in order that it
may be easier of digestion, so let what we read be committed
to the memory and reserved for imitation, not when it is in
a crude state, but after being softened, and as it were tritu-
rated, by frequent repetition.

For a long time, too, none but the best authors must be 20
read, and such as are least likely to mislead him who trusts
them; but they must be read with attention, and indeed with
almost as much care as if we were transcribing them; and
every portion must be examined, not merely partially, but a
whole book, when read through, must be taken up afresh, and
especially any excellent oration, of which the merits are often
designedly concealed; for the speaker frequently prepares his 21
audience for what is to follow, dissembles with them, and
places ambuscades; and states in the first part of his pleading
what is to have its full effect at the conclusion. Hence what is
advanced in its proper place often pleases us less than it
ought, since we are not aware why it is advanced; and all such
passages, accordingly, ought to be perused again after we have
read the whole. But one of the most useful exercises, is to
learn the history of those causes of which we have taken the 22
pleadings in hand for perusal, and, whenever opportunity
shall offer, to read speeches delivered on both sides of the

same question; as those of Demosthenes and Aeschines in opposition to each other; those of Servius Sulpicius and Messala, of whom one spoke for Aufidia and the other against her; thoes of Pollio and Cassius when Asprenas was accused; and 23 many others. Even if the pleaders seem unequally matched, yet some of the speeches may be reasonably consulted in order to ascertain the question for decision, as the orations of Tubero against Ligarius and of Hortensius on behalf of Verres, in opposition to those of Cicero. It will also be of advantage to know how different orators pleaded the same causes; for Calidius delivered a speech concerning the house of Cicero. Brutus wrote an oration in defense of Milo, merely as an exercise; Cornelius Celsus, indeed, thinks that Brutus spoke it, but he 24 is mistaken. Pollio and Messala, too, defended the same persons; and, when I was a boy, there were in circulation celebrated speeches of Domitius Afer, Crispus Passienus, and Decimus Lælius, in defense of Volusenus Catulus.

Nor must he who reads feel immediately convinced that everything that great authors have said is necessarily perfect; for they sometimes make a false step, or sink under their burden, or give way to the inclination of their genius; nor do they always equally apply their minds, but sometimes grow weary; as Demosthenes seems to Cicero sometimes to nod, and 25 Homer himself appears to Horace to do so.[7] They are great men, indeed, but men nevertheless; and it often happens to those, who think that whatever is found in such authors is a law for eloquence, that they imitate what is inferior in them— for it is easier to copy their faults than their excellences—and fancy that they fully resemble great men when they have merely adopted great men's defects.

26   Yet students must pronounce with diffidence and circumspection on the merits of such illustrious characters, lest, as is the case with many, they condemn what they do not understand. If they must err on one side or the other, I should prefer that every part of them should please youthful readers rather than that many parts should displease them.

[7] The references are to famous passages in Cicero, *Orator* 29, and Horace, *Ars poetica* 359.

Theophrastus says that the reading of the poets is of the 27
greatest use to the orator. Many others adopt his opinion,
and not without reason, for from them is derived animation
in relating facts, sublimity in expression, the greatest power
in exciting the feelings, and gracefulness in personifying character; and—what is of the utmost service—the faculties of
the orator, worn out as it were by daily pleading in the forum,
are best recruited by the charms of the works of such authors.
Accordingly Cicero thinks that relaxation should be sought
in that sort of reading. But we must remember that poets are 28
not to be imitated by the orator in every respect—not, for
instance, in freedom of language, or unrestrained use of figures—that the style of poets is adapted for display, and, besides, that it aims merely at giving pleasure, and pursues its
object by inventing not only what is false, but even sometimes
what is incredible; that it enjoys certain privileges, inasmuch 29
as, being confined to the regular requirements of feet, it cannot always use proper terms, but, being driven from the
straight road, must necessarily have recourse to certain by-
paths of eloquence, and is obliged not only to change words,
but to lengthen, shorten, transpose, and divide them; but
that we orators stand in arms in a field of battle, contend for
concerns of the highest moment, and must struggle only for
victory.[8]

8 Here begins a lengthy discussion of particular orators and writers.
Since these figures would be virtually unknown to modern readers, his
comments on them are omitted here.

CHAPTER TWO

1 FROM THESE authors, and others worthy to be read, must be acquired a stock of words, a variety of figures, and the art of composition. Our minds must be directed to the imitation of all their excellences, for it cannot be doubted that a great portion of art consists in imitation—for even though to invent was first in order of time and holds the first place in merit, it is nevertheless advantageous to copy what has been invented
2 with success. Indeed, the whole conduct of life is based on the desire of doing ourselves that which we approve in others. Thus boys follow the traces of letters in order to acquire skill in writing; thus musicians follow the voice of their teachers, painters look for models to the works of preceding painters, and farmers adopt the system of culture approved by experience. We see, in short, that the beginnings of every kind of study are formed in accordance with some prescribed rule.
3 We must indeed, be either like or unlike those who excel; and nature rarely forms one *like,* though imitation does so frequently. But the very circumstance that renders the study of all subjects so much more easy to us than it was to those who had nothing to imitate, will prove a disadvantage to us unless it be turned to account with caution and judgment.
4 Undoubtedly, then, imitation is not sufficient of itself, if for no other reason than that it is the mark of an indolent nature to rest satisfied with what has been invented by others. For what would have been the case, if, in those times which were without any models, mankind had thought that they were not execute or imagine anything but what they already
5 knew? Assuredly nothing would have been invented. Why then is it unlawful for anything to be devised by us which did exist before? Were our rude forefathers led, by the mere natural force of intellect, to the discovery of so many things, and shall not we be roused to inquiry by the certain knowl-

edge that those who inquired did find new things? When 6
those who had no master in any subject have transmitted so
many discoveries to posterity, shall not the experience which
we have in some things assist us to bring to light others, or
shall we have nothing but what we derive from other men's
bounty, as some painters aim at nothing more than to know
how to copy a picture by means of compasses and lines?

It is dishonorable even to rest satisfied with simply equaling 7
what we imitate. For what would have been the case, again,
if no one had accomplished more than he whom he copied?
We should have nothing in poetry superior to Livius Andro-
nicus, nothing in history better than the Annals of the Pon-
tiffs; we should still sail on rafts; there would be no painting
but that of tracing the outlines of the shadow which bodies
cast in the sunshine. If we take a view of all arts, no one can 8
be found exactly as it was when it was invented; no one that
has confined itself within its original limits; unless, indeed,
we have to convict our own times, beyond all others, of this
unhappy deficiency, and to consider that now at last nothing
improves; for certainly nothing does improve by imitation
only. But if it is not allowable to add to what has preceded 9
us, how can we ever hope to see a complete orator, when
among those whom we have hitherto recognized as the greatest no one has been found in whom there is not something
defective or censurable? Even those who do not aim at the
highest excellence should rather try to excel, than merely
follow, their predecessors; for he who makes it his object to
get before another, will possibly, if he does not go by him,
at least, get abreast of him. But assuredly no one will come 10
up with him in whose steps he thinks that he must tread, for
he who follows another must of necessity always be behind
him. Besides, it is generally easier to do more, than to do precisely the same; exact likeness is attended with such difficulty
that not even nature herself has succeeded in contriving that
the simplest objects, and such as may be thought most alike,
shall not be distinguished by some perceptible difference.
Moreover, everything that is the resemblance of something 11
eles must necessarily be inferior to that of which it is a copy,

as the shadow to the substance, the portrait to the natural face, and the acting of the player to the real feeling. The same is the case with regard to oratorical composition; for in the originals, which we take for our models, there is nature and real power, while every imitation, on the contrary, is something counterfeit, and seems adapted to an object not its own.

12   Hence it happens that declamations have less spirit and force than actual pleadings, because in one the subject is real, in the other fictitious. In addition to all this, whatever excellences are most remarkable in an orator are inimitable—natural talent, invention, energy, easiness of manner, and

13   whatever cannot be taught by art. In consequence, many students, when they have selected certain words or acquired a certain rhythm of composition from any orator's speeches, think that what they have read is admirably represented in their own sentences. However, words fall into desuetude, or come into use, according to the fashion of the day, so that the most certain rule for their use is found in custom. They are not in their own nature either good or bad (for in themselves they are only sounds), but only as they are suitable and properly applied, or otherwise; and when our composition is best adapted to our subject, it becomes most pleasing from its variety.

14   Everything, therefore, relating to this department of study, is to be considered with the nicest judgment. First of all, we must be cautious as to the authors whom we would imitate, for many have been desirous to resemble the worst and most faulty originals. In the next place, we must examine what there is, in the authors whom we have chosen for models, that we should set ourselves to attain, for even in great writers there occur faulty passages and blemishes which have been censured by the learned in their remarks on one another. I wish that our youth would improve in their oratory by imitating what is good, as much as they are deteriorated in it by copying what is bad.

15   Nor let those who have sufficient judgment for avoiding faults, be satisfied with forming a semblance, a mere cuticle, if I may so express myself, of excellence, or rather one of

those images of Epicurus, which he says are perpetually flying [16] off from the surfaces of bodies. This, however, is the fate of those who, having no thorough insight into the merits of a style, adapt their manner, as it were, to the first aspect of it; and even when their imitation proves most successful, and when they differ but little from their original author in language and harmony, they yet never fully attain to his force or fertility of language, but commonly degenerate into something worse, lay hold on such defects as border on excellences, and become tumid instead of great, weak instead of concise, rash instead of bold, licentious instead of exuberant, tripping instead of dignified, careless instead of simple. Accordingly, [17] those who have produced something dry and inane, in a rough and inelegant dress, fancy themselves equal to the ancients; those who reject embellishment of language or thought, compare themselves, forsooth, to the Attic writers; those who become obscure by curtailing their periods, excel Sallust and Thucydides; the dry and jejune rival Pollio; and the dull and languid, if they but express themselves in a long period, declare that Cicero would have spoken just like themselves. I have known some, indeed, who thought that they [18] had admirably represented the divine orator's manner in their speeches, when they had put at the end of a period *esse videatur*.[1] The first consideration, therefore, for the student, is, that he should understand *what he proposes to imitate,* and have a thorough conception *why it is excellent.*

Next, in entering on his task, let him consult his own pow- [19] ers—for some things are inimitable by those whose natural weakness is not sufficient for attaining them, or whose natural inclination is repugnant to them—lest he who has but a feeble capacity, should attempt only what is arduous and rough, or lest he who has great but rude talent should waste his strength in the study of refinement, and fail of attaining the elegance of which he is desirous; for nothing is more ungraceful than to treat of delicate subjects with harshness. I [20] did not suppose, indeed, that by the master whom I instructed

---

1 That is, by using an admired Ciceronian phrase. See Quintilian's citation of this term (from Cicero's *Pro Ligario*) in *Institutio* IX.iv.73.

in my second book,[2] those things only were to be taught to which he might see his pupils severally adapted by nature; he ought to improve whatever good qualities he finds in them; to supply, as far as he can, what is deficient; to correct some things and to alter others; for he is the director and regulator of the minds of others; to mold his own nature may
21 be more difficult. But not even such a teacher, however he may wish everything that is right to be found in the highest excellence in his pupils, will labor to any purpose in that to which he shall see that nature is opposed.

There is another thing also to be avoided, a matter in which many err; we must not suppose that poets and historians are to be the objects of our imitation in oratorical composition,
22 or orators and declaimers in poetry or history. Every species of writing has its own prescribed law, each its own appropriate dress; for comedy does not strut in tragic buskins, nor does tragedy step along in the slipper of comedy—yet all eloquence has something in common, and let us look on that
23 which is common as what we must imitate. On those who have devoted themselves to one particular kind of style, there generally attends this inconvenience, that if, for example, the roughness of some writer has taken their fancy, they cannot divest themselves of it in pleading those causes which are of a quiet and subdued nature; or if a simple and pleasing manner has attracted them, they become unequal to the weight of their subject in complex and difficult causes; when not only the nature of one cause is different from that of another, but the nature of one part of a cause differs from that of another part, and some portions are to be delivered gently, others roughly, some in a vehement, others in an easy tone, some for the purpose of informing the hearer, others with a view to excite his feelings—all which require a different and
24 distinct style. I should not, therefore, advise a student to devote himself entirely to any particular author, so as to imitate him in all respects. Of all the Greek orators Demosthenes is by far the most excellent, yet others on some occasions may

2 That is, Chapter Eight of Book II.

have expressed themselves better; and he himself has expressed many things better on some occasions than on others.
But he who deserves to be imitated most, is not therefore the
only author to be imitated. "What then?" the reader may ask,   25
"is it not sufficient to speak on every subject as Cicero spoke?"
To me, assuredly, it would be sufficient if I could attain all his
excellences. Yet what disadvantage would it be to assume, on
some occasions, the energy of Cæsar, the asperity of Cælius, the
accuracy of Pollio, the judgment of Calvus? For besides that it   26
is the part of a judicious student to make, if he can, whatever
is excellent in each author his own, it is also to be considered,
that if, in a matter of such difficulty as imitation, we fix our
attention only on one author, scarcely any one portion of his
excellence will allow us to become masters of it. Accordingly,
since it is almost denied to human ability to copy fully the
pattern which we have chosen, let us set before our eyes the
excellences of several, that different qualities from different
writers may fix themselves in our minds, and that we may
adopt, for any subject, the style which is most suitable to it.   27
    But let imitation (for I must frequently repeat the same
precept) not be confined merely to words. We ought to contemplate what propriety was observed by those great men
with regard to things and persons; what judgment, what arrangement, and how everything—even what seems intended
only to please—was directed to the attainment of success in
their cause. Let us notice what is done in their exordium;
how skillful and varied is their statement of facts; how great
is their ability in proving and refuting; how consummate
was their skill in exciting every species of emotion; and how
even the applause which they gained from the public was
turned to the advantage of their cause; applause which is
most honorable when it follows unsolicited, not when it is
anxiously courted. If we gain a thorough conception of all
these matters, we shall then be such imitators as we ought to
be. But he who shall add to these borrowed qualities excel-   28
lences of his own, so as to supply what is deficient in his models and to trim off what is redundant, will be the complete
orator whom we desire to see; and such an orator ought now

surely to be formed, when so many more examples of eloquence exist than fell to the lot of those who have hitherto been considered the best orators: for to them will belong the praise, not only of surpassing those who preceded them, but of instructing those who followed.

CHAPTER THREE

SUCH, THEN, are the means of improvement to be derived 1
from external sources. But of those which we must secure for
ourselves, *practice in writing,* which is attended with the most
labor, is attended also with the greatest advantage. Nor has
Cicero without reason called the pen *the best modeler and
teacher of eloquence;* and by putting that opinion into the
mouth of Lucius Crassus in his Dialogues on the character of
the Orator,[1] he has united his own judgment to the authority
of that eminent speaker.

We must write, therefore, as carefully, and as much, as we 2
can; for as the ground, by being dug to a great depth, becomes more fitted for fructifying and nourishing seeds, so improvement of the mind, acquired from more than mere super-
ficial cultivation, pours forth the fruits of study in richer
abundance, and retains them with greater fidelity. For without this perseverance the very faculty of speaking extempore
will but furnish us with empty loquacity, and with words
born only on the lips. In writing are the roots, in writing are 3
the foundations of eloquence; by writing resources are stored
up, as it were, in a sacred repository, whence they may be
drawn forth for sudden emergencies, or as circumstances require. Let us above all things get strength, which may suffice
for the labor of our contests, and may not be exhausted by
use. Nature has herself appointed that nothing great is to be 4
accomplished quickly, and has ordained that difficulty should
precede every work of excellence; she has even made it a law
with regard to gestation, that the larger animals are retained
longer in the womb of the parent.

But as two questions arise from this subject, *how* and *what* 5
we ought principally to write, I shall consider them both in
this order. Let our pen be at first slow, provided that it be

1 *De oratore* I.xxxiii.150.

accurate. Let us search for what is best, and not allow ourselves to be readily pleaesd with whatever presents itself; let judgment be applied to our thoughts, and skill in arrangement to such of them as the judgment sanctions; for we must make a selection from our thoughts and words, and the weight of each must be carefully estimated; and then must follow the art of collocation, and the rhythm of our phrases must be tried in every possible way, since any word must not take its

6 position just as it offers itself. That we may acquire this accomplishment with the more precision, we must frequently repeat the last words of what we have just written; for besides that by this means what follows is better connected with what precedes, the ardor of thought, which has cooled by the delay of writing, recovers its strength anew, and, by going again over the ground, acquires new force; as is the case, we see, in a contest at leaping: men run over a certain portion of ground that they may take a longer spring, and be carried with the utmost velocity to the other part on which they aim at alighting; as in hurling a javelin, too, we draw back the arm; and, when going to shoot an arrow, we pull back the

7 bowstring. At times, however, if a gale bear us on, we may spread our sails to it, provided that the license which we allow ourselves does not lead us astray; for all our thoughts please us at the time of their birth; otherwise they would not be committed to writing. But let us have recourse to our judgment, and revise the fruit of our facility, which is always to be

8 regarded with suspicion. Thus we learn that Sallust wrote; and his labor, indeed, is shown in his productions. That Virgil wrote very few verses in a day, Varus bears testimony.[2]

9 With the speaker, indeed, the case is different; and I therefore, enjoin this delay and solicitude only at the commencement of his course; for we must make it first of all our object, and must attain that object, to write as well as we can; practice will bring celerity; thoughts, by degrees, will present themselves with greater readiness, words will correspond to

---

[2] It was reported that Virgil used to say of himself that he licked his verses into shape as bears lick their cubs.

them, and suitable arrangement will follow; and everything, in a word, as in a well-ordered household, will be ready for service. The sum of the whole matter, indeed, is this: that 10 by writing quickly we are not brought to write well, but that by writing well we are brought to write quickly. But after this facility has been attained, we must then, most of all, take care to stop and look before us, and restrain our high-mettled steeds with the curb—a restraint which will not so much retard us as give us new spirit to proceed.

Nor, on the other hand, do I think that those who have acquired some power in the use of the pen should be chained down to the unhappy task of perpetually finding fault with themselves. For how could he perform his duty to the public, 11 who should waste his life in polishing every portion of his pleadings? But there are some whom nothing ever satisfies, who wish to alter everything, and to express everything in a different form from that in which it first occurs to them. Some, again, there are, who, distrustful of themselves, and paying an ill compliment to their own powers, think that accuracy in writing means to create for themselves extraordinary difficulties. Nor is it easy for me to say which I regard as 12 more in the wrong—those whom everything that they produce, or those whom nothing that they produce, pleases; for it is often the case even with young men of talent, that they wear themselves away with useless labor, and sink into silence from too much anxiety to speak well. In regard to this subject, I remember that Julius Secundus—a contemporary of mine, and, as is well known, dearly beloved by me, a man of extraordinary eloquence, but of endless labor—mentioned to me something that had been told him by his uncle. This uncle 13 was Julius Florus, the most celebrated man for eloquence in the provinces of Gaul (for it was there that he practiced it) and in other respects, an orator to be ranked with few, and worthy of his relationship to Secundus. He, happening one day to observe that Secundus, while he was still working at school, was looking dejected, asked him what was the reason of his brow being so overcast. The youth used no conceal- 14 ment, but told him that that was the third day that he had been vainly endeavoring, with his utmost efforts, to find an exordium for a subject on which he had to write; whence not only grief had affected him in respect to the present occasion, but despair in regard to the time to come. Florus immediately replied with a smile. *Do you wish to write better than you* 15 *can?* Such is the whole truth of the matter: we must endeavor to speak with as much ability as we can, but we must speak according to our ability. For improvement there is need of application, but not of vexation with ourselves.

But to enable us to write more, and more readily, not *practice* only will assist (and in practice there is doubtless great effect) but also *method,* if we do not, lolling at our ease, looking at the ceiling, and trying to kindle our invention by muttering to ourselves, wait for what may present itself, but, observing what the subject requires, what becomes the character concerned, what the nature of the occasion is, and what the disposition of the judge, set ourselves to write like reasonable beings—for thus nature herself will supply us not only 16 with a commencement but with what ought to follow. Most points, indeed, are plain, and set themselves before our eyes if we do not shut them; and accordingly not even the illiterate and untaught have long to consider how to begin; and therefore we should feel the more ashamed if learning produces difficulty. Let us not, then, imagine that what lies hid is always best; or, if we think nothing fit to be said but what we have not discovered, we must remain dumb.

17　A different fault is that of those who wish, first of all, to run through their subject with as rapid a pen as possible, and, yielding to the ardor and impetuosity of their imagination, write off their thoughts extemporaneously, producing what they call a rough copy, which they then go over again, and arrange what they hastily poured forth; but though the words and rhythm of the sentences are mended, there still remains the same want of solid connection that there was originally in 18 the parts hurriedly thrown together. It will be better, therefore, to use care at first, and so to form our work from the beginning that we may have merely to polish it and not to mold it anew. Sometimes, however, we may give loose to our feeling, in the display of which warmth is generally of more effect than accuracy.

From my disapprobation of carelessness in writing, it is [19] clearly enough seen what I think of the fine fancy of dictation;[3] for in the use of the pen the hand of the writer, however rapid, as it cannot keep pace with the celerity of his thoughts, allows them some respite, but he to whom we dictate urges us on, and we feel ashamed at times to hesitate, or stop, or alter, as if we were afraid to have a witness of our weakness. Hence it happens that not only inelegant and casual expressions, but sometimes unsuitable ones, escape us, [20] while our sole anxiety is to make our discourse connected— that is, expressions which partake neither of the accuracy of the writer nor of the animation of the speaker; while, if the person who takes down what is dictated should prove, from slowness in writing, or from inaccuracy in reading, a hindrance, as it were, to us, the course of our thought is obstructed, and all the fire that had been conceived in our mind is dispelled by delay, or sometimes, by anger at the offender. Besides, those gestures which accompany the stronger excitements of the mind, and which, in some degree, rouse the [21] imagination, such as waving of the hand, alteration of the features, turning from side to side, and all such acts as Persius satirizes when he alludes to a negligent species of style (the writer, he says,

> *Nec pluteum cædit, nec demorsos sapit ungues,*
> Nor thumps his desk, nor tastes his bitten nails),

are utterly ridiculous except when we are alone. In short, to mention once for all the strongest argument against dictation, [22] privacy is rendered impossible by it; and that a spot free from witnesses, and the deepest possible silence, are the most desirable for persons engaged in writing, no one can doubt.

Yet we are not therefore necessarily to listen to those who think that groves and woods are the most proper places for

---

[3] Oral dictation had become so common among the wealthy even by Cicero's time that he says in one place that it is a special mark of favor to a friend to send him a letter written in one's own handwriting.

study, because the free and open sky, they say, and the beauty of sequestered spots, give elevation to the mind and a happy 23 warmth to the imagination. To me, assuredly, such retirement seems rather conducive to pleasure than an incentive to literary exertion; for the very objects that delight us must, of necessity, divert our attention from the work which we designed to pursue; for the mind cannot, in truth, attend effectually to many things at once, and in whatever direction it looks off, it must cease to contemplate what had been in24 tended for its employment. The pleasantness, therefore, of the words, the streams gliding past, the breezes sporting among the branches of the trees, the songs of birds, and the very freedom of the extended prospect, draw off our attention to them; therefore all such gratifications seem to me more adapted to 25 relax the thoughts than to brace them. Demosthenes acted more wisely, who secluded himself in a place where no voice could be heard, and no prospect contemplated, that his eyes might not oblige his mind to attend to anything else besides his business. As for those who study by lamplight, therefore, let the silence of the night, the closed chamber, and a single 26 light, keep them as it were wholly in seclusion. But in every kind of study, and especially in such nocturnal application, good health, and that which is the principal means of securing it—regularity of life—are necessary, since we devote the time appointed us by nature for sleep and the recruiting of our strength, to the most intense labor; but on this labor we must not bestow more time than what is too much for sleep, 27 and what will not leave too little for it; for weariness hinders application to writing; and daylight, if we are free from other occupations, is abundantly sufficient for it; it is necessity that drives men engaged in business to read at night. Yet study by the lamp, when we come to it fresh and vigorous, is the best kind of retirement.

28   But silence and seclusion, and entire freedom of mind, though in the highest degree desirable, cannot always fall to our lot; and therefore we must not, if any noise disturbs us, immediately throw aside our books, and deplore the day as lost, but we must strive against inconveniences, and acquire

such habits that our application may set all interruptions at defiance—for if we direct our attention, with our whole mental energy, to the work actually before us, nothing of all that strikes our eyes or ears will penetrate into the mind.

Does a casual train of thought often cause us not to see per- 29 sons in our way, and to wander from our road, and shall we not attain the same abstraction if we resolve to do so? We must not yield to excuses for idleness; for if we fancy that we must not study except when we are fresh, except when we are in good spirits, except when we are free from all other cares, we shall always have some reason for self-indulgence. In the 30 midst of crowds, therefore, on a journey, and even at festive meetings, let thought secure privacy for herself. Else what will be the result, when we shall have, in the midst of the forum, amid the hearing of so many causes, amid wranglings and casual outcries, to speak, perhaps on a sudden, in a continued harangue, if we cannot conceive the memoranda which we enter on our tablets, anywhere but in solitude? For this reason Demosthenes, though so great a lover of seclusion, used to accustom himself, by studying on the seashore where the breaker dashed with the loudest noise, not to be disconcerted at the uproar of public assemblies.

Some lesser matters also (though nothing is little that re- 31 lates to study) must not be left unnoticed. One of these is that we can write best on *waxen tablets*, from which there is the greatest facility for erasing, unless, perchance, weakness of sight[4] requires the use of parchment; but parchment, though it assists the sight, yet, from the frequent movement of the hand backwards and forwards, while dipping the pen in the ink, causes delay, and interrupts the current of thought. Next 32 we may observe, that in using either of these kinds of material, we should take care to leave some pages blank, on which we may have free scope for making any additions— since want of room sometimes causes a reluctance to correct, or, at least, what was written first makes a confused mixture

---

4 Apparently the letters would be plainer and more legible on parchment than on wax tablets.

with what is inserted. But I would not have the waxen tablets extravagantly broad, having found a youth, otherwise anxious to excel, make his compositions of too great a length, because he used to measure them by the number of lines, a fault which, though it could not be corrected by repeated admonitions, was at last removed by altering the size of his tablets. There should also be a portion of space left vacant on

33 which may be noted down what frequently occurs *out of order* to persons who are writing, that is, in reference to other subjects than those which we have in hand; for excellent thoughts sometimes start into our minds, which we cannot well insert in our pages, and which it is not safe to delay noting down, because they sometimes escape us, and sometimes, if we are anxious to keep them in memory, divert us from thinking of other things. Hence they will be properly deposited in a place for memoranda.

CHAPTER FOUR

NEXT FOLLOWS *correction,* which is by far the most useful part
of our studies—for it is believed, and not without reason,
that the pen is not least serviceable when it is used to erase.
Of correction there are three ways: to *add,* to *take away,* and
to *alter.*

In regard, however, to what is to be *added* or *taken away,*
the decision is comparatively easy and simple; but to com-
press what is tumid, to raise what is low, to prune what is
luxuriant, to regulate what is ill-arranged, to give compactness to what is loose, to circumscribe what is extravagant, is a
twofold task, for we must reject things that had pleased us,
and find out others that had escaped us. Undoubtedly, also
the best method for correction is to lay by for a time what we
have written, so that we may return to it after an interval as
if it were something new to us, and written by another, lest
our writings like newborn infants compel us to fix our affec-
tions on them.

But this cannot always be done, especially by the orator,
who must frequently write for present purposes; and correction must therefore have its limits; for there are some that
return to whatever they compose as if they presumed it to be
incorrect; and, as if nothing could be right that has presented
itself first, they think whatever is different from it is better,
and find something to correct as often as they take up their
manuscript, like surgeons who make incisions even in sound
places; hence it happens that their writings are, so to speak,
scarred and bloodless, and rendered worse by the remedies
applied. Let what we write, therefore, sometimes please, or at
least content us, that the file may polish our work and not
wear it to nothing. To the time, too, allowed for correction,
there must be a limit: for as to what we hear about Cinna's
Zmyrna, that it occupied nine years in writing, and about the

Panegyric of Isocrates, which they who assign the shortest period to its production assert to have been ten years in being finished, it is of no value to the orator, whose aid would be useless if it were so long in coming.

CHAPTER FIVE

THE NEXT point is, to decide *on what we should employ* 1
ourselves when we write. It would be a superfluous labor,
indeed, to detail what subjects there are for writing, and what
should be studied first, or second, and so on in succession; for
this has been done in my first book, in which I prescribed
the order for the studies of boys, and in my second, where I
specified those of the more advanced. What is now to be considered, is whence copiousness and facility of expression may
be derived.

To translate Greek into Latin our old orators thought to 2
be a very excellent exercise. Lucius Crassus, in the well-known
books of Cicero's *De Oratore*,[1] says that he often practiced it;
and Cicero himself, speaking in his own person, very frequently recommends it, and has even published books of
Plato and Xenophon translated in that kind of exercise. It
was also approved by Messala; and there are extant several
versions of speeches made by him, so that he even rivaled the
oration of Hyperides for Phryne in delicacy of style, a quality
most difficult of attainment to Romans. The object of such 3
exercise is evident, for the Greek authors excel in copiousness
of matter, and have introduced a vast deal in art into the
study of eloquence; thus in translating them we may use the
very best words, for all that we use may be our own. As to
figures, by which language is principally ornamented, we may
be under the necessity of inventing a great number and variety of them, because the Roman tongue differs greatly from
that of the Greeks.[2]

[1] *De oratore* I.xxxiv.

[2] Quintilian discusses the "figures" at some length in Books IX and X
of the *Institutio* under the rubric of style, as is common in Roman rhetorical theory. His treatment of the figures is one of the most complete
in ancient rhetoric since he includes various viewpoints about individual

4   But the conversion of Latin writing into other words will also be of great service to us. About the utility of turning poetry into prose, I suppose that no one has any doubt; and this is the only kind of exercise that Sulpicius is said to have used; for its sublimity may elevate our style, and the boldness of the expressions adopted by poetic license does not preclude the orator's efforts to express the same thoughts in the exactness of prose. He may even add to those thoughts oratorical vigor, supply what has been omitted, and give compactness to that which is diffuse, since I would not have our paraphrase to be a mere interpretation, but an effort to vie with and rival our original in the expression of the same thoughts.

5   I therefore differ in opinion from those who disapprove of paraphrasing Latin orations on the pretext that, as the best words and phrases have been already used, whatever we express in another form must of necessity be expressed worse. But for this allegation there is no sufficient ground, for we must not despair of the possibility of finding something better than what has been said; nor has nature made language so meager and so poor that we cannot speak well on any subject except in one way; unless we suppose, indeed, that the gestures of the actor can give a variety of turns to the same words, but that the power of eloquence is so much inferior that when a thing has been once said, nothing can be said

6   after it to the same purpose. But let it be granted that what we conceive is neither better than our original nor equal to it; yet it must be allowed, at the same time, that there is a

7   possibility of coming near to it. Do not we ourselves at times speak twice or oftener, and sometimes a succession of sentences, on the same subject, and are we to suppose that though we can contend with ourselves we cannot contend with others? If a thought could be expressed well only in one way, it would be but right to suppose that the path of excellence has been shut against us by some of our predecessors; but in reality there are still innumerable modes of saying a thing,

---

devices and makes frequent reference to the Greek origins of many of them.

and many roads leading to the same point. Conciseness has its charms, and so has copiousness; there is one kind of beauty in metaphorical, another in simple expressions; direct expressions become one subject, and such as are varied by figures another. In addition, the difficulty of the exercise is most serviceable. Are not our greatest authors by this means studied more carefully? For in this way we do not run over what we have written in a careless mode of reading, but consider every individual portion, and look, for necessity, thoroughly into 9 their matter and learn how much merit they possess from the very fact that we cannot succeed in imitating them.

Nor will it be of advantage to us only to alter the language of others; it will be serviceable also to vary our own in a number of different forms, taking certain thoughts for the pur- 10 pose, and putting them, as harmoniously as possible, into several shapes, just as different figures are molded out of the same wax. But I consider that the greatest facility in composition is acquired by exercise in the simplest subjects; for in treating of a multiplicity of *persons, causes, occasions, places, sayings,* and *actions,* our real weakness in style may readily escape notice amidst so many subjects which present themselves on all sides, and on some of which we may readily lay hold. But the great proof of power is to expand what is nat- 11 urally contracted, to amplify what is little, to give variety to things that are similar, and attraction to such as are obvious, and to say with effect much on a little.[3]

---

[3] Quintilian concludes this chapter with some general remarks on practice in oratory (sections 12–23).

CHAPTER SIX

1 NEXT TO writing is *meditation,* which indeed derives strength from it, and is something between the labor of writing and the trial of our fortune in extempory speaking. I know not whether it is not more frequently of use than either, for we cannot write everywhere and at all times—but there is abundance of time and room for thought. Meditation may in a very few hours embrace all points of the most important causes. When our sleep is broken at night, meditation is aided by the very darkness. Between the different stages in the pleading of a cause it finds some room to exercise itself, and never allows itself to be idle. Nor does it only arrange within

2 its circle the order of things (which would itself be a great assistance to us) but forms an array of words, and connects together the whole texture of a speech, with such effect that nothing is wanting to it but to write it down. That, indeed, is in general more firmly fixed in the memory, on which the attention does not relax its hold from trusting too securely to writing.

But at such power of thought we cannot arrive suddenly or

3 even soon. In the first place, a certain *form* of thinking must be acquired by great practice in writing, a form which may be continually attendant on our meditations; a *habit* of thinking must then be gradually gained by embracing in our minds a few particulars at first, in such a way that they may be faithfully repeated; next, by additions so moderate that our task may scarcely feel itself increased, our power of conception must be enlarged, and sustained by plenty of exercise—power which in a great degree depends on memory, and I shall consequently defer some remarks on it till I enter on that head

4 of my subject.[1] Yet it has already been made apparent that he

[1] Quintilian discusses memory in Book XI.

to whom nature does not obstinately refuse her aid, may, if assisted only by zealous application, attain such proficiency that what he has merely meditated, as well as what he has written and learned by heart, may be faithfully expressed in his efforts at oratory. Cicero indeed has acquainted us that, among the Greeks, Metrodorus of Scepsis and Empylus of Rhodes, and Hortensius among our own countrymen, could, when they pleaded a cause, repeat word for word what they had premeditated. 5

But if by chance, while we are speaking, some glowing thought, suggested on the instant, should spring up in our minds, we must certainly not adhere too superstitiously to that which we have studied; for what we meditate is not to be settled with such nicety, that room is not to be allowed for a happy conception of the moment—when thoughts that suddenly arise in our minds are often inserted even in our written compositions. Hence the whole of this kind of exercise must be so ordered that we may easily depart from what we arranged and easily return to it; since, though it is of the first importance to bring with us from home a prepared and precise array of language, yet it would be the greatest folly to reject the offerings of the moment. Let our *premeditation,* therefore, be made with such care that fortune, while she is unable to disappoint, may have it in her power to assist us. But it will depend on the strength of our memory, whether what we have embraced in our minds flows forth easily, and does not prevent us, while we are anxious and looking back, and relying on no hope but that of recollection, from casting a glance in advance; otherwise I should prefer extemporary venturesomeness to premeditation of such unhappy coherence. It has the very worst effect to be turning back in quest of our matter, because, while we are looking for what is in one direction, we are diverted from what is in another, and we derive our thoughts rather from mere memory than from our proper subject. Supposing, too, that we had to depend wholly on premeditation or wholly on the conceptions of the moment, we know very well that more may be imagined than has been imagined. 6

CHAPTER SEVEN

1   BUT THE richest fruit of all our study, and the most ample recompense for the extent of our labor, is *the faculty of speaking extempore;* and he who has not succeeded in acquiring it will do well, in my opinion, to renounce the occupations of the forum, and devote his solitary talent of writing to some other employment; for it is scarcely consistent with the character of a man of honor to make a public profession of service to others which may fail in the most pressing emergencies, since it is of no more use than to point out a harbor to a vessel, to which it cannot approach unless it be borne along by the gentlest breezes. There arise indeed innumerable occasions where it is absolutely necessary to speak on the instant, as well before magistrates, as on trials that are brought on before the appointed time; and if any of these shall occur, I do not say to any one of our innocent fellow-citizens, but to any of our own friends or relatives, is an advocate to stand dumb, and, while they are begging for a voice to save them, and are likely to be undone if succor be not instantly afforded them, is he to ask time for retirement and silent study, till his speech be formed and committed to memory, and his voice and lungs be put in tune? What system of pleading will allow of an orator being unprepared for sudden calls? What is to be done when we have to reply to an opponent? For that which we expected him to say, and in answer to which we composed our speech, often disappoints our anticipations, and the whole aspect of the cause is suddenly changed; and as the pilot has to alter his course according to the direction of the winds, so must our plan be varied to suit the variation in the cause. What profit does much writing, constant reading, and a long period of life spent in study, bring us, if there remains with us the same difficulty in speaking that we felt at first? He, assuredly, who has always to encounter the same labor,

must admit that his past efforts were to no purpose. Not that I make it an object that an orator should prefer to speak extempore; I only wish that he should be able to do so.

This talent we shall most effectually attain by the following means. First of all, let our method of speaking be settled; for no journey can be attempted before we know to what place, 5 and by what road, we have to go. It is not enough not to be ignorant what the parts of judicial causes are, or how to dispose questions in proper order, though these are certainly points of the highest importance, but we must know what ought to be first, what second, and so on, in each department of a pleading; for different particulars are so connected by nature that they admit no alteration of their order, nor allow any thing to be forced between them, without manifest confusion. But he who shall speak according to a certain method, will be led forward, most of all, by the series of particulars, as 6 by a sure guide; and hence even persons of but moderate practice will adhere with the greatest ease to the chain of facts in their narratives. They will also know what they want in each portion of a speech, and will not look about like persons at a loss; nor will they be distracted by ideas that present themselves from other quarters, nor mix up their speech of ingredients collected from separate spots, like men leaping hither and thither, and resting nowhere. They will likewise have a certain range and limit, which cannot exist without 7 proper division. When they have treated, to the best of their ability, of everything that they had proposed to themselves, they will be sensible that they have come to a termination.

These qualifications depend on *art;* others on *study;* thus we must acquire, as has been already directed, an ample store of the best language; our style must be so formed by much and diligent composition, that even what is poured forth by us unpremeditatedly may present the appearance of having been previously written; so that, after having written much, we shall have the power of speaking copiously. For it is 8 *habit* and *exercise* that chiefly beget facility, and if they are intermitted, even but for a short period, not only will our fluency be diminished, but our mouth may even be closed.[2]

. . . .

But this talent requires to be kept up with no less practice than it is acquired. An art, indeed, once thoroughly learned, 24 is never wholly lost. Even the pen by disuse loses but very little of its readiness, while promptitude in speaking, which depends on activity of thought, can be retained only by exercise. Such exercise we may best use by speaking daily in the hearing of several persons, especially of those for whose judgment and opinion we have most regard—for it rarely happens that a person is sufficiently severe with himself. Let us however rather speak alone than not speak at all. There is also another kind of exercise, that of meditating upon whole sub- 25 jects and going through them in silent thought—yet, so as to speak, as it were within ourselves—an exercise which may be pursued at all times and in all places, when we are not actually engaged in any other occupation. It is in some degree more useful than the one which I mentioned before it; for it is more accurately pursued than that in which we are afraid to interrupt the continuity of our speech. Yet the other method, again contributes more to improve other qualifica- 26 tions, as strength of voice, flexibility of features, and energy of gesture, which of itself, as I remarked, rouses the orator, and, as he waves his hand and stamps his foot, excites him as lions are said to excite themselves by the lashing of their tails.

But we must study at all times and in all places, for there is scarcely a single one of our days so occupied that some prof- 27 itable attention may not be hastily devoted during at least some portion of it (as Cicero says that Brutus used to do) to writing, or reading, or speaking. Caius Carbo, even in his tent, was accustomed to continue his exercises in oratory. Nor must we omit to notice the advice, which is also approved by 28 Cicero, that no portion even of our common conversation should ever be careless; and that whatever we say, and wherever we say it, should be as far as possible excellent in its

---

[2] Sections 9–23 are repetitions of general speaking advice repeated several times elsewhere, and so are omitted here.

kind. As to writing, we must certainly never write more than when we have to speak much extempore; for by the use of the pen a weightiness will be preserved in our matter, and that light facility of language, which swims as it were on the surface, will be compressed into a body as husbandmen cut off the upper roots of the vine (which elevate it to the surface of the soil) in order that the lower roots may be strengthened by striking deeper. And I know not whether both exercises, 29 when we perform them with care and assiduity, are not reciprocally beneficial, as it appears that by writing we speak with greater accuracy, and by speaking we write with greater ease. We must write, therefore, as often as we have opportunity; if opportunity is not allowed us, we must meditate; if we are precluded from both, we must nevertheless endeavor that the orator may not seem to be caught at fault, nor the client left destitute of aid. But it is the general practice among pleaders 30 who have much occupation, to write only the most essential parts, and especially the commencements, of their speeches; to fix the other portions that they bring from home in their memory by meditation; and to meet any unforeseen attacks with extemporaneous replies.

That Cicero adopted this method is evident from his own memoranda. But there are also in circulation memoranda of other speakers, which have been found, perhaps, in the state in which each had thrown them together when he was going to speak, and have been arranged in the form of books; for instance, the memoranda of the causes pleaded by Servius Sulpicius, three of whose orations are extant; but these memoranda of which I am now speaking are so carefully arranged that they appear to me to have been composed by him to be handed down to posterity. Those of Cicero, which were in- 31 tended only for his particular occasions, his freedman Tiro collected; and, in saying this, I do not speak of them apologetically, as if I did not think very highly of them, but intimate, on the contrary, that they are for that reason more worthy of admiration.

Under this head, I express my full approbation of short notes, and of small memorandum-books which may be held

in the hand, and on which we may occasionally glance. But
the method which Lænas recommends, of reducing what we
32 have written into summaries, or into short notes and heads, I
do not like; for our very dependence on these summaries
begets negligence in committing our matter to memory, and
disconnects and disfigures our speech. I even think that we
should not write at all what we design to deliver from memory, for if we do so it generally happens that our thoughts fix
us to the studied portions of our speech, and do not allow us
to try the fortune of the moment. Thus the mind hangs in
suspense and perplexity between the two, having lost sight of
what was written, and yet not being at liberty to imagine anything new.

Appendix

Suggestions for Further Reading

Index

APPENDIX: EDITIONS AND TRANSLATIONS OF THE *INSTITUTIO ORATORIA*

The *Institutio oratoria* has undergone many complete editions since it was first printed in Rome in 1470 by Campanus. Among frequently used modern editions are those of Charles Halm (Leipzig, Germany: Teubner, 1863) and Ludwig Radermacher, 2 vols. (Leipzig, Germany: Teubner, 1907 and 1935). H. E. Butler uses the Halm text as the basis for his Loeb Classical Library edition of 1921.

The best modern edition, however, is that of Michael Winterbottom, *Institutionis oratoriae libri duodecim* (Oxford, UK: Clarendon, 1970). Winterbottom has also published an extensive series of editorial comments on individual passages from the text, *Problems in Quintilian* (London: University of London Institute of Classical Studies, Bulletin Supplement no. 25, 1970). The third section ("Noctes Quintilianae" 61–218) may be of interest even to non-Latin readers since Winterbottom often discusses general questions in relation to the technical points involved in editing the text. See also *The Minor Declamations Ascribed to Quintilian* edited with commentary by Michael Winterbottom (Berlin: Walter de Gruyter, 1984). Again, Winterbottom's lucid notes are extremely valuable.

Single books have been edited several times. Perhaps the most useful for the general reader would be F. H. Colson, ed., *M. Fabii Quintiliani institutionis oratoriae liber I* (Cambridge, UK: Cambridge UP, 1924). In addition to the text of the first book with elaborate notes, Colson provides an invaluable introduction to the life, influence, and theory of the Roman author.

Another edition of the first book is that of Charles Fierville, *M. F. Quintiliani de institutione oratoria liber primus* (Paris: n.p., 1890). Among several useful appendixes in this version is the Latin text of the twelfth-century abstract that Étienne de Rouen made of the *Institutio oratoria*. Fierville's text of this piece is transcribed from Bibliothèque Nationale Ms. Fonds Lat. 14146.

Book 10 has been edited separately with commentary by William Peterson, *M. Fabii Quintiliani institutionis oratoriae liber decimus* (Oxford, UK: n.p., 1891). Peterson's introduction is notable for its excellent discussion of literary criticism in the *Institutio oratoria* and for its treatment of Quintilian's own writing style. The book has now been reissued (New York: Sophron, 2013) with a foreword by James J. Murphy.

R. G. Austin has edited the final book, *Quintiliani institutionis oratoriae liber XII* (Oxford, UK: Clarendon, 1948; revised edition, 1953). The introduction contains a useful bibliography.

Selections from Quintilian have been published by several translators. Perhaps the most important of these is William Smail, *Quintilian on Education, Being a Translation of Selected Passages* (Oxford, UK: Oxford UP, 1938). Catherine R. Smith also uses the title *Quintilian on Education: Selections from the Institutes of Oratory* (New York: New York University Store [multigraphed], 1936). A miscellany of partial translation, partial paraphrase is presented by Charles Little, *Quintilian: The Schoolmaster*, 2 vols. (Nashville, TN: George Peabody, 1951). One of the declamations once ascribed to Quintilian has also been translated: Robinson Ellis, *The Tenth Declamation of the Pseudo-Quintilian* (London: H. Frowde, 1911).

A useful French translation is that of Henri Bornecque, 4 vols. (Paris: Garnier Freres, 1933–34), with an accompanying Latin text. See also Jean Cousin, *Quintilien, Institution oratoire, I-VII* (Paris: Les Belles Lettres, 1975–80). Mieczyslaw Brazok published a Polish version of Books 1, 2, and 10, *Ksztakenie M OlVCY* (Wroclaw, Poland: n.p., 1951).

There is a useful German translation by Helmut Rahn, *Ausbildung des Redners: Zwölf Bücher*, with a critical edition of the Latin text (Darmstadt, Germany: Wissenschaftliche Buchgesellschaft, 1972).

Adriano Pennacini has used a unique method in his *Quintiliano* (Turin, Italy: Einaudi, 2001), providing Italian translations of the twelve books of the *Institutio oratoria*, each by a separate author.

Quintilian's book was first translated into English in 1755 by W. Guthrie under the title of *Quintilian's Institutes of Eloquence: The Art of Speaking in Public in Every Character and Capacity*, 2 vols. (London: R.

Dutton, 1755). It should be noted that Guthrie takes some liberties with the text, including idiosyncrasies of translation and a tendency to omit whole passages without notice to the reader.

J. Patsall translated the work nineteen years later under the title *Institutes of the Orator*, 2. vols. (London: B. Law, 1774). This translation also omits some passages.

One of the most popular translations and the basis of the text printed here, was that of the Reverend Watson, completed in 1856 and published in two volumes by George Bell and Sons of London under the title *Quintilian's Institutes of Oratory, or, Education of an Orator*. The work was included in the Bohn's Library series published by Bell and was reprinted several times up to 1903. Watson used the Latin text of G. Spalding, published between 1798 and 1811.

The translation of H. E. Butler, with accompanying Latin text, was published in the Loeb Classical Library series in 1921, *The Institutio oratoria of Quintilian with an English Translation*, 4 vols. (London: William Heinemann; Cambridge, MA: Harvard UP, 1921). See also H. E. Butler, trans., *Quintilian as Educator: Selections from the Institutio oratoria of Marcus Fabius Quintilianus* (New York: Twayne, 1974).

The most recent text and English translation is that of Donald A. Russell, *Quintilian: The Orator's Education*, 5 vols. (Cambridge, MA: Harvard UP, 2001), Loeb Classical Library. This improved edition has many more explanatory notes than the preceding 1921 Loeb Library edition by Butler.

An extremely useful re-edition of Book 2 by Tobias Reinhardt and Michael Winterbottom (Oxford, UK: Oxford UP, 2006) includes extensive commentaries on the text and a thorough exploration of sources.

For a concise treatment of the current state of Quintilian studies, see Jorge Fernandez Lopez, "Quintilian as Rhetorician and Teacher," in *A Companion to Roman Rhetoric*, ed. William Dominik and Jon Hall (Oxford, UK: Blackwell, 2007), 307–22.

Also, for an appreciative treatment of the way Quintilian uses his sources, see the rather mistitled chapter "The Rhetoric of Rhetorical Theory" by Erik Gunderson in *The Cambridge Companion to Ancient Rhetoric*, ed. Erik Gunderson (Cambridge, UK: Cambridge UP, 2009), 109–25. The essay is entirely about Quintilian, despite the title.

SUGGESTIONS FOR
FURTHER READING

Agnew, Lois. "The Classical Period." In *The Present State of Scholarship in the History of Rhetoric: A Twenty-First Century Guide*. Ed. Lynée Lewis Gaillet with Winifred Bryan Horner. 3rd ed. Columbia: University of Missouri Press, 2010. 7–41.

Baldwin, Charles Sears. *Ancient Rhetoric and Poetic*. New York: Macmillan, 1924. Rpt. Gloucester, MA: Peter Smith, 1959.

Bonner, Stanley F. *Education in Ancient Rome: From the Elder Cato to the Younger Pliny*. Berkeley: University of California Press, 1977.

———. *Roman Declamation in the Late Republic and Early Empire*. Berkeley: University of California Press, 1949.

Clark, Donald Leman. *Rhetoric in Greco-Roman Education*. New York: Columbia University Press, 1957.

Clarke, Martin Lowther. *Rhetoric at Rome: A Historical Survey*. London: Cohen and West, 1953. Rpt. New York: Barnes and Noble, 1963.

Colson, F. H., ed. Introduction. *M. Fabii Quintiliani institutionis oratoriae liber I*. Cambridge, UK: Cambridge University Press, 1924.

Corbett, Edward P. J., and Robert J. Connors. *Classical Rhetoric for the Modern Student*. 4th ed. New York: Oxford University Press, 1998.

Crowley, Sharon, and Debra Hawhee. *Ancient Rhetorics for Contemporary Students*. 4th ed. White Plains, NY: Longman, 2009.

Dominik, William, and Jon Hall, ed. *A Companion to Roman Rhetoric*. Oxford, UK: Blackwell, 2007.

Erickson, Keith V. "Quintilian's *Institutio oratoria* and Pseudo-*Declamationes*" [A Bibliography] *Rhetoric Society Quarterly* 11 (1981): 45–62.

Fantham, Elaine, et al. *Women in the Classical World: Image and Text*. New York: Oxford University Press, 1994.

Fritz, K. von. "Ancient Instruction in Grammar according to Quintilian." *American Journal of Philology* 70 (1949): 337–66.

Gwynn, Aubrey. *Roman Education from Cicero to Quintilian.* Oxford, UK: Clarendon, 1926. Rpt. New York: Columbia University Teachers College, n.d. Classics in Education No. 29.

Haarhoff, Theodore. *The Schools of Gaul.* Oxford, UK: Clarendon, 1920.

Hoermann, Jacquelyn E. and Richard Leo Enos. "Vernacular Eloquence: What Speech Can Bring to Writing." *Composition Studies* 42.2 (Fall 2014): 163–70, 187–88.

Hubbell, Harry M. *The Influence of Isocrates on Cicero, Dionysius, and Aristides.* New Haven, CT: Yale University Press, 1913.

Kaster, Robert A. "Controlling Reason: Declamation in Rhetorical Education at Rome." In *Education in Greek and Roman Antiquity.* Ed. Y. L. Too. Leiden, Netherlands: Brill, 2001. 317–39.

———. *Guardians of Language: The Grammarian and Society in Late Antiquity.* Berkeley: University of California Press, 1988.

Kennedy, George A. *The Art of Rhetoric in the Roman World: 300 B.C.–A.D. 300.* Princeton, NJ: Princeton University Press, 1972.

———. *A New History of Classical Rhetoric.* Princeton, NJ: Princeton University Press, 1994.

———. *Quintilian.* 2nd ed. New York: Sophron, 2013.

Lausberg, Heinrich. *Handbook of Literary Rhetoric: A Foundation for Literary Study.* Ed. David E. Orton and R. Dean Anderson. Trans. Matthew T. Bliss and Annemiek Jansen. Leiden, Netherlands: Brill, 1998.

Little, Charles, ed. *Quintilian: The Schoolmaster.* 2 vols. Nashville, TN: George Peabody, 1951.

Lopez, Jorge Fernandez. "Quintilian as Rhetorician and Teacher." In *A Companion to Roman Rhetoric.* Ed. William Dominik and Jon Hall. Oxford, UK: Blackwell, 2007. 307–22.

Marrou, Henri-Irenée. *A History of Education in Antiquity.* Trans. George Lamb. New York: New American Library, 1964. Rpt. Madison: University of Wisconsin Press, 1982.

Murphy, James J. "'Data Don't Breathe': An Interview with Quintilian, the Master Teacher of Rome." *Writing on the Edge* 24 (2013): 94–105.

————. "The Modern Value of Ancient Roman Methods of Teaching Writing, with Answers to Twelve Current Fallacies." *Writing on the Edge* 1 (1989): 28–37.

————. "Quintilian's Advice on the Continuing Self-Education of the Adult Orator: Book X of His *Institutio oratoria.*" In *Quintilian and the Law: The Art of Persuasion in Law and Politics.* Ed. Olga Tellegen-Couperus. Leuven, Belgium: Leuven University Press, 2003. 247–52.

————. "Roman Writing Instruction as Described by Quintilian." In *A Short History of Writing Instruction: From Ancient Greece to Contemporary America.* Ed. James J. Murphy. 3rd ed. New York: Routledge, 2012. 36–76.

————, ed. *Quintilian in His Own Time.* Spec. issue of *Rhetorica* 13.2 (1995): 103–217.

————, ed. *Quintilian in Later Times.* Spec. issue of *Rhetorica* 13.3 (1995): 219–358.

Parks, Brother Edilbert P. *The Roman Rhetorical Schools as a Preparation for the Courts under the Early Empire.* Baltimore, MD: Johns Hopkins University Press, 1945. Johns Hopkins University Studies in Historical and Political Science Ser. 63, No. 2.

Quintilian. *Quintilian Book 2.* Ed. Tobias Reinhardt and Michael Winterbottom. Oxford, UK: Oxford University Press, 2006.

————. *Quintilian: The Orator's Education.* Ed. and trans. Donald A. Russell. 5 vols. Cambridge, MA: Harvard University Press, 2002. Loeb Classical Library.

Too, Y. L., ed. *Education in Greek and Roman Antiquity.* Leiden, Netherlands: Brill, 2001.

Welch, Kathleen E. *The Contemporary Reception of Classical Rhetoric: Appropriations of Ancient Discourse.* Mahwah, NJ: Lawrence Erlbaum Associates, 1990.

Wilkins, A. S. *Roman Education.* Cambridge, UK: Cambridge University Press, 1914.

INDEX

170   *Index*